The Soul Knows No Bars

Also by Drew Leder

Games for the Soul:
40 Playful Ways to Find Fun and Fulfillment in a Stressful World

Spiritual Passages: Embracing Life's Sacred Journey

The Absent Body

The Soul Knows No Bars

Inmates Reflect on Life, Death, and Hope

DREW LEDER
WITH
CHARLES BAXTER * WAYNE BROWN
TONY CHATMAN-BEY * JACK COWAN
MICHAEL GREEN * GARY HUFFMAN
H. B. JOHNSON JR. * O'DONALD JOHNSON
ARLANDO JONES III * MARK MEDLEY
"Q" * DONALD THOMPSON
SELVYN TILLETT * JOHN WOODLAND

ROWMAN & LITTLEFIELD PUBLISHERS, INC.
Lanham • Boulder • New York • Oxford

ROWMAN & LITTLEFIELD PUBLISHERS, INC.

Published in the United States of America
by Rowman & Littlefield Publishers, Inc.
4720 Boston Way, Lanham, Maryland 20706
www.rowmanlittlefield.com

12 Hid's Copse Road
Cumnor Hill, Oxford OX2 9JJ, England

British Library Cataloguing in Publication Information Available

The hardback edition of this book was previously cataloged by the Library of Congress as follows

Library of Congress Cataloging-in-Publication Data

Leder, Drew.
    The soul knows no bars : inmates reflect on life, death, and hope / Drew Leder, with
    Charles Baxter ... [et al.].
        p.   cm.
    Includes index.
    1. Prisoners—Education (Higher)—Maryland—Baltimore—Case studies. 2.
Philosophy—Study and teaching (Higher)—Maryland—Baltimore—Case studies. 3.
Prisoners—Maryland—Baltimore—Intellectual life—Case studies. I. Title.

HV8883.3.U52 M35 1999
365'.6'097526 21—dc21   99-045670

ISBN 0-8476-9290-6 (cloth alk. paper)
ISBN 0-7425-1247-9 (pbk. alk. paper)

Printed in the United States of America

⊖™ The paper used in this publication meets the minimum requirements of American National
Standard for Information Sciences—Permanence of Paper for Printed Library Materials,
ANSI/NISO Z39.48–1992.

For H. B. Johnson Jr.,
Gary Huffman,
Mark Medley,
and all those in prison
who truly seek to be free

Contents

PART FOUR—SEX AND RACE

PART FIVE—JOURNEYS

PART SIX—BEGINNINGS AND ENDINGS

Foreword

How rare and refreshing to see a passionate philosophy professor engaged in serious and substantive dialogue with challenging and talented fellow citizens behind bars! Drew Leder has taught—and been taught by—incarcerated men in Baltimore for many years. He is a kind of latter-day Socrates who embodies and enacts an intellectual spirituality that critically questions and lovingly serves others in an atmosphere of mutual respect.

When I visited Professor Leder's course and lectured in the prison, I was struck by the genuine camaraderie and the intense intellectuality of the class. Martin Buber would have approved of our dialogues—dynamic I-Thou exchanges that touched heart, mind, and soul. How I wish such high-quality pedagogical experiences could be had in schools and prisons across this nation and world! Yet Professor Leder never lost sight of the different plight and predicament of those outside and inside the oldest prison in America. His class promotes an intellectual and spiritual freedom that even bars cannot contain, yet these bars still divide, degrade, demean, and dishonor. The delicate dialectic of personal responsibility and societal accountability, of individual choice and limited social options, informed our philosophical discussions of evil, injustice, and social misery.

This book is a timely lifting of the veil on the *human* doings and sufferings within one of the fastest growing industries in America—a prison industry that literally warehouses disproportionately black and brown peoples due mainly to social neglect, poverty, lovelessness, inequality, and sheer icy indifference to the suffering of the most vulnerable in our society. Professor Leder's ability to accent the profoundly *human* dimension of his intellectual dialogues stands in stark contrast to the stereotypical perceptions of prisoners rendered invisible in our midst.

In this way, this is philosophy at its best—the courageous love and quest for wisdom that sheds light and enlightens souls in the heart of American darkness.

Cornel West
Harvard University

Acknowledgments

More than most books, this one is the product of a communal effort. Consequently, there are many to thank.

First, I wish to acknowledge the unstinting support of Father Tim Brown, S.J., and the Center for Values and Service of Loyola College in Maryland. The Center provided funds for tape-transcriptions and is seeking to make copies of this book available to those whom it might benefit. Father Brown's friendship and participation in the project have meant more to me than I can say. Part of the book was written during a research sabbatical generously provided by Loyola College. The school's administration and my colleagues in the philosophy department have been consistently supportive of this unorthodox work.

This would have availed little without the cooperation of administrators at the Maryland Penitentiary. It is very hard to get out of a maximum security prison, but neither is it easy to get in. I wish to thank Wardens James Rollins and Sewall Smith, and the prison school's principal, Daniel Murray, for opening the doors (so to speak) to this challenging project. Mr. Murray, in particular, was a strong advocate of our work; he and his staff provided the logistical help without which we never could have proceeded.

Since so much of the book consists of inmate dialogues, I am indebted to those who painstakingly transcribed the audio tapes. This includes Molly Mitchell, Linda Petrelli, Ellan Thorson, and Lisa M. Flaherty. Ms. Flaherty, an invaluable associate on the project, also provided many other forms of help, as this complex manuscript was assembled and revised time and again.

Mike Bowler of the *Baltimore Sun* has been a wonderful friend and colleague in this prison work. I am also indebted to Wally Shug for an advance look at his history of the Maryland Penitentiary, forthcoming from the Maryland Historical Society.

Lynn Rosen of the Leap First Literary Agency played a special role in the birthing of this book. For minimal recompense, but with great generosity of time and spirit, she helped in finding the manuscript a home and ironing out the many details of publication. I also thank Joy James and Lewis Gordon, who helped steer the manuscript to Rowman & Littlefield, and Christa Acompora and her colleagues, who graciously took it on. Cornel West, a busy man if ever there was, found time not only to provide moral support, but to come to the penitentiary, meet with the inmates, and contribute the book's foreword.

I wish to recognize the many others who devote their time, often their lives, to inmates and prison issues, even while the social climate for such work remains forbidding: Bo and Sita Lozoff, whose Human Kindness Foundation has helped inmates around the world; the volunteers of the Quaker-sponsored Alternatives to Violence program who bring a healing message into the nation's prisons; and other such groups and individuals. I especially want to thank Natalie Sokoloff of the John Jay College of Criminal Justice and Stephen Steurer of the Correctional Educational Association for generously offering their expertise and assistance.

On a personal note, I am greatly indebted to my wife and fellow philosopher, Janice McLane. Not every wife would be so very supportive of a husband trooping off to a maximum security prison, and the multiple contacts that ensue. Moreover, Janice provided invaluable encouragement, ideas, and feedback on the evolving manuscript.

Finally, I wish to thank my co-authors, the men whose words are recorded here. The crimes that brought them to prison cannot be excused or fully amended. Yet I admire the courage, perseverance, and honesty they brought to the project as they shared deeply of their experience without the cover of anonymity. I believe they have something of great value to say to those both inside and outside prison walls.

Some readers, inspired by this book or personal commitments, may wish to take some practical action. There are many possibilities. You might consider volunteering skills and/or sending books (perhaps including this one) to a local prison. Equally important is political advocacy around criminal justice issues. To help provide inmates with the resources to support positive growth, you might also consider a donation to the Human Kindness Foundation. For more than twenty-five years, this committed group has reached out to tens of thousands of inmates, sending free materials to those who seek to use their prison time for personal and spiritual renewal. The organization can be reached at

Human Kindness Foundation
RR 1 Box 201-N
Durham, NC 27705
www.humankindness.org

CHAPTER ONE

Getting into Prison

The first time I entered the prison was the only time I saw it. From then on I was used to it all or had trained myself to see through it and beyond. The bars and guards had become just passing annoyances on the way to the classroom. But the first time I arrived they seemed everywhere.

I came in through the portals of a massive, Gothic building—a strange castle or dungeon incongruously plunked near the heart of downtown Baltimore. As I walked through the entry—I almost expected to see a moat and drawbridge—I encountered the first set of iron bars. With some convincing, the guard waved to another guard sitting inside a bulletproof room. When she pushed a button the gates slid open.

There were more barriers to surmount, physical, psychic, bureaucratic, in this passage to another world. I signed in at the visitor's registry. This was my first day as a volunteer instructor in the Pen. A call was made to the prison school for someone to accompany me. Then I waited along with a dozen others on a set of institutional benches in a dingy room—a couple of vending machines, a one-person bathroom whose door didn't lock (please knock before entering), posted signs everywhere (as of April 1, visitors to the prison will no longer be allowed to wear shorts or tank-top T-shirts). There were young women with me, black and white, waiting for a half-hour supervised visit with their inmate. A girl squirmed in impatience like any child forced to sit on a cold bench without toys. I wondered what it meant to a five-year-old to be visiting her father in the state penitentiary. That her daddy had done something wrong and been sent to his room, for twenty years? That my daddy's different, we're different too, or that this is just where all daddies go? Did the prison scene reappear in the child's nightmares—her father entwined in a cage by dream-serpents, or ever receding as the girl pursued? And when would *my* escort ever come to rescue me from this dismal dream? Everything was unfolding with glacial slowness—the movements of the guards, the gates, the promised redeemer who had never arrived. I was not just in a waiting room, but in a whole temple of waiting where time was all anybody did and there was plenty of it to kill.

1

Finally, my escort appeared. The guard in the plastic booth pressed a second button to slide open a second gate and I was frisked, signed in again, stamped, and banded. The guards were not rude, but neither were they friendly. They were doing their job, boring, repetitive, with its whiff of power but not quite enough to get drunk on. I went through the visiting room where inmates sat across tables from girlfriends, uncles, mothers, and lawyers. Everyone leaned forward but never touched.

As I descended a flight of stairs, voices echoed from the cell area to my right, resonating in the strange sound chamber made by so many cages in a row. It seemed a human zoo. I have been invited to visit that region of the prison, but in two years have never gone. Better to meet my students as men than to peer at them curiously through bars.

Walking on, I came into a sudden blaze of sun and space. The prison yard, about a football field in size, sported an occasional straggly tree. Inmates congregated here and there, talking against a fence or playing pick-up ball. High above in one of the Gothic turrets a guard with a high-powered rifle surveyed the scene. I didn't notice it then—not until several weeks later when one of the other teachers pointed out: "I like to know where they are just in case I get jumped crossing the yard." But I didn't find this armed surveillance too reassuring: if a free-for-all broke out with me in the middle, how discriminating would the marksman be?

I approached the school building, a two-story red-brick job. I was led to an upstairs classroom, not that different from any other, just smaller and dingier, where I sat alone. My students, I was told, would arrive from lunch *sometime*. It depended on which cell block was served first and how long the general count-out took (that process repeated six times a day of counting each of the 886 inmates). Finally, three or four filtered in, of the thirty-five who had signed up. No one had reminded inmates when my course was to begin; no one had prepared the paperwork for them to come to class. I did a slow boil at this incompetence that had wrecked my plans. I was not yet used to it. Later I learned that this was "the belly of the beast," at least for me—not so much the rage of murderers gathered around in evil mob, but the unending indifference and glitches of prison bureaucracy. What could I do? The guards and administrators had their anger, their modes of imprisonment and resistance, intertwining with those of the convicts. I had stepped on a new dance floor and was learning the moves.

I introduced myself to the few prisoners and we struggled to figure out what we wanted from one another. This was a world apart from my elite college environs. But I'd decided to render it familiar using two rules of thumb. (1) I was the teacher, they were the students—a role-play I had trained for over many years. (2) These were individuals to be addressed as courteously and respectfully as I would a colleague. I suspected that they would appreciate such treatment since it was not a part of their daily fare.

The next week I was excited by a flood of students, all by my requirement college-level or beyond. The thrill did not last. It was based on a mistake: instead of a class in *philosophy*, this had been billed by the school as a *psychology* course, a popular major in the prison's Coppin State University program. A number of inmates immediately melted away, and we were down to ten or fifteen hard-core guys. Many of them are still part of the class two years later, not a long time when you're serving double life. Yet the years did bring changes to our group: deaths, transformations, releases. But we'll get to all that.

I remember our first real class, studying Plato's *Apology*. They had read it in advance and were loaded for bear. I posed some standard questions: Was Socrates trying to win his trial, or convert the men of Athens to a better way of living even at the cost of his own life? Was he a masterful orator or did he needlessly alienate the jury? The discussion became quite intense, students raising their voices, leaping from seats to make a point as five other hands demanded recognition. They identified with Socrates; they knew what it was like to stand before a hostile jury. Yes, he was on trial for challenging Athens' gods and corrupting her youth, and they for Murder One. Same difference.

They certainly seemed to share Socrates' intellectual passion. Many had studied him before and had their own interpretations to defend. The convicts cared about ideas, more than many of my Loyola College students sentenced to serve out their required curriculum. I felt at home in this drab penitentiary classroom and so, seemingly, did the inmates.

Toward the end of the *Apology*, Socrates is condemned to death. Half serious, half in jest, he tells the jury:

> If . . . death is a removal from here to some other place, and if what we are told is true, that all the dead are there, what greater blessing could there be than this, gentlemen? . . . It would be a specially interesting experience for me to join them there, to meet Palamedes and Ajax the son of Telamon and any other heroes of the old days who met their death through an unfair trial, and to compare my fortunes with theirs—it would be rather amusing, I think—; and above all I should like to spend my time there, as here, in examining and searching people's minds, to find out who is really wise among them, and who only thinks that he is. (40e–41b)

There we sat in the midst of Hades, these castoffs comparing to that of Socrates their unfair trials (for almost to a man they were convinced it was so, at least in some specific way). And like Socrates they delighted in the search for wisdom.

Suddenly a guard appeared to call the class to a halt. Time to return to the cell block for the day's third count-out. The discussion's heat chilled as I remembered: we're in a maximum security prison here. It no longer seemed the underworld Socrates so praised, but that of dead, desolate

Achilles. When Homer's Odysseus visits him in Hades, Achilles laments, "I'd rather follow a plow as the serf of a land-hungry poor peasant, than be king over all these exhausted dead" (*Odyssey,* Book II: 579–81). Escorted across the bare yard, past the barred cells, through the many gates and guards, and out of prison, I am happy to be free.

Voices

I first decided to teach in prison while at a Jesuit seminary and retreat center in Wernersville, Pennsylvania. My own religious leanings are decidedly mixed: I'm a Jewish Quaker with Hindu beliefs in karma and reincarnation; I dabble in Buddhist meditation and teach at Loyola College, a Catholic school. It makes perfect sense to me. A believer in utilizing all avenues to the sacred, I seized on the Jesuit center available to Loyola folks. Its rolling hills and cloistered rooms, its vaulting dark-pooled sanctuary, all combined to create a deep stillness. It is written that "In the beginning was the word," but before that there had to be silence.

From the silence, I remember hearing two voices within, one addressing the past, the other, the future. I grew up in a storm-tossed house. Between my eighteenth and twenty-first birthdays my mother died of breast cancer, my father and brother, by suicide. I had always blamed much of this on Mom. I saw her as a puppet-master jerking us to her tune until all the strings broke. But that day in Wernersville I understood her a little better. She was first diagnosed and had her mastectomy when I was thirteen. It wasn't talked about—she'd gone to the hospital, returned, and that was that. But now the significance flooded in: my whole adolescence, that period of brutal fights between her and my brother, she was living under the shadow of death. No wonder her voice was shrill and controlling. She could envision us growing up without a mother. She had no God to save her from the gathering dark. She was rageful, and most of all she was scared. I could identify.

The other call I heard was of a totally different sort. (It wasn't until later that I saw the interconnection, but that, in many ways, is what this book is about.) I had been searching for some kind of service work to do, but had no idea what; that trip to Wernersville was partly to seek guidance. A friend had once described to me his experience teaching in prison. The idea appealed but I had long since put it on a shelf with a dozen other vague intents. In meditation, God seemed to take this one down, dust it off, and drop it back in my lap. I envisioned prison as an ideal place for philosophical work. Though the body is trapped, the spirit, I imagined, could roam freely through the realm of ideas. My own books had excoriated such mind–body dualisms but at heart I was a flighty Platonist. After all, was a prison setting so different from what I'd sought out at Wernersville? In one sense, yes, a thousand times yes. I was encompassed there in palatial style by the riches of the Catholic Church. Freely, I came to, and could leave, this retreat center and seminary for would-be priests. How opposite the condition of the criminal confined to a dilapidated cell.

Yet opposites may have much in common. The prison cell was originally modeled on the monastic cell. The very term penitentiary, coined in the 1770s, referred to a space set aside for monks in need of penitence and reform. Surely, our culture has wandered far from this vision. Imprisonment is seen as a way to quarantine and harshly punish the criminal. But might the inmates themselves not reclaim the original vision? When Mohandas K. Gandhi wrote from Yeravda Prison, his semipermanent home, he'd mark his letters "Yeravda Mandir"—Yeravda *Temple*. Why not convert the prison into a sort of temple or monastery, a place of deep reflection, learning, and spiritual transformation? And why should not I help direct this process? (It's embarrassing to recognize how the ego expands, particularly when we are at our most selfless.)

I called the nearby Maryland Penitentiary. The voice on the other end described a heavy-duty prison for the perpetrators of serious, usually violent crimes. For a long time, it had been Maryland's only maximum security prison. Willie Horton was in here—the man who helped elect George Bush in 1986. He raped a woman after being furloughed from a Massachusetts prison. Featured prominently in Bush's ad campaign, that pretty much did in his opponent, Massachusetts Governor Michael Dukakis. It was also here in May 1994 that John Thanos was given a lethal injection, Maryland's first execution in thirty-three years.

Speaking of firsts, I later learned from Wally Shug, author of a history of the Maryland prison, that it was the oldest continuing operating penitentiary in the Western world. Oh, there were older jails and dungeons the world over. But no other *penitentiary*, flowing out of the late eighteenth-century prison reform movement, had been active as long as the Maryland Pen, whose doors first opened (shut?) in 1811.

Some of the inmates probably felt they'd been there from the start. Most of them were lifers, yet still hopeful of a future. "Some guys just give up and waste away," I was later told. "They hear the judge say 'life,' and they actually think it means life." My students clung to their optimism, petitioning judges for reduction of sentence, building good parole records, and like eager college seniors, planning their post-graduate careers—whether realistically or not, I've never been that sure. In Maryland, lifers are first eligible for parole after seventeen years. But some of the prisoners caught more than life—"life plus twenty," or "double life." A strange concept, difficult to fathom.

When I first called, the prison school principal quickly accepted my offer to teach a volunteer workshop. During the summer there were no courses in the prison's two regular college programs. In humid Baltimore those months were often the most brutal with temperatures in the cell area reaching 120 degrees and tensions heating up in the baked dirt yard. "If there are riots," I was told, "they're gonna be in the summer."

I later learned this was far from hyperbole. While not a violent place compared to many prisons, the Maryland Penitentiary had seen its share of summertime riots going back to 1920. One in 1988 had sent eight correctional officers, three inmates, and a prison psychologist to the hospital. Another in 1991 included a failed escape attempt, inmates raping and assaulting one another, and a tense stand off involving an officer held hostage. Patient negotiation averted further bloodshed.

So the inmates could use something in the summer to keep them occupied. Such a course would also enable participants to maintain student status, for which they received five dollars and one and a half days off their sentence per month. I was reminded of my Loyola undergrads. Wearily they stumble to their required courses, chasing the promise of eventual release (graduation) and a future paycheck.

I started the prison course envisioning myself in and out before the fall. That summer we began with the topic of imprisonment and liberation. We argued about Socrates on trial, then Epictetus, the Stoic philosopher, crippled and a slave; Job suffering through divine abandonment; Jesus mocked on the cross; the searing account by James Bond Stockdale (remember Ross Perot's first running mate?) of his eight years in a North Vietnamese POW camp; and Martin Luther King Jr.'s clarion call for justice in "Letter from a Birmingham Jail." Like an eagle, the discussions would soar to speculative heights, then plunge into the dirt of prison life, retrieving some carcass for us to gnaw on together. It became clear that the students weren't there for the money or time off; many were already getting that deal through their prison jobs. Nor were they receiving college credit for the workshop. They were there because they *wanted to fly*. They also craved the food captured on our predatory missions. Epictetus's *Handbook* begins: "Some things are up to us and some are not up to us." They knew. Stoic detachment was a strategy of survival in harsh conditions. So, too, Job's acceptance, Martin's and Malcolm's defiance, Jesus' redemptive cross.

When summer ended we didn't. They weren't going anywhere, I thought, so how could I? This life-sentence stuff was proving ideal for teaching: I finally had a long-term captive audience. But I was captive too. The academic forces propelling students to other teachers, then out into the world, were here disabled. I felt bound, but joyfully, like a new mother suddenly realizing the extent of her commitment. Grace Paley writes of this ambivalence: "Then through the short fat fingers of my son, interred forever, like a black and white barred king in Alcatraz, my heart lit up in stripes."

My students welcomed me into this joyful incarceration. It's a funny thing to *receive* someone in prison; you can't exactly sit them on the living room couch and fetch a cup of tea. It would seem that to play host one needs a home. Yet I found quite the opposite; when striding through the nuclear wasteland of the yard, surrounded by barbed wire and prickly strangers, a friendly face was home incarnate. Donald or Charley or Wayne would keep an eye out. And when they caught sight of me, I would catch their smile; that was couch and tea enough. "How ya doin', Doc? How your week been?" They would escort me gallantly to the classroom, conversing politely as any Emily Post. "Those Loyola kids behaving?" Tony would fetch chalk or see about equipment; he seized on the least opportunity to be helpful, like a hungry man grabs for food. But it wasn't Uncle Tomism. It was an expression of dignity. When a person knows he has been given something, he wants to give something in return.

As we grew more familiar, politeness gave way to kidding. "Man, you looked lame today walking across the yard!" (Tray, who else.) "Your arms be flying in every different direction like a chump. You got some important dudes in this class, people knows us, we got a reputation to uphold. And it reflects poorly on us all when you don't know how to walk!" His prescription: three nights training at O'Dell's, a local hip disco where people for-damn-sure can move. But even though I secretly got a little pissed (what's the matter with the way I walk!?) I knew this meant I was family. If they could mock the white man's gait, I could do my impression of the ghetto-blaster jive-stride and we'd laugh together. I grew up a scrawny Jewish kid, always with his (big) nose in the books. It felt good to finally be accepted by the tough boys. One of the gang.

Everyone seemed to like me, but not always each other. Tray got powerfully on H.B.'s nerves with his twenty-six-year-old arrogant pose. I'm right, I'm cool, I'm brilliant, he'd seem to say. Or he'd just say it. And then H.B.—award-winning playwright, published poet and essayist—his hand would shoot up. Whatever point Tray just made, Skinny (as everyone called H.B.) would proclaim, "I disagree!" He'd show Tray a fool a dozen ways before Sunday. Later, after H.B. got out, I'd ask him if he had any message for the class. "Yeah. Tell Tray I disagree."

And Tray felt about the same way back. H.B. had a stately slow way of talking, allowing time for his thoughts to accumulate like clouds and then rain forth in just the right words. It drove Tray nuts. That old man droning on and on, like we got nothing better to do in this prison than sit and listen to him till count-out time.

We worked it through. We talked about mutual consideration—the importance of courteously hearing out each speaker, and the need for speakers to laser in, then shut up. We instituted the three-fingered sign; if you thought someone was hogging the stage, raise three fingers and discussion stopped—we'd pause to examine class dynamics and see who was in the right. But once we had that sign we never had to use it. The inmates worked to respect each other, even draw out the quieter guys like O'Donald, a teenage killer, thrown in lock-up for repeatedly attacking guards . . . but shy.

Lashed together thusly, we embarked on an ambitious world tour of philosophy. We studied Indian karma and Chinese wu-wei, finally alighting on African philosophy and folktales. Almost all my students were black. They knew "nigger" far too well. That voice echoed in hollow caves of self-hatred and despair. They needed a stronger foundation on which to build a self: great civilizations, world-historic discoveries, a proud philosophy teaching reverence to nature, tribe, and spirit. Western thought was filled with riches, but not quite theirs. "The more information I can get about myself, my culture, my history, the more powerful I become," Donald had said. John Woodland and Selvyn were already accomplished students in African history. I scrambled for something to teach, feeling very, very white.

But around then I also began to hear a new voice, gentle yet insistent. It felt like a God-nudge. Why not tape these discussions I was finding so compelling and publish a dialogue from edited transcriptions? "No," I told myself, "it's too exploitative. It has the stench of ego. I'd just be showing off what a good guy I am, using the guys while they rot in prison." Sounds convincing. But I had learned to distrust my own voices of distrust. Yes, I get off on attention, résumé material, and head-pats. But, no, that's not the sole motivation or result. I had a number of other agendas in mind: to encourage prison teaching, capture its insights, and help give voice to men who had long been muffled. Speech echoed and faded within our classroom walls. It was a different matter when put in print: the voice multiplies a thousand fold and clambers over walls, returning in hard copy to strengthen the speaker. The prisoners were serving life sentences—I thought of *sentences serving life*.

Lingua Franca, a national magazine aimed at college teachers, actually published our first foray. I was tickled. The inmates seemed vaguely amazed at their ideas distributed to tens of thousands of people. "Oh, we've been in the newspaper a lot," Tray later said. "But not the kind of stuff you feel real good about."

In the next issue of the magazine I was accused by an angry letter-writer of "Ledering the witnesses." He said I manipulated the conversation to fit my (bleeding-heart liberal) agenda. The class vehemently disagreed, God bless 'em. They muttered, with my encouragement, about dashing off a reply. But next week when I tried to hammer home a point, Tony piped up, "Ledering the witnesses again?" It was a joke, but the issue tugged at my sleeve. I wanted to draw out and capture each person's unique voice. But if I'm asking the questions, leading discussion, and then editing the transcripts, choosing what to keep and toss, condensing speeches and cleaning up syntax, how much is it all *my voice* in disguise? Good question. All I could do was keep asking it, and not only of myself. I would show the prisoners any manuscripts before publication. It was their words, fixed up for readability, but if they thought the fixing left it phony or skewed they were free to make changes. Mostly, they said I got it right. But were they just being polite? It relates to an old issue in philosophy. When we read Socrates' trial, are we hearing his voice or Plato's words placed in a dead man's mouth? Scholars have debated this for centuries. Maybe all philosophy is dialogue—the "logos" (speech, thought, reason) that emerges in the "dia"—Greek for "across" or "between." In that case, it's never been a question of my voice or theirs, but something that emerges only in the between.

Flush with our first triumph, I suggested we work on a book together. My students enthusiastically signed on. Over the next year-and-a-half we taped some forty-five class hours, of which only a small proportion appears in this book. (See the book's appendix for some further clarification of my method.) To the edited dialogues, I also added a brief introduction to the author and excerpts from the text, under discussion. From time to time, I break in to provide a "freeze-frame" biography of one of the inmates. Every person, with the exception of one—designated as "Q"—has chosen to go on record with his true name, photo, and history (though a couple preferred to withhold the specific nature of their crimes). Q, who has been released from prison and is now working two jobs and attending graduate school, does not want the label of ex-con hung around his neck.

But what was the book to be about? Again, that would only unfold in dialogue, the speech between. But I seized the initiative to set the agenda, guided by my academic training. I was educated in the school of philosophy known as "phenomenology." A phenomenologist seeks not so much to explain as to *describe*. Select a domain of human experience—let's say that of "time"—and the first move is to put out of play (as much as possible) one's scientific, moral, and metaphysical preconceptions. We're not starting with clock-time measured by chronometers, or Einstein's relativistic theory of time. No, we're seeking to lay bare time as it's experienced. This does not flow equally as on a clock. As I wait impatiently, lived-time slows down to a crawl, then speeds up when I get busy, and even leaps to past and future as I remember and anticipate. We discover the structure of experience when we don't presume to know it in advance.

I didn't presume to know much about the life-experience of these men. Growing up a Park Avenue doctor's son, I wanted to probe the voices of an alien world. I also hoped their self-reflection would prove helpful to these men. Perhaps history so explored would not need to be repeated. But as phenomenologists together, we would not set out to explain, pronounce moral judgments, or push a certain political agenda. Our first task would be simply to describe. And to try to get it right, doing justice to the complexity and contrasting currents of life. What was it like growing up in the inner city? What dreams, what heroes walked down these childhood streets? How did the men first get involved in criminal activity? What was the structure of this world, with its drugs, guns, and power games? Once caught, how did it feel to stand before judge and jury? And during the long years of imprisonment that followed, what happens to one's experience of space and time? What unfolds between inmates and guards, blacks and whites? Then too, what forms does sexuality take in this hothouse? And how, within its confines, do people ever change? Somehow I had to reconcile that image I received of friendly, bright, college students with their history of drug-dealing, murder, and rape.

Some of what the prisoners say I never would have expected. But even more surprising to me was what I had to say. I decided to pair with each dialogue chapter my own response. My mission, at first, was largely didactic: I would highlight key points, develop implicit themes, share some of my own thoughts and experience. What I wasn't prepared for was a deepening call to tell my life-story just as I asked them to do. And in the writing itself, I discovered that the men were not as alien to me as I had thought. I, too, knew of rage and violence; of death upon death, and the guilt and remorse that follow; of long years of incarceration, even if this be in a mental jail; and of a painful/joyful struggle for freedom, coated in blood and prayer. Writing this book became part of that freedom fight. At a certain point, I was no longer doing it just for or about *them*. This was *my* story too, my prison memoir, and I had to get it out no matter what the cost.

So the final product is a structure of alternating voices, sometimes phrasing a delicate intellectual point, sometimes unleashing a howl of pain. Yet along with these present voices are many that are absent. Their silence provides an horizon for all the words in this book. For example, we don't hear from the prison authorities. No doubt, the guards, staff, and administrators have a very different perspective on life in the joint. We also miss the voice of many ordinary inmates. My class involved only an educated elite. And what of women inmates or of men incarcerated under different conditions from the one prison I entered?

Then too, there are the absent voices of those who have died. My father, mother, and brother—as I tell my family's story I wonder what they would add or delete. I can't say: I can only hope that in some way they speak through me, and would assent to my attempt to tell the truth. And what of the inmates' victims, lives cut brutally short? We hear the pain of the murderers. But the pain they have inflicted echoes back from the void, screaming in its silence.

Another absent voice is that of you, the reader. This is the silent partner to all our dialogues. Plato portrays Socrates discussing with others, exposing falsities, illuminating issues, progressing toward truth, but never arriving at "the answer." It's frustrating, but also seductive. It invites the reader to continue the quest. What do you believe? Who did you agree with, and why? What might be the answer the discussants never found? You are drawn into the dialogue. And I hope the same will happen with this book. As you hear us talk, listen to your own voice responding.

TWO VIEWS OF THE MARYLAND
PENITENTARY, BALTIMORE.

CHARLES BAXTER

Charles Baxter is in his thirteenth year of serving life plus 10 years for first-degree murder and handgun violations. You wouldn't know it to talk with him today: he seems a gentle, smiling soul, well known in prison circles for his generosity. He grew up in South Baltimore, the oldest of three boys with an absent father, a mother on welfare. From an early age he was taught how to pick-pocket, steal jewelry, and deal drugs. Where he'd been making $20 a week selling newspapers, he found he could make $100 a day "boosting" with a friend. The butt of jokes about his dark skin, glasses, and beady hair, he found that his criminal activities also helped him to feel accepted by friends. But he writes, "Most of my friends are either dead, in between [prison] bits, dying of AIDS, or on crack, coke, or dope. Nobody ever came back and told us what the future held for us."

He came to prison with a fourth-grade reading level, never having finished junior high. But since then he has worked his way through a B.S. in business sciences. Introduced to Islam when in reformatory at age 14, he later part-owned a Muslim bookstore and grocery store, and now, at age 35, is an imam (spiritual leader) of the Sunni Muslim faith. He credits Allah (and Betty, whom he married in prison) with granting him a new life.

Whatever its source, this new Charles is easygoing and warm. I've always appreciated the big smile and hug I get each week as he greets "his Jewish brother."

WAYNE BROWN

Wayne Brown, at 37, is a big burly bear of a man. Only five feet six, he weighs in at 235 pounds but with nary an ounce of fat. He is a serious weightlifter with the bulging biceps and expansive chest to prove it. A recent bill has served to ban weightlifting equipment in prison—people had visions of murderers and looters beefing up at government expense, all the better to terrorize innocent citizens upon release. Perhaps . . . but it's difficult to connect Wayne with that image. A committed Christian with a theological degree, studying to be an ordained minister, he seems placid and good-humored no matter what the provocation.

He grew up in a family of eleven, with a father who "pulled long disappearing acts," but a mother and aunt he greatly admires for struggling to bring up the huge family. Wayne does not have the career criminal history of many of the men. But he had a juvenile incarceration for attempted murder (when someone spoke ill of his mom) and, later, was sentenced for car theft. He's now in his eleventh year of a life term for rape. He claims that he's not guilty, that the victim was using the system for revenge. The jury obviously concluded otherwise.

TONY CHATMAN-BEY

When Tony Chatman-Bey was only 19 months old his grandmother took him to Beaumont, Texas. At the time both his parents were in the L.A. County Jail, his mother for prostitution, his father, a pimp and drug dealer, for pandering. From age 13 on he lived on the streets, until four years later a man named Lloyd took Tony into his home. Tony writes that along with his grandmother and daughter, "Lloyd is the only other person in this world that I have really loved. They were my positive influences, however I never really could remove myself from those negative ones that I knew in the streets."

It was there he learned to steal, and at age 22 he was jailed for two counts of armed robbery. Released after five years, he enrolled in college and worked three jobs, but as he says above, he went back to crime and was arrested again for robbery. According to Tony, he was then confused with another similar-looking man who was both a robber and a rapist. "The crazy part of this whole thing is I was given life for the rapes which I didn't do and only got twenty years for the five robberies that I did. I guess that's what they call justice."

But Tony says prison's one of the best things that have happened to him—otherwise "I'd most likely be dead now." In jail he has completed a double degree in psychology and criminal justice and sees himself as much wiser, calmer, and better off for escaping the fast track to the grave. I'd have to agree. Tony seemed the resident sage of the class, amiable in personality and thoughtful in his comments. He appears to be a man, at age 36, who's finally grown comfortable in his skin. Too bad it wasn't sooner.

JACK COWAN

Jack Cowan is a 46-year-old African American, a steady, quiet, and industrious man who helped administer the prison's college program. Maybe his discipline had early origins: he grew up with three sisters and a brother, in a strict and "well-scripted" environment, receiving constant beatings when he became rebellious. In high school, he had "intermittent forays into the world of criminal activity, but once I was in Vietnam I jumped in with both feet." He started selling drugs to other GIs and, upon return, continued dealing, supplemented by burglary. He has served twenty years so far for murder and armed robbery.

In prison, at first he was afraid to enter the college program—maybe he wouldn't, couldn't, make it. When he decided to take the risk, he found out quite the opposite. He graduated with honors and a double degree in sociology and management science and was cited four straight years in a national registry of honors students.

MICHAEL GREEN

Michael Green, 44 years old, reflects: "My childhood was typically American: I had a boxer puppy who grew up with me; I was a Cub Scout and later a Kadet." While his father worked nine-to-five (with some gambling on the side), his mother stayed home to raise the children in a mostly white neighborhood. Mike was small and frail for his age, and he first started hanging out with a local gang to prove his toughness. He broke into stores with them, then graduated directly into armed robbery. During an incarceration in the late '70s he met a convict who opened him to a new world of the mind, and he resolved to go straight. But when a friend turned him onto cocaine he relapsed: "unknown to me I had become an addict. I know if not for that my life would have been far different." He's now in the fifteenth year of a life plus 45 sentence for armed robbery and murder.

Mike looks every part the sullen tough guy. At first, he would sit in class wearing a Walkman or reading a newspaper, but with a countenance that said, "Don't mess." I didn't. But as I got to know him better, I realized here's a thoughtful man. The Walkman, the newspaper, he explained, was so he could always be taking in information even during the down times. (Down times in my class?!) He has a B.A. in sociology from Morgan State; in jail he writes poetry, plays basketball, and works with Project Turnaround.

H. B. JOHNSON JR.

H. B. Johnson Jr., 47 years old, grew up in a strict Christian home, his father a somewhat tyrannical Baptist minister. From an early age, H.B. rebelled against the harsh discipline, and as a teenager he embarked on a life of drug use and armed robberies that has brought him in and out of prison ever since. Some thirteen years ago he and a friend, high on gin and cocaine, held up an insurance agency. H. B. shot one of the employees, he says by accident. He was sentenced to 35 years for attempted murder and handgun possession, 25 of those nonparolable.

Entering prison with an eighth-grade education, H.B. studied the works of James Baldwin, Richard Wright, Albert Camus, and Samuel Beckett, and was inspired to become a writer. He would fashion and refashion his work long into the prison night, telling stories of the inner city through the poetry of jive street-talk. A slew of plays, poems, and essays spilled from his pen, and his unique voice began to gain attention in the outside world. In 1992 and 1994 he won the WMAR-TV Black Playwrights contest. Profiled on the NBC *Today* show, his work has twice been honored by the PEN American Center and it has appeared in a variety of venues.

But while in prison, during a less successful time, H.B. became HIV-positive from shooting up with a dirty needle. He has since progressed to full-blown AIDS. This, along with his writing career, became the basis of a request for commutation of sentence by the governor. But that's a story for later. . . .

O'DONALD JOHNSON

O'Donald Johnson, the "baby" of the class, just turned 20. His problems in life started early. Diagnosed at age six with a behavioral disorder, he was placed on medication and seen at numerous clinics. He made the street his primary home, fearful to be alone with a tormenting older brother. But out there he tormented others, embarking on a spree of theft, drug dealing, and armed robbery. By the time he was 13 he had done time in seven different juvenile facilities. But "no matter who I took my anger out on, the true anger inside of me was not quenched." And I'm not sure it is yet. Now serving a 55-year sentence for first-degree murder committed at age 15, O'Donald has been in and out of solitary lock-up for his aggressive behavior.

But changes have begun. In prison, he's become religiously inclined and an avid reader, hungry to learn. He's completed his GED. If he still steals, it's now mainly books for his shelf. I marvel at O'Donald: he seems so innocent for one so guilty, so young for the past he's accumulated. I hope he has a future.

ARLANDO (TRAY) JONES III

Arlando (Tray) Jones III is a tall and slender 26-year-old. (The "Tray" refers to the fact that he's the III'rd.) When he was just 18 months old, his father was killed by the police; thereafter he was raised by his aunt and grandmother. As a pre-teen, he became involved in dealing drugs for the money, power, and acceptance. Unlike some of the other guys, early on he decided on a criminal career and never wavered. His greatest dream was to become a successful gangster. But he didn't get too far; at age 16 he began serving life plus 20 years for first-degree and second-degree murder related to drugs. (As he wrote me from solitary, "It's times such as now that overwhelm me with regret . . . being a gangster isn't going too well.")

He's developed a different side of himself in prison. Performing at the top of his class, he's completed a B.A. in psychology; co-directs Project Turnaround (in which problem kids are brought into the prison to discourage them from crime); and is the head of the Inmate Advisory Council.

As you'll see, Tray likes to play the cynic, showing other prisoners why they're full of bull. In contrast, he's quick to proclaim his own genius, good looks, and general greatness. But always with a smile. Does he mean it? Or is he mocking his own ego, ever the jokester? Some of both, I think. But he always makes me laugh. And his personal letters betray a softer, even modest, side he goes to great lengths to hide.

DONALD THOMPSON

Donald Thompson, 38 years old, grew up in a row house with his parents and six siblings. He was a good kid and excelled in school: his father, despite a drinking and gambling problem, helped him with his studies every night and even made them seem fun. But his father was murdered outside their house when Donald was 12. Life took a marked turn for the worse. "Unfortunately, my mentors became drug dealers, sneak-thieves, stick-up boys, would-be pimps, etc." Donald embarked on a life that included "almost every crime imaginable," most drug-related. He's now serving life plus 100 years for armed robbery, attempted murder, and murder in the first degree.

As with many of the other men, things only turned around once he was in prison. There Donald converted to Islam. "It gave me the strength to see the monster I had become," to pray for forgiveness and seek to make amends. A Twelve Step program helped him kick a 15-year heroin habit and then earn his B.S. in management science.

The Donald I know today seems a warm but introspective man. He spoke of our class as a kind of therapy; he wanted to explore and purge any violence left in him and would approach me through letters or personal chats. I still sensed the 12-year-old boy in there, seeking healing, frozen at the moment of his father's death. Maybe that's why I feel particularly close to him.

SELVYN TILLETT

Selvyn Tillett is a 35-year-old Muslim. Once a black nationalist skeptical about studying with a white teacher, he has mellowed over the years, and I've found him a gracious and friendly man. He grew up in the Central American country of Belize, raised by his grandmother and aunt who were strict Jehovah's Witnesses. As a teenager he "started to crave the other life outside the church. First came the girls . . . then came the drugs . . . and then came the guns. After that, everything fell apart." Jailed regularly for smaller crimes, he is now in his fourteenth year of a life plus 20 sentence.

In jail, he not only has pursued his college degree, but has become a good poet and essayist and editor of a prison journal. Renewed relations with his family seem to have sparked a fire of hope and transformation. After years of rebellion against his religious upbringing, he's even turning into a praying man again.

JOHN WOODLAND

John Woodland's life started out pretty good. He came from a middle-class African American family, his father a dentist, his mother a schoolteacher. But his father died when he was 12, and his mother, who became an alcoholic, passed away six years later, leaving John "an angry self-centered person." His criminal career began when he was 13 with shoplifting, breaking into warehouses and flatcars, and dealing drugs.

While continuing to sell drugs (marijuana, pills, heroine, cocaine), John pursued success in the legitimate world. He was cruising through Morgan State University and had a law school acceptance in hand when he was incarcerated. His intention had been to use his criminal activities to build a nest egg for the law school years. But that never happened. Now 39 years old, he's in the twelfth year of a life sentence for first-degree murder related to drugs.

Since entering prison, John has completed his college degree in management science, and developed, along with Tray, into one of the prison leaders. He co-directs Project Turnaround, tutors in the school, and teaches within the Muslim community. Of all my students, he seems one of the most serious and self-motivated, assigning himself extensive study programs. If Tray likes to play court jester, John values his dignity. If Tray is upbeat, John can get downhearted, I suspect especially when he thinks about his three kids growing up without a father. But a friendly gesture, or a good debate, pulls him out of himself and you discover a man fiercely alive.

Back row: O'Donald Johnson, Donald Thompson, Michael Green, Wayne Brown, John Woodland, Selvyn Tillett. *Front row*: Tony Chatman-Bey, Arlando (Tray) Jones III, Drew Leder, Charles Baxter. *(Not in the photo*: Jack Cowan, Gary Huffman, H. B. Johnson Jr., Mark Medley, Q.)

PART ONE

Power

CHAPTER TWO

Fields of Force

Simone Weil was a French philosopher and religious thinker who lived from 1909 to 1943. André Gide called her "the most spiritual writer of this century." An intellectual par excellence, Weil was also passionately committed to social justice. Her thinking was shaped by a Christian sensibility deepened by mystical experience.

Her essay "The Iliad, Poem of Might" was published in 1940–41. On the surface, it is an exploration of the centrality of force in Homer's epic. However, it was also addressed to her French compatriots living under Nazi occupation. (She was to die in London in 1943 after refusing to eat any more than the scanty rations given in occupied France; her death was ruled a suicide from self-starvation.) This essay treats in depth the rule of force in human affairs—its ability both to intoxicate the one with power and to dehumanize the victim. As such, it seemed an appropriate vehicle to use in exploring the role of force in the prisoners' lives.

Power Makes You Stupid

He who possesses strength moves in an atmosphere which offers him no resistance. Nothing in the human element surrounding him is of a nature to induce, between the intention and the act, that brief interval where thought may lodge. Where there is no room for thought, there is no room either for justice or prudence. This is the reason why men of arms behave with such harshness and folly. . . . They never guess as they exercise their power, that the consequences of their acts will turn back upon themselves. (Simone Weil, "The *Iliad*, Poem of Might," 163)

Tray: I used to have this aura from being in so many gun battles. I could be dead wrong but people would do what I wanted because they feared me. "You can't sell nothing in this neighborhood—you're on my turf!" It made me feel *grand.*

Drew: It sounds almost like a drug you get high on.

Tray: Indeed.

13

John: Once I whipped a guy who had treated me wrong in a drug deal. When you get into that kind of rage it shocks everybody. I could see the looks on everyone's faces, watching. And for me, it was a mixed feeling. You like the respect. You don't worry about guys pushing you around. But you see people looking at you different than they would a normal person. And that didn't make me feel particularly good.

Tony: Another thing—if you're smart, then in the back of your mind you know that sooner or later somebody's going to want that power you have. The only way you get to be king is to knock the king off. That's why you have a lot of killing out there.

John: But there's also another side to it—in a hostile environment sometimes you need force just to survive. People will set out in increments to take advantage of you until you draw a line in the sand. If you draw that line you might be able to live out your existence peacefully. I don't know if this environment would be considered the same as the one the Trojan War was set in—I don't think so. But growing up in hostile environments, we had to make it clear that some things couldn't be done to me nor my family.

Tray: It's like when you come through this penitentiary door, if you have a reputation of being soft, people will take your commissary stuff and kick you in the butt. But if you draw the line in the sand, you can live peacefully. And it's the same on the street. Even for the judge in his courtroom, the president of the country, the business man—for anyone to enjoy their life anywhere, they have to embody some kind of force.

But Weil's right that power makes you stupid. I could relate to what she said but I didn't like it. I was thirteen or fourteen when I was made to believe I had more power than I actually had. Older men feared me. If I told somebody "Run here! Do this!" people *obeyed.* I started feeling bigger than God. I wouldn't pay my associates. I would go to Atlantic City and blow fifty grand, mess up my partners on sharing the money. I could do whatever I wanted and wasn't nobody going to buck my authority.

I didn't see it at the time but I was losing their loyalty. So when I came to prison, when I met a power bigger than me ("I fought the law and the law won"), I needed them and they weren't there for me. Because when I had the power I would talk to 'em *greasy.*

If somebody had had a force greater than mine, I would have *considered*—considered before going to the crap parlors, to the motels with prostitutes, messing everybody up. But I did whatever I wanted because couldn't nobody stop me. Power makes you stupid.

I'm not saying it isn't true. I just resent her saying it.

Drew: It's not a truth you enjoy contemplating.

Tray: There you go.

Donald: When I was thirteen I beat a guy with a two-by-four. I think I was intoxicated with that experience because I overdid it. I beat him unconscious. And the thing is, while I was beating him I felt sorry for him in a way. But I just continued.

John: I remember starting to make a lot of money in drugs, and that money really gets you intoxicated. You have at your disposal most things you want. And when my trial date came up I just said, kindly and politely, "Call my lawyer and bail bondsman, call the judge, and tell them *I'm not coming in.*" It was around Christmas so I thought I'll stay out and take care of my kids. *After* Christmas we'll talk about coming in.

So legally speaking I was a fugitive from the law, wanted on a capital offense. But I still ran around and did my business. If police pulled me over—at that time they weren't so hot on photo ID cards—all I had to do was tell a person's name, address, driver's license number, and they would check it and let me go.

And it got to a point where I was intoxicated with what I was doing. I paid no mind to the fact that I was a fugitive. Where initially I would lay in the house all day, only coming out at night, eventually I just did what I wanted. Went to all the clubs, visited my family, stopped going from hotel to hotel, and just stayed in one. I stopped being cautious.

One day I went to visit my daughter in Pittsburgh, drove back, and went to sleep in a hotel room. The police woke me up. I wasn't really interested in staying out much longer because I was meeting my goals— but I could have if I hadn't become so ignorant. I was saying "Stuff that may apply to everyday persons no longer applies to me. *I'm above that.*"

Drew: There was an article in the *New York Times* last Sunday. The basic theme was that criminals are *dumb*, to put it bluntly. Like the two people who shot Michael Jordan's father—they took his cell phone and made calls that were easily traceable. Why would they behave in this fashion? The article said it's because most criminals haven't made it in life and, honestly, are not that bright.

But as I listen to you talk I hear a different analysis. Maybe it's not that these guys were stupid, but that they were intoxicated by being able to blow someone away. You begin to lose the sense of your own mortality and vulnerability. It's as if you're in a magically protected place.

Selvyn: Yeah. I lived in a black community surrounded by all-white, where we got into a lot of scrapes with white guys, making them walk in the mud, or just outright attacking them. One morning I had nothing better to do than walk up to a guy's house and kick the door in. It wasn't like I was trying to rob him—I just wanted to kick the door in and walk all through the house.

When the police came, I was one of the spectators watching them look for the person. I stood there laughing, and asked them, "Did you *see* it?

Did you *catch* him?" And I knew they were looking for me! I did get caught eventually, but at that time I felt invincible.

Drew: As Simone Weil says, that sense of unlimited power is what ultimately leads people to overreach themselves. In the *Iliad,* first Agamemnon goes too far, and then Achilles, then Patroclus, then Hector. Everybody, all the invincible warriors, fall victim to a kind of drunkenness that leads them one step over the boundaries of their power.

Tray: Weil says everybody's going to succumb to force. But you still have to make up your mind what side of it you want to be on. The victim or victimizer.

Drew: You'd still prefer to be on the victimizer side?

Tray: Indeed!

Under the Thumb

Might is that which makes a thing of anybody who comes under its sway. When exercised to the full, it makes a thing of man in the most literal sense, for it makes him a corpse. . . . The might which kills outright is an elementary and coarse form of might. How much more varied in its devices, how much more astonishing in its effects is that other which does not kill, or which delays killing. It must surely kill, or it will perhaps kill, or else it is only suspended above him whom it may at any moment destroy. This of all procedures turns a man to stone. From the power to transform him into a thing by killing him there proceeds another power, and much more prodigious, that which makes a thing of him while he still lives. . . . The soul was not made to dwell in a thing, and forced to it, there is no part of that soul but suffers violence. (Weil, "The *Iliad,* Poem of Might," 153–55)

Drew: This passage raises the question of what happens when you're totally under the power of another, feeling force bearing down upon you. When have you been in that position?

Donald: I was playing in the street and a guy in his car almost hit one of my friends. We started pounding on the car, and I stuck my head in and started cussin' at him. He pulled a gun, put it directly on my head, and said, "*I could kill you right now.*" And it was like my whole world was suspended. I never felt that feeling before in my life.

It seemed like I was there for a long period before my friend (he tells me) pulled me out of the car and the guy continued on.

I think I did become a corpse at that time. Since then I've tried my best to make sure that *nobody* is in a position to bring that much force on me. I tried to carry a gun most of my life so if I was placed in that situation I'd be able to bring equal force.

O'Donald: One time I was banked. Now before they banked me, about fifteen of them surrounded me in a circle.

Drew: You were what? Banked?

Tony: Operationally defined, jumped on by more than one person.

O'Donald: When you get banked, they don't really jump on you. *They wait a few minutes.* And this was the scary part for me, the waiting. After they jumped on me, the fright was gone and the anger took over. But as I was getting banked, though I was helpless I felt power because it took fifteen people to jump on one man. That tells me I'm a *threat,* that alone they wouldn't have a chance. So I felt powerful and also, at the same time, powerless.

Tray: Every time I came under a greater force, it kind of angered me. In here a couple of times, I had an altercation with the police in the kitchen and they dragged me out and threw me in the cell, and each time I felt humiliated. So I never let it happen again.

And then there was times when I tried to establish a [drug] shop in a certain neighborhood and dudes would tell me I had to go. They'd be so much more powerful than my crew that we'd move. But I'd say, "Never again. It can't happen again." I didn't feel scared. The only thing I been afraid of was this could happen again.

Like once a guy had a shotgun on me. When you're looking through the barrel you can actually see the bullet. And the shotgun was cocked. I noticed all this but it seemed like I stepped outside my body. I thought, "Goddamn chump! This ain't supposed to happen to *me.* I'm a king!" And I tried to make my life where I won't ever have to go through that again.

Right now I'm under this force, and I feel the strength of it everyday, every time I look at them bars. The humiliation of it—shit, I feel it. And all I think of is I *never* want to go through it again. That's why I study so hard. I study economics, psychology, everything, so I'll know the ways of the world and I won't have to succumb to this might again.

Drew: It's a different kind of power from the kind you were seeking out on the street. It's not the power you got from selling drugs or having guns.

Tray: No, it's the *same* power. It's the same power, but I went for it the wrong way. I think everybody's searching for everlasting peace, happiness, financial security. And that's all I wanted. You know, the respect of my peers, being able to protect my loved ones, that's all I ever wanted. But I used the drugs and all that stuff to do it. Now I don't have to. All I have to do is know how to function inside American society, to become an educated person who can make it in *your* ring.

Selvyn: For me, the most helpless I ever felt was about halfway through my trial. It hit me: "You're going to jail. It don't matter what you do or what you say to these people. You're going to jail for a *long time.*" The attorney, he turned his back on the judge and laughed. He said, "I don't care whether you did it or not, you going." From then on, I just gave up. The next four years was the lowest part of my life.

I had cut my family loose; I didn't call or write them or nothing. But one day I got a letter in the mail. It was my sister and she said, "I'm look-ing for my big brother. Regardless of what happened in your past I still love you. If you're that person, call me and let me know. If you're *not*, write or call to let me know you're not my brother so I can continue look-ing." That's basically what the letter said. And I was touched. That was like a light at the end of the tunnel.

I started pulling myself up by my bootstraps. All the drugs, I stopped all that, and smoking cigarettes and messing around. I realized, hey, there is something for me to live for. Now the light keeps getting closer and closer, and as it does I'm getting some of my humanity back.

John: What Selvyn said brought something to mind. For me, and I guess for a lot of African American men, coming in contact with police and the criminal justice system is really where we see ourselves most powerless. The first time I can remember this is in high school. Two security guards walked up to me and told me, "Where're you going?" And I said, "I've been suspended. I have to leave the school." And they said, "Nah, you don't go to this school." And one of them knew I did. He was the main one that grabbed me. I was struggling with them and they picked me up and slammed my face into the wall. I had to turn, hoping that my nose didn't get broken. And that's when I began having a problem with the justice system.

As I got older, when I was up to something wrong I never felt that what the police were doing was out of hand. But I remember times I was just walking, ain't doing nothing, and the police would pull their guns out and yell "Freeze!" One of them would have a gun to my head and was patting me down against the wall. That's a very miserable feeling—I know from experience that it don't take anything for a gun to go off.

But the worst was like Selvyn said. When I was convicted—and I'm not going to argue the innocence or guilt aspect of it—I knew in that situation that I'm being taken advantage of and *there's nothing I can do.* The jury comes back and says you're guilty. You want to say, "Wait a minute! All the facts didn't come up. Everybody listen!" But you can't do that. You got to sit there and accept it.

When I was walking out of the courtroom, my son's mother looked at me and I could see her kind of cry. I said, "Don't do that. Don't let these people see you cry. That's the *last* thing you want to do." When you come out of the neighborhoods we're from, you learn you can't show weakness. But this all had such an impact on me that I remember sitting in diagnos-tic for ninety days. I felt like I'd been beaten with a baseball bat. I didn't have no physical bruises, but I just lost the will to live. I couldn't think. I kept putting on a front, but inside I was walking around in a daze. I could not put two and two together to save my life. Any suggestion that popped up in the air, like a rope to life, I was ready to grab it. But inside, I said, "Man, you done *lost* something here."

Karmic Forces

Thus it is that those to whom destiny lends might, perish for having relied too much upon it . . . they go beyond the measure of their strength, inevitably so, because they do not know its limit . . . and here they are, exposed, naked before misfortune without that armour of might which protected their souls, without anything any more to separate them from tears. . . . This retribution, of a geometric strictness . . . punishes automatically the abuse of strength. . . . (Weil, "The *Iliad*, Poem of Might," 164)

Drew: Simone Weil says that exactly the same kind of thing you experienced under the foot of the criminal justice system—powerless, delivered over, your life taken away—would reflect back the same power you inflicted on others as a criminal. This retribution is called *karma* in the East. What do you think about this concept of karmic payback?

John: I can understand it in an individual sense. I may have done things that then come back. But the criminal justice institution does these things and never experiences them back. Being part of the system lets you abuse so many others but walk away looking a hero.

Drew: Well, Simone Weil would probably say that the people who are misusing their force in that fashion—it could be cops, maybe there are guards here—

John: Prosecutors, judges, everybody. . . .

Drew: —that they, in turn, at some point will fall victim to force. They too will receive a karmic payback.

John: That's something we never see.

Donald: When John was talking I was thinking about the first experience I had with the criminal justice system. I couldn't imagine anything I perpetrated on anyone so terrible to suffer the kind of pain I experienced in that courtroom. It's like each day they take a part of your soul away. After my trial, I had to—it's hard to even find words to articulate it—I had to reestablish my humanity all over. I had to sell myself that I was worth something. The last day of the trial, the sentencing, they got all these different names for you.

Drew: What kind of names?

Selvyn: Heinous monster.

Donald: That's one of their favorites—heinous monster. The judges use that when they're sentencing you. So I had to rename myself.

Drew: Ordinarily when we think of force, as in the Weil article, we're thinking about *physical* force. But this brings up the idea that certain things that are non-physical, like words, are also embodiments of force that can do violence to an individual.

Charles: Y'all talking about names—in court they called me a "notorious gangster," Charles "Lucky Luciano." And for a while I actually tried to live that name out. But now I'm at a point in my life where I hate that name. It's a dead person's name and I'm not a dead man at all. I'm well and alive.

But you know there's something that happened to me, Doc. When I was about fifteen, right, I followed this woman all the way up to Eastern Avenue and snatched her pocketbook. And man, this woman screamed and hollered. Out of all the robberies that I ever did in my life, sometimes when I make my prayers I think about that woman. I say, "God, *please* forgive me." And that's been almost twenty years ago.

Wayne: I only recall one instance like that; this old lady, she had asked me to see whether her watch was ticking. She said her husband had bought it for her a long time ago. When I got the watch, I took off with it but in the process of running, something began to tell me "This is wrong." Later, I come to find out it's a *conscience.* We've been talking about going through the legal system—but, you know, your conscience has a built-in legal system. If you do wrong it's always nagging until you straighten it out.

And so in the process of running I felt like a victim to some unidentified force. I didn't know what was going on, but it had me in its grasp. I had to stop, think, run back. This force was growing so much, there was nothing I could do. I went all the way back, but the lady wasn't there. I wondered how many buses took off within the last five minutes. I knew if I felt the weight of this force now, imagine what it's going to be like if I never catch this woman! I chased down four buses. When I found her and returned the watch she said, "Oh thank you. You're so kind, young man."

Drew: So that's also a different force from the physical one Weil focuses on—a *spiritual* force or a *moral* force of conscience. In this case, instead of it robbing us of our humanity, it restores our humanity.

Wayne: But the two forces can work the same way. If you're afraid—you're surrounded by people and about to be pounded on—it causes you to sweat, your heart to palpitate. The force on the inside does the same thing. It causes you to *sweat.*

CHAPTER THREE

Victim / Victimizer

Donald mentions a gun pointing straight at his head. John speaks of another, wielded by cops. Tray goes one step further: he can even see the bullet. And it doesn't seem to matter whose hand the gun is in. An irate motorist, a suspicious cop, a drug dealer—same thing. A gun trained at your head makes such subtleties fade.

These men had come under the rule of force. Here was a moment when all the forces circulating in their lives had crystallized into a single diamond-like node that would leave its mark forever. As Tray says, "I tried to make my life where I won't ever have to go through that again." He would fight force with force. But his response brought what he most feared upon him. Now a man hovers above him in the guard tower with a shotgun, perhaps for the rest of his life. Sometimes our worst nightmares come true.

Does that make Tray and his fellow inmates victims? According to the dictionary, a victim is a person who suffers from a destructive or injurious action or agency. These men clearly had so suffered. For many of them, inner-city streets, busted-up families, impoverished schools, all had taken their expectable toll. Prison was but the fuller expression of such confining forces.

And it's hard not to see a racial dimension to this victimization. Most, though not all, of the inmates I taught were black, not surprising in Baltimore, a city with a black majority. John says, "For me, and I guess for a lot of African American men, coming in contact with police and the criminal justice system is really where we see ourselves most powerless." He's not kidding about "a lot of African American men." Fully one-third of black men between twenty and twenty-nine are caught up in the criminal justice system, whether incarcerated or on work release, parole, or probation. An astounding figure. If you're black in the United States, you're eight times more likely to end up in prison, at some point, than if white. Or to put the figures in perspective, our country jails its blacks at a *fourfold greater rate than South Africa under apartheid.* Whether you deem this the result of discriminatory sentencing, or of the poverty, restricted opportunity, and despair that drive so many African Americans to crime, it's hard not to see in such figures a pattern of racial victimization. But whatever the ultimate causes of their crimes, the men I taught were not simply victims. They were *victimizers* as well. Through their criminal activity these men had brutally violated others. Most, I knew, had *killed.*

Victim/victimizer. I had been trained to see these as irreconcilable opposites. The victim is in a relatively powerless position; the victimizer is a possessor of force. The victim suffers; the victimizer perpetrates an injury. The victim is worthy of compassion; the victimizer is deserving of contempt. Like light and dark, good and evil, the two terms gain meaning by their opposition. But how then should I react to meeting these men, who seemed to me victims and victimizers both?

It is wondrous what the mind can do in the face of seeming contradiction. Denial is always an option—make one side of the contradiction go away. And I was guilty of that, I admit. The problem was I *liked* these guys. I liked it when Charley gave me a big hug, showed me pictures of his wife, called me his "main man." I liked Tray's curious mixture of the Ego-from-Hell and self-deprecating humor. I liked Wayne's cheerful Christianity, and John's fierce intelligence, which he used like a knife for stripping arguments to the bone. In one way or another I liked them all.

This made it easier to see these men as victims and to blank out the other side. Though I knew they were in for serious offenses, I usually didn't inquire too much about these. Then too, there seemed an unbridgeable gap between the men I saw now and their criminal histories. Mark, who appeared such a gentle soul and scholar, was in for a double murder. Whither the difference, I wondered? Was it getting off drugs? Undergoing religious conversion? The fact that we were meeting in a guarded classroom rather than on the mean streets? Whatever, I found myself experiencing more of compassion than condemnation.

But should I have? Within my mind, a cynic kept blasting away at the bleeding-heart liberal within. "You're such best buddies with these guys, so concerned for their plight. Cruel prison system. Poor victims of racism and poverty. But what about the folks they terrorized? The kids dead from crack? The merchants looted? People snatched from the street, a gun held to their head? And the bleeding corpses after your buddies pulled the trigger? What about those corpses? Where's your compassion for them?"

The voice was right, I couldn't deny it. I didn't focus much energy on compassion for these crime victims. It made me feel almost complicitous in their murder. But I attribute it to something other than moral failing: maybe a failure of imagination. The word compassion means to "suffer with." And it was simply easier for me to suffer with the prisoners (and they with themselves and each other) than with their victims. After all, I knew these guys. I could see the harshness of their confinement and the ghetto neighborhoods they had walked. I could hear their tangled stories unweave themselves in pain. Perhaps the book's reader will find himself or herself in the same position. It's harder to imagine the unspoken tales of the dead victims. Gone, they are gone. My imagination remains woefully insufficient. Maybe when I myself am terrorized, or a loved one, God forbid, I will better know.

I would get a glimpse crossing the prison yard. That guy over there throwing the football—if I were alone in a dark alley with him, what might he have done? How about this mean-looking skinny dude, or that weight-lifter type? Suddenly I would realize myself surrounded by two hundred men who in other circumstances might have slit my throat. It was the luxury of my protected surroundings, guards everywhere, that enabled me to feel disdain for the guards and open my heart to killers. I was artificially safe. So artificially compassionate.

As I had my mental blank-spots, so did the prisoners. They often seemed to minimize their crimes. I wondered why and came up with several theories. Perhaps acts of violence appeared inevitable within their world. After all, people sometimes refer to the inner city as a "war zone." And as Tolstoy writes,

> The aim of war is murder, the methods of war are spying, treachery, and their encouragement, the ruin of a country's inhabitants, robbing them or stealing to provision the army, and fraud and falsehood termed military craft. The military life is characterized by absence of freedom, that is, discipline, idleness, ignorance, cruelty, debauchery and drunkenness. And in spite of all this it is the highest class, respected by everyone . . . and he who kills most people receives the highest rewards. (*War and Peace*, Book 3, Part 2, Chapter 25, p. 831)

Such is the power of war's field of force, whether in the *Iliad* or the inner city. Good and evil become ambiguous or reversed.

Then too, I think many of the prisoners experienced what could be called the "fallacy of intention." They looked inside themselves and did not find some kind of malicious, hateful intent we've all come to associate with the *bad man.* "I was just doing what I had to. I didn't want to hurt anybody." But there's no limit to the evil that men can perpetrate with a sense of justification in their hearts. You can't judge the act by reference to how you *feel.*

I think a time factor also comes into play. You blow someone away in an instant, only to receive a life sentence. Fifty years behind stone walls for one flick of the trigger finger? It seems wrong that something so evanescent should be punished in such an enduring way. Sure, one can intellectually grasp the logic. One can point out the equal years of life, and more, the murderer rips away from the victim. But perhaps it will always feel to the perpetrator that this argument rests on a sleight of hand. How can you weigh what *doesn't* exist (the dead man's might-have-been future) against what certainly *does* exist (my life wasting away in prison)?

Yet, truly, these men were victimizers. They had willingly engaged in violent crime. But just as truly, I believe, many of these men were victims, subject to injurious forces throughout their lives. What happens when you try to hold both perspectives at once? Like the optical illusion created by a Necker cube, you see first one cube-face, then the other, leaping out of the page. It's almost impossible to view both together.

But unless we do, our sight remains partial. Just see the *victim* and you arrive at what might be called the "liberal fallacy." Taken to the limit, this is the notion that a human being has no free will, bears no responsibility for choices, but is simply a victim of external forces. We've seen this defense in some well-publicized trials. Abuse, or TV violence, or Twinkies, or racism *made me do it.* We want to say, "No, own your own acts."

But on the other hand, to see just the *victimizer* is to arrive at what might be called a "conservative fallacy." This is the notion that we as individuals are wholly responsible for the course of our life. If *you* ended up a criminal and *I* became an upstanding Loyola College professor, it is because of your depravity and my moral superiority. The more I spoke with the prisoners, the more this contrast seemed simplistic. I shared the same human drives and dreams as did the inmates. If I had been subject to the same web of forces they were caught in, I was doubtful that I, myself, would have escaped.

If I saw these men only as victimizers, I could not understand or feel compassion for their lives. But if I see them only as helpless victims, I was robbing them of responsibility. Either view reduces a human being to something less.

The truth, I believe, is that humans can be victim/victimizers; that we often abuse in precisely the areas and ways we have ourselves been abused. A large proportion of sex crimes are perpetrated by those who were sexually violated. Most child abusers were abused as children. How to loathe the victimizer and feel compassion for the victim when we discover they are one and the same? For violence, finally, is circular. A man grows up in violent circumstances. He adopts violent measures to survive and escape. He is caught and subjected to violent punishment. Embittered, he leaves with violence in his heart. Shall the circle ever go unbroken? What power is capable of setting us free?

CHAPTER FOUR

Hooked on Power

Friedrich Nietzsche (1844–1900) is considered one of the most significant and controversial philosophers of the modern era. Recognized early for his genius, he was awarded a professorship at the University of Basel when just twenty-four. Ten years later he resigned for reasons of poor health (he suffered from horrendous migraines and digestive problems), and to pursue his writing. During the next decade, in a fit of productivity interrupted by constant illness, he wrote a number of famous works including Thus Spake Zarathustra *and* Beyond Good and Evil. *In 1889 he suffered a mental collapse, possibly from syphilitic infection. He was thereafter cared for by his family, remaining an insane invalid until his death.*

Nietzsche fiercely criticized Judeo-Christian morality and religion, regarding its values as sickly and hypocritical. In his later work, he develops the hypothesis that, although it takes many forms, there is a single basic drive dominating all human beings, even all life—the will to power. Using this notion, I explore with the inmates the complex ways power plays out in the world of drugs and prisons.

Dealers and Addicts

Not necessity, not desire—no, the love of power is the demon of men. Let them have everything—health, food, a place to live, entertainment—they are and remain unhappy and low-spirited: for the demon waits and waits and will be satisfied. Take everything from them and satisfy this, and they are almost happy—as happy as men and demons can be.

The striving for distinction keeps a constant eye on the next man and wants to know what his feelings are: but the empathy which this drive requires for its gratification is far from being harmless or sympathetic or kind. We want, rather, to perceive or divine how the next man outwardly or inwardly *suffers* from us, how he loses control over himself and surrenders to the impressions our hand or even merely the sight of us makes upon him; and even when he who strives after distinction makes and wants to make a joyful, elevating or cheerful impression, he nonetheless enjoys this success not inasmuch as he has given joy to the next man or elevated or cheered him, but inasmuch as he has *impressed* himself on the

25

soul of the other, changed its shape and rules over it at his own sweet will. (Friedrich Nietzsche, *A Nietzsche Reader,* 221, 217–18; aphorisms from *Daybreak,* sections 262 and 113)

Drew: Nietzsche is presenting a thesis here that's sometimes called "the will to power." Among other things, it's a philosophical or a psychological doctrine that all human activities are really motivated by a drive to gain and experience *power*—not just survival, wealth, sexual pleasure, or whatever else you might consider most important. Let's explore and test Nietzsche's theory a bit; see if we agree or disagree with it and whether we can gain insight from it about our behavior.

Were the criminal activities that you personally engaged in motivated by the will to power?

H.B.: I suppose in all cultures we have what's called crimes of attraction. So in the African American culture, dope dealing became the crime of attraction—years ago it was, perhaps, chicken stealing, then bootlegging, now drug dealing. The money's good. The money is *extremely* good. Then you can tell yourself, "Well, I'm not making anybody take it. If I don't sell it somebody else will." All these little trapdoors where one thinks one can find some escape from responsibility.

Then people can take the drug and live a wonderful illusion that says everything's alright. I know personally from using cocaine that when you inject it you feel like a king. Everything is fine in the whole universe. I don't care what you going through, I don't care how bad it is, when that drug hits your system you're a winner.

I don't think anyone who has ever sold drugs, who has turned people on with the intent to get them hooked, was not in a quest for power. And I don't think that anybody who's ever used drugs was not on a quest for power too—the power of independence, self-realization, joy. So there's so many different power plays all twisted up in there.

Tray: When you're a dealer, nobody gives you more power than the dope fiend. But my pride and power also came from my family. I come from a household where the finances wasn't there, especially when the primary caregiver in my household, who was my aunt, was strung out on narcotics. She eventually died from an overdose in '89. When my father passed away, I went to live with her and her two daughters who was like my sisters. And when Christmas came around, or birthdays, I was able to make them feel happy. With the money from drugs I got them extravagant gifts, and I felt so much pride and power from being able to pay all the bills in the house. Okay, I'm not doing good in school—but here I'm a giant, I'm a *king.*

John: I think, for most people, the initial involvement in crime has more to do with economics than the will to power. You're poor. You can't meet your bills. You don't see anyone concerned about your plight so you decide, "Hey, I don't owe these people *anything.* If I have to get on top by stepping on a couple of them then I'm going to do it, because people are stepping on *me.*" You're just trying to get some money.

But once you see the power you have, it becomes addictive. You can't see yourself anymore just being the everyday person, the *powerless* person. You become addicted to people looking for you, seeing if you have drugs, and recognizing you 'cause of the clothes you wear, the car you drive. Then the will to power keeps you involved.

But I don't think the dealer's really got the power: the power is the *drug.* 'Cause whatever direction it goes, that's where the power goes. They can like me today because I got something that's smoking, but tomorrow it might fall off and the other guy's got the power 'cause he has the drug.

Tony: When I started into drugs I was basically doing a favor for my father. He had just got out of the federal penitentiary and had a rap sheet. I'd just got out of the service, clean as a whistle, so he wanted me to sell drugs for him. I was his front. But like the guys say, after a while the money gets so good, and when you see some of the things people'll do for drugs, you get hooked yourself.

Like I remember there was a young lady came to my house about three in the morning for Quaaludes. In Texas they sold for fifteen dollars a piece. And she had fifteen dollars' worth of change. So I joked, "Damn, girl, what'd you do? Rob your little boy's piggy bank?" And she said, "Yes." She was serious. I was like, "Damn, you taking your own kid's money for dope?" I kicked her out of the house. I wouldn't even sell to her. But, see, that's the power. I could do that. I could afford to do it. Because I knew as soon as she walked out the door. . . .

After I got out of jail in Texas I came back to Maryland, and for the first six months all I did was work. I had three jobs and made about three, four hundred dollars a week. When I was selling drugs I made that in an hour! So it wasn't long before I was selling a little dope here, doing a little robbery there. 'Cause you do, you get hooked on that prestige, that money, and that power the fast money brings.

H.B: Thinking about the will to power of the criminal, something very significant popped out in me: there's a difference between a *criminal* and a *fool.* I sit up here wondering why I just don't feel that some of the younger guys in here are criminals. They weren't criminals, man, they were fools. Some older guy grabbed the kid when he was about twelve and groomed him, right? Used him, had him running around breaking the law. You know, he's only a juvenile: "Get caught, all they'd do is take you down to the station and call your mother to come and pick you up. But if they catch me doing this same act they'd lock me up and throw the key away." The older guy is the criminal. But this kid is just out there *playing.*

Tray: I can respect what H.B. says. I'm the quintessential youngster he spoke about. But even before I started doing what I was doing, I knew the consequences. I knew that if I killed people I'd get life in prison. Being a youngster don't make you a fool.

John: These kids are being used—they have no concept of the total picture. But we counsel a lot of kids, and we see that once they're involved they get the will to power. At the Narcotics Anonymous program, older drug addicts tell us how different it is now with these young kids. They're completely on a power trip, the way they talk to you, the way they carry their guns. But when they finally run into the justice system, they turn up little kids again. Wanting protection, wanting comfort, wanting their mommy! For the last year or so you been out there acting like Adolf Hitler or Attila the Hun, now all of a sudden you want your mommy? Naw. *You're going to prison.*

Tony: I agree. Look at the way the new breed of drug dealers handle their business. Like these drive-by shootings. You got a beef with someone about his corner and instead of walking up there like in the old days to fight him or stab him, you gonna stand thirty feet across the street with a semi-automatic rifle and just Derrrrrrrr! Don't care what you hit. There's a baby sitting on the front porch trying to play jacks, and this fool across the street with an AK-47 sprayin'. If that ain't a power trip I don't know what it is.

O'Donald: I'll be in defense of the young 'uns. We learned this from you older guys. We want to be noticed, we want people to see us and say, "I know him." So if the older guys did it a certain way, we say, "Well, damn, if we do it *this way*, we can get even more noticed."

Tony: You got that!

Prison Power

> The first effect of happiness is the *feeling of power:* this wants to *express itself,* either to us ourselves, or to other men, or to ideas or imaginary beings. The most common modes of expression are: to bestow, to mock, to destroy—all three out of a common basic drive. (Nietzsche, *A Nietzsche Reader,* 222; aphorism from *Daybreak,* section 356)

Drew: To bestow, to give somebody something, how does that exercise the will to power?

Charles: When you're able to help someone who's not able to help themselves, that gives you power. In this country and a lot of places, that's how you make a person dependent upon you. Every time they need assistance you're the person they come to, and then you have the ability to put conditions and set rules for being so benevolent, and that's how you start to control.

Drew: Maybe I'm doing something like that. On the surface, I'm volunteering my time and that's really nice. But from Nietzsche's point of view I'm doing this because I get to feel so important—I'm fantasizing about taking murderers and rapists and converting them to philosophers, getting off on the power trip. [*laughter*]

Tray: It's coming out ain't it?!

Drew: And how about "to mock," how is that the will to power?

Mark: I can think of an example: when the courts sentence someone to multiple life sentences without parole, all running consecutive. To satisfy the government's requirement you'd have to die and then be resurrected to serve another sentence. I think that's a mockery of the concept of God. The government doesn't have the power to resurrect you.

Tray: In the drug game I was able to fulfill all the elements that Nietzsche talked about. If my little sister wanted a pair of new shoes for school I could get it for her and it made me feel powerful. And then I was able to destroy people if I didn't like them. Don't want you selling dope in my neighborhood?—knock you all out, burn the house up. And I could mock people, like "Man, you're looking rough, I don't want to see you around here, you're nothing but an old dope fiend." After the first week I was able to buy what I wanted, so it was no longer the money. It was being able to bestow, mock, and destroy.

Drew: How about within a prison? It's a setting where, at least in the eyes of society, people are in a relatively powerless position. But if Nietzsche's correct, that drive for power will still be very much alive.

Tray: I don't think no group of people could validate Nietzsche's philosophy as much as in a prison setting. We convicts are always striving for distinction. For example, I try to distinguish myself—I'm an *honorable* criminal, you know. There's different degrees of murderers—we're all not the same kind. *He* hit the old lady in the head just to take ten bucks out of her wallet so I'll look down on him. At least *I* tried to run a corporation. It was a criminal one, but a corporation nonetheless.

Most of the time, to be considered important in a prison situation, you had to have been notorious on the street. You sold a lot of drugs, had a few people murdered. And when you come in here a red carpet is laid out.

Donald: I think power in a community is whatever the community accepts as being power. I'm going to give an example. A young guy came in here from my neighborhood. He got his high school equivalency GED in here and *scored the highest of anybody in the state*. And very few people in this prison knew that. This person had a problem with another guy who was playing with him too much, and he came to me and said, "I'm going to hurt this guy, man." I recommended he take the guy in the gym and they do fisticuffs. He said, "No. I want people to respect me in this prison. I'm going to stab him, and once I stab this dude everybody will look up to me." And he did. He stabbed the guy up, almost killed him.

He didn't get any recognition for having the type of mind that could score three hundred plus on the GED. But he got recognition for the stabbing and it's held up to this day, ten years later. Young guys like O'Donald that don't know him, somebody might pull them aside and say, "He stabbed a few people." And most of the young guys will hold him in high esteem.

If he felt he could be accepted as powerful for scoring real high on the GED, then maybe he would have gone another route.

H.B.: I think that in a prison, power is an illusion that's passed around among the prisoners for the sole reason of helping them hold each other up. But there is the *reality* of power in prison, and over these past twenty years I've seen that power always in the hands of somebody who didn't want it. Because it had nothing to do with material possession, it had nothing to do with how violent the person could be. Believe it or not, it always seemed to radiate from a person who *cared* about those prisoners, and those prisoners *knew* it. That person wielded more power than any dope dealer I ever seen.

Drew: Can you give an example?

H.B.: Okay. It's usually a prisoner. But it's the type of person who the prisoners knew would give his life for them, would be carted off in chains trying to protect them. I saw Ben Chavis with that in North Carolina. George Jackson had it out in California. That's power. But a little ole guy dope dealer? He's always going to have some flunkies around. But he's in here for doping up a whole community and wiping out half a generation. Now he's doing the same with the young men in the penitentiary who are trapped in confusion. This cat wears an *illusory* badge of power. But when you get an individual who cares about the prisoners and they know it . . . now that's power.

Drew: This might also suggest that Nietzsche's analysis is incomplete or flawed. He's asserting that pretty much all behavior falls under the will to power, but maybe what you're talking about can't be reduced to that drive. I think a lot of people who are Christians, Muslims, Jews, whatever, would think and hope that there's certain forms of behavior—giving behavior, spiritual behavior, moral behavior—that are not simply based on the will to power.

Donald: Yeah, you could go crazy thinking that everything you were doing—like you teaching in prison—is just for the power.

Drew: When I was reading Nietzsche I was getting really depressed. I thought, "Man, this guy is right. The only reason I'm volunteering in this penitentiary is because I'm on an ego trip! I'm getting off on pretending to help these guys. Maybe I should just quit." I finally decided, "Wait a second, Nietzsche's probably right about *part* of my motivation. And I need to watch that part because it could turn destructive. But there's some other stuff going on too that's real positive. So let's not throw the baby out with the bath water."

Donald: It could be the other way around, couldn't it, Doc? Did you think about that?

Drew: What do you mean?

Donald: *We* could be on a power trip and you could be the victim. [*laughter*]

Drew: That's true. . . .

Donald: Just joking, Doc.

CHAPTER FIVE

Kind Power

We'd been talking about power in its many forms: the power of dealer over addict, of the drug itself, of guns and knives in the hands of insecure men seeking reputation. In one form or another this is *violent power*. Then H.B. gave it a flip—the truer power emanates from a person who cares. Is there, then, *kind power*? And are the two powers at root the same, as Nietzsche claims, or opposed in nature?

Violent power refers to the superior strength that enables one to *violate*. That is, to break, infringe, trespass, destroy. The Maryland Penitentiary was filled with violators. Men who had murdered, robbed, and raped, gathered here like worshipers of a common god in their holy temple.

The penitentiary as a temple to violence? Isn't it quite the opposite, built to punish and eradicate violence? On the surface, yes. But underneath, I sensed another message. If the thug had more power than the victim he stabbed, then the state must exert its *even greater power* over the transgressor. The penitentiary's tall walls and barbed wire bore eloquent testimony to superior force. When John Thanos was executed on the premises, it merely brought this point home with a flourish. This was surely not a matter of eradicating violence, but of redirecting it in ways "protective to the community." And such is one purpose of any temple. Turn the god's dangerous energies to use.

In fact, our country is in the midst of an orgiastic celebration of violent power turned on the criminal. The numbers of executions are soaring. So too, and perhaps more significantly, are our incarceration rates. In 1970 the United States had fewer than two hundred thousand inmates. As I write this, there are now *about 1.8 million.* This is the highest rate in the Western world, with the exception of Russia, which we should soon surpass, and is some six to ten times greater than that of most industrialized nations. The state of California alone holds more inmates than France, Germany, Great Britain, Japan, Singapore, and the Netherlands combined. What accounts for our massive and anomalous drive to incarcerate our citizens? It's not simply a response to rising crime. As I write this, the crime rate has now declined for six straight years. Murder rates are lower today than twenty years ago. Still, our prison population increases. In the words of a *New York Times* report, "The imprisonment boom has developed a built-in growth dynamic independent of the crime rate," the result of longer sentences, mandatory jail terms for drug offenders, reduced use of parole, and other factors. We're engaged in a bizarre social experiment, as we imprison ever more of the population. And the more we pour resources into this violent power, the less is available for "kind power" endeavors. We're spending some forty billion dollars a year on housing and feeding inmates (more than three times what is spent on the much vilified welfare program, Aid to Families with Dependent Children). What if you took the twenty thousand dollars a year or more it takes to incarcerate a person, and used that instead for education, drug treatment, family counseling, and job training? Instead we worship the violent god of the prison-temple.

The inner sanctuary of this particular temple was ringed by many walls. It's extremely hard to get out of a maximum security prison, but it's not much easier, I found, to get in. Of course not. You don't want people smuggling things to the prisoners. But beyond that, to seek entry was to be put in your place. If this was a temple to violent power, everything conspired to illustrate to me that I was but a lowly sycophant in its precincts.

This was demonstrated through frustrations and delays. I was a prison school instructor with proper ID, yet it wasn't unusual for me to be turned away at the door. The paperwork wasn't prepared. Or classes were canceled today. Or something. In fact, I write these words having just been turned away the second week in a row from my scheduled class.

Guard: "We don't have your count-out."

Me: "But I called the principal yesterday to confirm it would be prepared."

Guard: "We never got it."

Me: "But in the past I haven't even needed a count-out, since I have a state ID."

Guard: "On this shift, the shift commander says no one gets in without a count-out."

Me: "Oh."

Most class days I would be admitted, but at their own sweet time. I might wait at the front gate; then wait at the middle gate; then wait to be frisked; then wait at the inner gate that finally led to the yard. The guards, to their credit, were never cruel. It's just that, despite all the concern with count-outs, I just didn't *count*. My time, my educational mission, was of little import in this temple. And being made to wait is one way we clarify to one another who holds power and who doesn't. The same ritual is enacted in government offices, corporate headquarters, doctors waiting rooms, the world over. So, too, in prison. What is a prison, after all, but a place where we drop all frills and *just make people wait?* Imagine being sentenced to thirty years in a waiting room run by a callous bureaucracy and overcrowded with other angry and unwilling customers. That's prison.

The prisoners were subject not only to the power of the institution, but that of the other inmates as well. If you showed weakness, you were liable to suffer violation. Someone might steal your commissary stuff. Lend out cigarettes—forget about getting them back. Or you're taking a shower and a strange guy cozies up from behind. Soon you're a "fuck-boy."

The only way to counter this violent power is to grab some yourself. Tray talks about the prisoner who wins respect because he "had a few people murdered. And when you come in here a red carpet is laid out." The mark of a king. Or we see this in Donald's story about the young guy who excelled on the GED and found out it meant nothing. It wasn't coin of the realm. When he stabbed someone he acquired hard currency that was still paying interest a decade later.

But here's where H.B. put his spin on things. "[Real power] had nothing to do with how violent the person could be. Believe it or not, it always seemed to radiate from a person who *cared* about those prisoners, and those prisoners *knew* it." Believe it or not—I did. I had witnessed a lot of kindness in the penitentiary, and its profound effects upon men.

I had been told, "You don't make many friends in prison. You watch your back." That may be true, but I also witnessed tight friendships within our class. Just about everyone seemed to count Charley their main man; this Muslim imam had a generosity that John had been working for years to restrain. "It gets you into trouble here. You can't keep giving people the shirt off your back. They'll use you like a chump." Charley had learned to keep his shirt on, but he kept giving away the buttons. And his generosity was a force-field of its own, protecting him and lightening other's burdens.

People looked out for one another. If someone from the class was on solitary lock-up they sneaked in food, letters, readings. "Was it legit?" I asked. Yeah. Well, sort of. Just don't do it in front of a guard. I watched people help each other out as they might have in my great grandparents' Russian shtetl. Tight times, and the "us versus them" mind, breeds community. The prisoners knew they would be together for a long, long time in a closed-in place and they had only each other to make it habitable. Observing rules of politeness was far more crucial here than in elite society.

Then too, people seemed bound by an empathy born of common home and fate. Most of the world doesn't care, but the prisoners all knew what it's like serving time—that noise always blasting through the cell block—the guards' contempt, and how they don't do what they're supposed to do even when they say they do, and there's nothing you can do about it—the long nights with a bad case of *thinks*—the poor excuse of a dead carcass they serve up as chicken. They all knew and it linked them for life.

But even before prison, these people were woven together. So many came from the same places, East Baltimore, West Baltimore, that you met schoolmates, cousins, friends from down the street. It was like a twisted-up reunion in Hades: "Hey, I didn't know you were in here too—so how ya doin'?!" If you were lucky there were homies smoothing your way from the moment you arrived, offering protection and the inside scoop. In Hades, but embraced. Simone Weil has written of the *Iliad*'s grim world, "Justice and love, for which there can hardly be a place in this picture of extremes and unjust violence, yet shed their light over the whole without ever being discerned otherwise than by the accent" (p. 177). I discerned justice and love between prisoners despite the brutality of their crimes and surroundings.

And I, too, was the recipient of love. I was made welcome, praised for my teaching, given useful tips, and in every way looked after. H.B. would call sometimes on the prison phone. He was serving a thirty-five-year sentence, twenty-five nonparolable, and was sick from AIDS. This meant skin blotches, throat thrush, night sweats, times when it was a chore to breathe or his lower body went all limp. "You gotta take better care of yourself," he told me. "Don't work so hard. Enjoy life!" My Jewish mother.

And I would receive kind letters in the mail. A sample of one from Donald:

> First of all I must say *I love you and your wife*. You wouldn't be the person you are without a supportive wife. Dr. never mind the fact that you exposed me to Western Philosophy on master level. And that you also went out your way to expose me to Black Philosophy. But it is the fact that you treated all of us like Human Beings. You accepted us unconditionally.

Such comments suggest that the prisoners experienced their kindness as a response to mine. But the reverse was true as well: I felt well treated, and responded in turn. Just as violent power circulates and multiplies, so, seemingly, does the power of kindness.

But we again approach the Nietzschean challenge. Aren't these two powers, at root, the same? Wasn't my own kindness just a way "to bestow," to "impress myself on the soul of the other"? After all, what greater power than to transform the heart of a murderer, exerting a force greater than that of his crime, or even that of his punishment?

If we can give a Nietzschean reading of my behavior, so, too, that of the inmates. I can imagine a voice saying: "Don't be fooled by their kindness. It's just one way of surviving in the joint. They've got to be civil with their cellmate or maybe they'll wake up dead. They've got to stay out of trouble or they'll never make parole. And they see in you a way to increase their chances: you offer the power of knowledge, credentials, maybe a letter to the parole board. Naturally, they're going to stay on your good side."

True, all true, but only up to a point. I can't help but believe there's an element in kindness that is *different*, irreducible to Nietzsche's will to power. Weil identifies this power with the Divine. In addition to "gravity," the downward pull of the world's cruel mechanics, she refers to "grace"— another kind of energy that lightens and liberates.

My own introduction to this grace came through the Twelve Step program first pioneered in Alcoholics Anonymous. Some fourteen years ago I started using that approach for a slew of obsessive problems; compulsive eating, co-dependency (as it's now fashionably called), and compulsive fear and guilt. For years this thinking had kept me trapped in a prison of misery and self-destructiveness. How to escape? As it says in the book *Alcoholics Anonymous*,

> Our human resources, as marshalled by the will, were not sufficient; they failed utterly. Lack of power, that was our dilemma. We had to find a power by which we could live, and it had to be a *Power greater than ourselves*. (p. 45)

Thus the notion of God is introduced in that book. Not as Truth. Not even as Love. But as *Power*.

And so God came to me. As I worked the Twelve Step program I began to experience power over my obsessions. My life gradually, but immeasurably, improved. Today I'm proud to declare myself kind of sane. Each Passover, it's this liberation that comes to mind. *"We were slaves to Pharaoh in Egypt, and God freed us from Egypt with a mighty hand."* The compulsive illness I suffered had been a violent Pharaoh, countering every attempt to escape with a new load of bricks. But I experienced God as a *greater* power, liberating the prisoner with kindness.

And I'm not the only one. The other day I received a letter from Charles Baxter that began:

> In the Name of Allah, Most Gracious, Most Merciful, In Control of all affairs
> As–Alaama–Aliakum,
>   Greeting my dearly beloved Teacher, doctor, brother and friend. I must first give praise to (Allah-God   ) he is the provider for us all; then I must give honor to you and those in the class.

Enclosed was a copy of his college diploma in management science, just completed after several hard years.

And what, I puzzled, did he mean by (Allah-God   )? Then I realized. He knew that many Jews believed the sacred name of God couldn't and shouldn't ever be written. Charley had left a blank space to honor my God, and in kindness to me.

There, too, is a power.

PART TWO

Architecture

CHAPTER SIX

Living in the Panopticon

Michel Foucault was a French philosopher who lived from 1926 to 1984. Although his death from AIDS was fairly recent, and his work is still being assimilated, he is already considered one of the most important of contemporary thinkers. While emerging, to a degree, from the "structuralist" tradition, his writings are also influenced by Friedrich Nietzsche's analysis of power. Foucault has especially focused on the operation of power and knowledge in a number of modern institutions: for example, the asylum (Madness and Civilization), *the hospital* (The Birth of the Clinic), *and in the work discussed below, the prison. Therein, Foucault argues that the power to "discipline and punish" takes genuinely new forms in the modern world. It shapes both the procedures and the architecture characteristic of the contemporary prison. But the prisoners will test his thesis through reference to their own experience.*

Docility–Utility

Methods which made possible the meticulous control of the operations of the body, which assured the constant subjection of its forces and imposed upon them a relation of docility–utility, might be called "disciplines." Many disciplinary methods had long been in existence—in monasteries, armies, workshops. But in the course of the seventeenth and eighteenth centuries the disciplines became general formulas of domination. . . . What was then being formed was a policy of coercions that act upon the body, a calculated manipulation of its elements, its gestures, its behaviour. . . . Thus discipline produces subjected and practiced bodies, "docile" bodies. (Michel Foucault, *Discipline and Punish: The Birth of the Prison*, 137–38)

Drew: "Discipline," according to Foucault, is how power mainly operates in our current society and institutions, be it a prison, the military, a hospital, a school. The goal is to control in a detailed way the behavior and body of the individual. The ultimate object is to increase "docility"—keep the individual submissive, obedient—and, at the same time, maximize "utility"—make the worker, student, whoever, productive and useful.

John: You can try to create an individual that's docile to take advantage of them. But I don't think you could ever get the maximum utility. Like here in prison. We may, to a degree, become docile because we decided this isn't the time to be aggressive or make a stand. But you're not getting no utility out of us. I mean, we're walking through the motions. We do half a job—soon as there's a chance to break, we're *gone.*

I do share Foucault's idea that you need a docile body in order to have utility. Like the military—you won't get any use out of your soldiers unless you make them docile with all that rigorous routine. But in a prison situation it's alright with them if we don't complete our tasks. Because in prison they don't want utility; they *want* to produce lazy people.

Drew: Or, in a sense, the more passive you are, the more useful—since the goal is to get rid of your power.

H.B.: The weapon they use here to promote docility is the "ticket." Say you're going up tomorrow to get transferred or make parole. Perhaps you were up sick all last night so you overslept a little bit this morning. The guard gives you a ticket: you were supposed to make count and didn't. Then when you go up for your transfer or parole hearing, you're turned down 'cause of this one ticket. They take the ticket, which was your darker day, and use it like a scouring pad during the entire interview, rub away all your brighter days. That's how you get your docility.

As far as your utility goes, they have a thing called state-used industries. In essence, the guys make products that would be more expensive for the state to obtain from private industry. So the state makes it themselves and also sells it to private industry. They're making a pretty good buck off the prisoners' work. But the guys, themselves, are only getting about sixty dollars a month. Yet you hear them say with a tremble in their voice, "Man, I'm going to lose my job! And I don't get any help from home. . . ."

John: For what H.B.'s talking about to function, you have to persuade people they have something to gain. These guys actually believe through propaganda ('cause it's not true) that working in the printshop might help them get released early.

Drew: Foucault argues that discipline is enforced through a system of graded punishments and rewards. It sounds like the reward–punishment system here involves the promise of earlier or later release.

Selvyn: In this jail there's another thing used to keep us docile. They allow us to wear our own clothes, have radios and appliances. But at the first sign of trouble, there's "You won't be allowed to get that package through the mail." So guys say, "I'm not trying to blow my package opportunity!" It's a way of keeping us in check without using a billy club.

Tony: And they have a *mental* billy club. Like in A block, they've got you to the point of controlling exactly where you have to stand and shower. You don't even have the power to be modest. But if a female guard passes by and sees you nude, she can give you a ticket and say you're exposing yourself.

Drew: Foucault says that discipline reverses the traditional logic of "visibility." Earlier, it would have been the *people in power* who were visible in society—like the king who had his picture on stamps and portraits. But now it's the other way around. The *people being controlled* are made to be visible.

The Panopticon

Bentham's Panopticon is the architectural figure of this composition. . . . Each individual, in his place, is securely confined to a cell from which he is seen from the front by a supervisor; but the side walls prevent him from coming into contact with his companions. He is seen, but he does not see; he is the object of information, never a subject in communication. . . .

[The Panopticon] is polyvalent in its applications; it serves to reform prisoners, but also to treat patients, to instruct schoolchildren, to confine the insane, to supervise workers, to put beggars and idlers to work. . . . In each of its applications, it makes it possible to perfect the exercise of power. . . . Because it is possible to intervene at any moment and because the constant pressure acts even before the offenses, mistakes or crimes have been committed. . . . Because, without any physical instrument other than architecture and geometry, it acts directly on individuals; it gives "power of mind over mind." (Foucault, *Discipline and Punish*, 200, 205–6)

Drew: Foucault is saying that the architecture of public spaces is a key mechanism for enacting power relations and controlling individuals. He describes how a British philosopher, Jeremy Bentham, came up with the architectural idea of a "panopticon," meaning to "see all." There's a central control tower with a guard, someone keeping surveillance, and surrounding it are the cells arrayed in a circle. This supports the disciplinary mechanisms we've been discussing, because everyone knows they're being watched. Do you see something like that here?

John: In this prison—you might not notice this—but the chief of security's office sits right up in the corner of the facility. And if he wants to look out his window he can cover about sixty-five percent of the yard. He can sit there and monitor: "What's this guy doing over there on that bench? Who are those two, and why are they sitting together? Are these guys getting ready to start a fight?" He can get on his walkie-talkie, say "Go check that out," and take control.

Donald: I wasn't really aware of that window until I came off lock-up and the security chief called me into his office. When I went in there, first thing I did was look out at everything. And I remembered the times I was in the yard trying to go in the kitchen and an officer was sweating, pressing me about "You aren't supposed to go in here!" I couldn't understand why. I'm thinking, "God, this broad is kinda crazy. She's giving me a lot of problems about something *small*—I'm just trying to get me a milk and some cereal." But now, after being in the security chief's office, I realize the officers know just what that man can see. So they act out roles.

Drew: In a panopticon not only are the prisoners under surveillance, but somebody could be watching the guards as well. The total institution is being watched.

Donald: I was thinking about the visiting booth. That's like a panopticon; they even have three or four mirrors where the officers can see you. So when I go in there for a visit, I'm very self-conscious. When my son comes in, or my family, they may touch me and that's frowned on, so I'll hold back. I like to touch, but my hands are, like, tied.

H.B.: The panopticon in this prison is not just an architectural structure, or the way an office is located—they use *human beings* to serve the same purpose. You have more informers in the prison system today than ever before. There was a time when being an informer was considered totally corrupt; now it's acceptable 'cause of plea bargaining, copping out, looking out for number one. It's not even necessary to build a guard tower in this particular yard because there are so many informers. And some of them do it simply because they don't have anything else to talk about, no ideas handy. You've heard the expression, "Big men talk about ideas. Little men talk about each other."

John: But the panopticon's only as effective as the person in control. Not all chiefs know how to use the tools. And you got blind spots everywhere. We show kids from Project Turnaround the blind spots around the penitentiary where you could lose your life and no one would ever see.

Also you become *very crafty.* You can time the police shifts, you know you got an hour before someone's coming by your cell. I remember when I first came here I wasn't able to pick up a vibe: I'd see guys running different ways but it didn't make any sense. Now when I step into that yard, I pick it right up—I see how guys are standing in little groups or moving, and I say there's something going on. Being observed creates a sense of observing—your ability to see things is enhanced.

Mark: When you're virtually under twenty-four-hour surveillance—like the new prison in Jessup—there's also a way you can *resist* or *escape.* Autistic thinking. Total absorption in fantasy. "I'm building an island and this is what my water source will be, and the kind of plants I'll have. . . ." You can absorb yourself in this for hours and hours and resist being conditioned by the discipline.

Charles: I was in Supermax, and a lot of the brothers in there, they escape by a lot of reading and studying—African history, the Bible, the Koran. They realize they're being watched, but they escape to something that gives them, you know, hope and inspiration.

Donald: But there's another side. Before I came here I was very violent. It didn't take much for me to strike out at another person—different ways—a baseball bat, a brick, a gun. But since I came in here I've had one fight. Knowing that I'm being watched has made me control this violence. And as time went on it helped me discipline myself, 'cause my intellect eventually kicked in.

Selvyn: Different people react differently to the discipline. It might make you or break you.

H.B.: The best is living a life where you don't have anything to hide. You don't care if the state's looking at you or not. *You've done nothing wrong.*

John: I have to agree. One of the things they have for monitoring a person is urinalysis, what they call a piss test, to determine if you've been using any drugs. When I *was* using, that piss test was one of my greatest fears. I'd say, "Wow, I've been high twenty-four hours. If they don't come piss me in two days I'm safe." But for that period of time I'm in a state of anxiety. I don't want nobody to see my eyes, my dilated pupils.

So I came to the realization that "Man, you gotta stop playing games with yourself and these people. Leave this stuff *alone.*" And now, because I don't do drugs, I laugh at them when they try to intimidate me about a piss test. And that makes me feel a lot better as a person. I'm not doing anything wrong so I got nothing to fear.

Donald: But to me, for instance, masturbation is not doing anything wrong. Yet I could get a ticket for it if a female guard saw me.

Drew: Foucault would say that a panopticon operates most effectively if it can get people to internalize the structure of discipline. It sounds like there are certain values, such as not being violent, or going clean, that you can internalize *positively* as a self-discipline. But then sometimes there's a conflict between your own values and the values of the institution.

Donald: You have to ask: What are the goals of the administration? Like was it even their goal to get John to stop using drugs? Maybe they don't care, they want to use the piss test to put him in Supermax or lock-up so they can get his cell for another individual.

John: A lot of times we're doing musical chairs in the cells because they don't have enough space. Some of us get phony tickets. We get sent to high security not 'cause we did anything wrong but 'cause they need cells. We see these fool games and say, "Man, these people, what they're doing is a joke!" There's nothing reformist about what's going on.

Mark: They have to liquidate their inventory. It's a matter of storage space.

Prison, Projects, Church

John: One thing I noticed when I first came to the penitentiary, is that the design is similar to the high-rise projects in West or East Baltimore. If in prison you got tiers, in projects, it's different floors. In prison, the cell's not really big enough for one person, but they put in two. Same thing with projects; they're not big enough, but they stick entire families in there.

It seems like someone wants to control the people who live there. And they also try to make as efficient use of space as possible. Every inch is for you to have just enough room to live in. *No more.* Nothing for relaxation, nothing for comfort.

And you walk down the inner-city streets and feel indifference to everything: "This isn't really a part of me. I'm just existing here. This is *nothing* I should care about, protect, or build up. I just gotta deal with it until I get out." It's the same way we look at prison. There's nothing in this building we think is particularly worth taking care of.

H.B.: At the heart, a prison building is about *size.* When we drive by a church, it dwarfs man. Drive by a prison and it's the same thing, plus a sense of fear, apprehension, revulsion—even, with some people, shame—and submission to a power outside yourself.

Prison and church—they're both symbols of authority. One's an authority that protects you from the bad guy. The other's an authority supposed to protect you from yourself.

Donald: The architecture of the Gothic church, the prison, the projects, is so vast that it makes a man feel dwarfed. Small and powerless.

John: As soon as you come around this type of structure, you feel the best you can do is *submit.*

Drew: In a church, what are we meant to submit to?

H.B.: To what authority are we submitting? As far as the church building is concerned, it serves two purposes. In time of peace you get sweet music from the bells in the belfry. In time of war it has always been a lookout post. What authority are we submitting to?—*we don't know.*

Tony: It's supposed to be a spiritual submission.

Charles: I don't believe religion is spiritual. Religion has separated us. The Protestants, Seventh-Day Adventists, Muslims, Jehovah's Witnesses,

Nation of Islam, all these people profess to believe in one God. But looking at church structures, you see authority, humans, *ego*.

Drew: But isn't the size of the church building meant to emphasize our smallness in relation to *God*? It gives a sense of an ultimate source of authority and justice. Whereas the prison building draws our eyes up to the majesty of the state and *its* power.

Donald: I think it's the same thing. History bears me out. The people running the church mostly wanted power; they didn't want no power to go to God.

Charles: I look at the churches in America as a slave institution, the same as the prison. Our people have submitted themselves—and I'm not being racist—to the Europeans. Because you go in the churches and you see a white Jesus. I just don't believe that Jesus was white.

Wayne: But there's a new wind blowing through the church. People are beginning to become conscious. Take the A.M.E. Church for one.

And I wanted to say concerning the church, that the building and its size is of no consequence. It's just a place where people can come together as one, learn how to interact socially and perfect that interaction. It's like a pivotal point. What starts in the church then begins to move out through the community.

I don't compare the church to a prison. Under the banner of Christ, we are one. There is no hierarchy. There are particular functions an individual has in the church, but that doesn't make you better than anyone else.

Drew: Wayne seems to have touched on a difference between prison and church buildings. Prison cells keep people in separate compartments for control, whereas the interior of a church tries to bring people together as a community. And its doors do open out into the larger world. Haven't there been occasions, like the civil rights movement, where the church has brought together a community and formed them into a political force?

Donald: The structure does bring people together collectively. You create a sort of a political power. But at the same time, there's a kind of hidden trick.

Take the courtyard in Baltimore projects: all the doors and houses face each other. But instead of giving people some sort of common power, it actually *takes* power away from them. When you come in and out, people can see you. The people in the project townhouses I've been around, they talk all day about how "Miss So-and-So is sittin' at her window watchin' and waitin' to see who Miss Sally comes in with." So Miss Sally keeps private by using the back door.

The architecture of the church might do the same thing. Instead of giving people power, maybe it takes power away.

CHAPTER SEVEN

The Visible and the Invisible

With its high stone walls, its Gothic towers and spires, the penitentiary reminds me of a medieval castle. I think of those movies where soldiers pour boiling oil from the ramparts onto attackers. It appears the technology for keeping people *out* and for keeping people *in* isn't that different, and hasn't progressed much over the past millennium.

But if Michel Foucault is right, the logic of power *has changed*. A medieval castle symbolized the power of the feudal lord. Ultimate power was embodied in the royal personage, of which all the walls, weapons, soldiers, and laws were but an extension. The ruler's power and image were everywhere visible.

By contrast, those exercising power in the modern-day panopticon do so by virtue of their *invisibility*. The security chief watches all, but himself is hidden. I only once met this mysterious man. Nor do the prisoners know where he is or what he's watching; hence the threat of his gaze is everywhere. However, to be *visible* within this system is to be *powerless*. One is under constant surveillance (from the French for "watching over"). The prison's walls, open yard, and exposed cell seek to ensure that the inmates cannot escape being seen.

I understand there's good reason for this surveillance. These men have a history of things they do while unseen. And *still* do. As John says, "We show kids from Project Turnaround the blind spots around the penitentiary where you could lose your life and no one would ever see." The invisible spells danger for the potential victim. And it also does, in a way, for the victimizer. Donald says, "Knowing that I'm being watched has made me control this violence." I can hear his relief, even his gratitude.

But I also heard how constant visibility plays havoc with a man's mind. I'm used to a zone of privacy when it comes to excretion, grooming, sex. But in a prison, as a zoo, all these are placed on display. Tony speaks of having to take showers in full view, though he might get a ticket if seen by a female guard. So too, Donald complains, if she sees you masturbating. At another time, the prisoners explained to me how the toilet in their cell is shielded only by a makeshift drape. It's embarrassing, especially when you have a cellmate subject to all the sounds and smells. And each cell is fully exposed, except for a few hours at night when you can close a curtain. Even then a guard passing each hour can pull it open.

Tray told me of how insecure this made him feel. Though called a "maximum security prison," that name refers to the security of those who build the prisons, not the prison's inhabitants.

I experienced some of this insecurity each time I entered the prison. I was caught in a zone not only of power, but of mandatory disclosure. People would pat me down, check my pockets, empty my briefcase. I'd have to remember to discard in advance anything the least bit suspicious. Once, I overlooked a little plastic bag of vitamin C that I'd carried around on a weekend trip. It was immediately confiscated for testing. I forgot all about it. But weeks later I found out I was almost banned from the prison for that one oversight. I was told by the school principal that the chief of security suspected me of smuggling drugs. Even when it came back from the lab as vitamin C, he thought I might just be testing the system before bringing in the real stuff. I suppose you have to think that way if you're the security chief. But this gave me a taste of what the prisoners must experience; you are *seen*, though you cannot see who sees you.

But if being in prison makes you visible, in other ways it makes you disappear. H.B. and Donald note the sheer size of prison buildings; it causes a man to feel tiny and powerless. But there's also the matter of the prison wall. It not only confines people, but keeps them hidden away from the gaze of the outside world. Dante's sign over Hades read, "Abandon all hope, ye who enter here." Once incarcerated, you could all but abandon hope that someone would see, pity, pardon, protect. You're invisible now. You don't exist.

This kind of invisibility, I imagine, has multiple effects. For one thing, it can lead to a lack of accountability on the part of prison authorities. Many a guard has beaten up, even killed an inmate when assured that no one's watching. Rights can be stripped away, living conditions deteriorate. That's why it's so important, I believe, that oversight committees, prisoners' rights organizations, mass media, be allowed in to *see*.

But this only works to the extent the public cares to see. We have become so angry at the violence visible on our streets, visible on TV every night, that we'd just as soon render the criminal invisible. "Three strikes, you're out!" is the battle cry toward repeat felons. "Lock 'em up and throw away the key!" It seems to me more than just wanting protection from the criminal. It's wanting him or her completely and permanently *disappeared.* In order to rehabilitate a felon we must keep watch, pay attention to the process and results. Simply jailing (or executing) the miscreant relieves us of that chore.

Yet now and then the media do peek behind prison walls. A couple of days ago I saw a feature on national news about an Oregon prison program. All the inmates had to work forty-hour jobs where, among other things, they made bluejeans that had become quite the rage in local stores. Watching, I remembered H.B.'s (and Foucault's) mistrust of state-extracted utility. But on the whole it seems like a good program; the prisoners had something to fill their day, learned marketable skills, and took pride in their accomplishments. They said so on camera. And so they, and this program, were made visible in a way that evoked concern. I can imagine this TV show leading to tangible benefits.

I had some experience of that sort of thing in my own contact with the media. A nice feature about my work appeared in the *Baltimore Sun.* Celebrity for a day! There was even a color photo of me posed in front of my 1967 candy-apple-red Mustang (translation: though he's a philosophy professor, he's a *regular guy* too). And the article led to letters and calls from people interested in prison work. One, Chris Daly, started his own class at the Maryland Penitentiary. Then too, I had a piece in the *Washington Post* supporting the continuation of Pell Grant funding for college education in prison. This was followed by a Pacifica News Radio feature on the issue including taped excerpts from our prison class. All this press coverage provided ways to place our work before the public and garner support.

But if the media giveth, the media taketh away. One reason Pell Grant funding for prison education was so in jeopardy was because of TV snippets that had recently appeared. They exposed the "scandal" of felons receiving federally funded education that crime-victims themselves could not afford. Looks pretty unfair! But, not surprisingly, the media treatment was brief and distorted. Inmates were not receiving special privileges or funding unavailable to others. Moreover, the money that went into such programs was minuscule, and the payoff impressive in terms of reduced crime and recidivism. No matter. The entertainment/news magazine TV vignette had little time for details, little appetite for balance. The sensational image grabs more viewers.

This form of visibility was perceived as a threat even by prison authorities. Photographers and reporters were not particularly welcome at the Maryland Penitentiary, and they met continual obstructions to their work. When we brought in a *Chicago Tribune* reporter to observe our class without having gone through all proper procedures, I was summarily ordered out of the prison (see chapter 25). It took six months to get a toe back in the door. Among other things, I was told that my timing had been really bad. "Everyone's very nervous about media coverage until April 15. That's when the state legislature goes home." Prison officials had been burned too often by some inflammatory feature seized on by politicians.

The inmates were equally wary of publicity. They knew how TV images of crime had helped provoke new "get-tough" sentencing laws, and how exposés of the "luxuries" of prison (weightrooms, classrooms, access to TV itself) can lead an incensed public to strip these away—the very things that made life in a cage bearable. As I mentioned earlier, at the time of this writing, the crime rate has actually been going down for six straight years. But many people, inundated by local news images of violent crime, don't realize it and are left in a frightened and rageful mood. In a later discussion I ask the men if they thought the general public remained concerned with their fate. Tray's response: "With the current political climate, I wish that some people would just stop being so concerned." Sometimes it's better to be forgotten, invisible, just plain left alone.

Yet there seems a paradox in the above reflections. Foucault suggests that prisons express power by making people *visible*. The inmates are constantly under surveillance and control. But, for better or worse, a prison also tends to make people *invisible*; men are dwarfed by its size, hidden behind its walls. How can both be true, and even act in concert?

The answer, I think, is simple. To be visible or invisible is not just opposite in kind. The two share a common frame of reference. They both presume a *looker*, before whom one is visible or not. In both cases one is defined according to one's status as an object.

We don't tend to regard inmates as fellow *subjects*. Rather, we figure out what to do with them as things. (Execute them? Employ them? Box them up for life?)

Yet in their dialogue I hear the men seizing back the position of subject. Even in a panopticon, John says, you can be the one who looks, keeping an eye on the yard. Mark reclaims subjectivity through mental escape. He transports himself to an imagined island where he alone watches, the king of his domain.

For Charles, it's books that provides this power: African history, the Bible, the Koran. You're both the reader and the person referred to in the text—that proud inheritor of African history, that soul constructed in the image of God.

Donald found a way to make even the gaze that rendered him object into his own. "Knowing that I'm being watched has made me control this violence . . . it helped me discipline myself, 'cause my intellect eventually kicked in." Foucault might call this the ultimate subjugation, as discipline inserts itself and operates from within. How better to gain power over people than to have them discipline themselves? But Donald experiences this as a freeing act. "*My* intellect kicked in," not some alien force.

So, too, with H.B.'s decision: "The best is living a life where you don't have anything to hide." From one point of view, the state has won. All criminal tendencies have been eradicated through surveillance. But H.B. experiences the opposite. By going straight, he has reclaimed his freedom. The state's surveillance is rendered impotent.

So it seemed to me that the prisoners were not trying to be visible or invisible but simply to be *men*. I recognize that this self-empowering move is not without its attendant dangers. After all, we know what these men have done in the past, and how they have misused their power and subjectivity.

Still, I support their move to claim themselves as subjects, not objects of another's gaze. Some will always remain under prison surveillance, but many will be returned to the streets. (On average over 40 percent of inmates are released each year.) In either case, if they are to make something of their lives, this must at some point involve taking responsibility, making sound choices, operating as men. Prison might be a place to practice these skills.

Might be, but usually isn't.

CHAPTER EIGHT

The Home
That Is Not a Home

O. F. Bollnow is a contemporary German philosopher who lived from 1903 to 1991. Though not a groundbreaking thinker such as Friedrich Nietzsche or Michel Foucault, he had a long and distinguished career. Working largely in the fields of existentialism, phenomenology, and the philosophy of education, he published more than twenty books. Though most of his work is untranslated, the prisoners and I used an article in English focusing on the experience of space and, particularly, what it is to have a "home." I wanted to know what happened to one's sense of lived-space when enduring conditions of extreme confinement.

Can a Prison Be a Home?

Thus as a rule the space lived by man arranges itself around a determining center, which is conditioned by his place of residence. . . . To *dwell* is not an activity like any other but a determination of man in which he realizes his true essence. He needs a firm dwelling place if he is not to be dragged along helplessly by the stream of time.

The second characteristic of the house is that by means of its walls man carves out of universal space a special and to some extent private space and thus separates an *inner space* from an outer space. . . . He needs the space of the house as an area protected and hidden, an area in which he can be relieved of continual anxious alertness, into which he can withdraw in order to return to himself. To give man this space is the highest function of the house. (O. F. Bollnow, "Lived-Space," 33)

Drew: Bollnow suggests that to have a house, or we might say a *home*, to build a home, to feel a sense of *being-at-home*, is essential to being human. But can a prison constitute a home in this sense?

Selvyn: I'd say yes and no. I don't want it to be a home because I don't want to be here. I consider home what I left on the street. But since I have to be here for a long time, the cell is somewhere I can go and keep unto myself. So I might fix it up a bit, paint the wall just to get a different color.

Charles: And the cell's where you actually get your schoolwork done, or work for organizations you're in, or work to get out of prison. Man is created from one cell, right, and as man grows he adapts into another cell, and that cell's also a place for growth and development. When you read the Koran and the Bible you'll see that different prophets went to the *cave* for comfort and isolation. And the cell's like that cave.

Tray: With a cell, you have a little space in the wall, you can put things in an orderly fashion and bolt the door so you feel safe. It can seem like a home.

But you can never really have a home in here. Because the officers could come with the key anytime they want and uproot you. Like right now, everything that I own I brought out with me (my toothbrush and all) because *I'm the cell*, my own body, rather than some hole cut out of space. My cell was just shook down two nights ago about three o'clock in the morning. Bam! That's how it goes.

Drew: Of course, society has made a judgment—if *we* want to have a home, a sense of protection and security, we have to have boundaries against people like you. So a prison establishes a home for society. But I hear that you've lost your sense of having a protected home. Having been judged a violator, you're now having the experience of being violated.

Tray: Yeah, we're always subject to violence. Maybe you're beefing with somebody, or some zap-out just loses his mind and jumps on you. And the guards might not like you, and then threaten you with tickets or convince another prisoner to pop you.

We're like in some kind of forest where everybody's a predator. Even when there's no actual danger, you always feel like there is. You don't get that sense of safety like when you're home on Sunday watching the ball game with the doors locked. All you can do is *long* for that feeling.

Drew: True. But I've heard that some people find more security, protection, privacy—more of a *home*—here in prison, than out. Are there people who try to get back into prison because it is easier or more familiar than being on the street?

Mike: There's the case of Joe who'd been in here upwards of twenty years and he finally dug his way out with a spoon. But when he got out, the world that he was familiar with no longer existed. Since I've been in prison, the outside world got microwaves, computers, and all that. If you haven't prepared yourself you'd be so out of touch that you have to go back to the world you're accustomed to.

Tray: And in prison it's easy to find a certain security—when you're going to eat, a warm bed to lay down in, medical treatment, and so forth. Once you're here for a while, you get a certain pseudo-respect thing. Dudes admire you for your typing abilities, recognize you for your intelligence if you have any. You sell sandwiches and your financial needs are secure.

But then you get out. How am I going to get this rent paid? They don't buy sandwiches out here. Nobody will hire me. It doesn't help to put together a petition.

I always pray to God that won't be my fate; that's the purpose of communicating with children, learning about computers, always reading, so I won't fall in love with *this* and have it become the only safety I know.

Drew: In a way, you don't want to feel too much at home in this environment. . . .

John: Never, never.

Drew: But on the other hand, the old home you knew may no longer be there. You have to start forming an extended "at-homeness" in the new world out there.

John: We always had a concept around here about keeping yourself distant from prison activities and the prison mentality. Don't participate in a whole bunch of prison groups, don't get caught up in playing football, basketball, don't think about fixing no cell up to make it comfortable. Let it stay raggedy. You want to keep a mindset that this is not some place for me to get comfortable.

Mike: I agree. I got a friend that every cell he moves into he paints to the max. I *refuse* to paint one of these cells or lay it out like it was home. To me it's just a place where you exist.

Charles: [*laughing*] I understand what Mike's saying because I'm one of those dudes—I call my cell my *palace*. As a matter of fact I just got it painted last week and paid the dude four packs to do it. He painted the floors, my ceiling, the whole thing. I got my Oriental rugs laid down. I don't care where I'm at, I'm going to make it heaven while I'm there. Even in this hellhole, I'm going to find some heaven.

Wayne: It's different being in a double cell. I could feel at home laying on my bunk. But when I got up and took one step to the wall, I felt like I'm in a danger zone 'cause I had somebody else on the top bunk. I was under their scrutiny. There's somebody watching.

But my cell buddy moved out this week. I finally have the cell all to myself and space has gotten bigger. I sleep better at night, I'm happier and relaxed. The whole cell has took on a different atmosphere. I read better, things soak in more 'cause I don't have to fight somebody looking over my shoulder.

Drew: Bollnow writes: "Where the spirit of envy and rivalry take hold of many, everyone stands in the other's way, and there is painful narrowness and friction. But when men come together in the true spirit of colleagues, friction disappears. One does not deprive the other of space; he rather *increases* the acting space of the other by working with him."

Tray: Yeah, when I used to sleep in a double cell, if I was in there with a person I didn't like, I felt like Wayne. But when I was in the cell with T—, the only cell buddy that I really got along with—a bond developed, and in our closeness we were so brotherly—when he came in the cell I didn't feel like my space was being violated. It seemed like I had *more* room in that cell with him than I do now when I'm alone. We'd play cards and talk, and it felt like there was a lot of room!

Drew: By the way, what's the size of an average cell here?

Tray: Usually nine by twelve. But dormitory is only fifty-two square feet and you got two people living there. In the West Wing, the cells are forty-nine square feet. I know the size because we was arguing a court battle—each person is supposed to have sixty square feet.

Charles: It's about the size of a small bathroom in an old house.

The Innermost Sanctum

To build a house is to form a cosmos in a chaos. Every home, as Eliade maintains on ethnological grounds, is a picture of the world as a whole, and therefore every house construction is the repetition of the creation of the world, the complement of the work once performed by the Gods. . . . therefore ultimately house building signifies a world-creating, world-sustaining activity which calls for sacred rites. (Bollnow, "Lived-Space," 34)

So they are finally razing the Maryland Penitentiary's notorious South Wing, probably the most hellish place in the Free State. I say hooray! Tear it down, tear it down! tear it down!

At least we *know* the roof is gone. A crane swooped down from above, opened its mouth and gripped the top of the South Wing in its teeth. It bit and pulled. The roof came away, while I stood in the yard and applauded. Smut and rust flakes burst from the corners of the crane's mouth as it chewed on the South Wing's head. . . .

I could see the South Wing's dead: all those who didn't make it: the mental patients; the rebels born to die with their boots on; the collaborators swinging from bars, sheet ropes around their necks. I could see the many eyes: the eyes of the innocent, tortured and wet; the hollow eyes of the guilty; the eyes of the truth-seekers, penetrating, perhaps a bit too open and sincere.

I also thought I heard something. I listened again. Yes it was there. I heard screams: the rage threatening to choke a nation to death, the cries of those being bludgeoned in the South Wing. (H. B. Johnson Jr., "At Last, the South Wing Falls!" *Baltimore Sun*, May 13, 1993, 21)

Drew: Bollnow talks about how the dwelling is a kind of sacred space that you mark by a series of rites—in our society there's the housewarming party, the dedication of the house, whatever. But if the prison is a home and its opposite, the place where you are never at home and never *want* to be at home, then maybe instead of these joyful ceremonies around the *construction* of the prison, you're more apt to have these ceremonies around the *destruction* of it. That's what I see in H.B.'s piece; it's a celebration of the razing of the South Wing.

Tony: Every time that crane would take a big ole bite, I'd smile.

Selvyn: Guys would be at the window and just stand there watching all day.

Drew: Why was the South Wing so hated?

Tray: It was the lock-up wing, detention. And a lot of people lost their lives over there. Both by their own hands and probably by the hands of others.

John: They'd lock you up "for thirty days" but leave you over there for three years. That's how they played it back then.

Charles: A dude spent seven years on lock-up confined to one cell.

Donald: A lot of people lost their minds over there.

Mike: I knew a guy named G— who cut his throat.

Selvyn: They had a guy popping his own eyeball out. They'd put it back in, and he pop it out again.

Donald: One guy got his nose bit off, half of it. He's still in here.

Mike: Someone called it *the innermost sanctum of hell.* You had four landings up, and there was trash constantly being thrown to the ground. There were smoke fires and floods, water coming down like waterfalls.

John: It was like you lived in an abandoned building and nobody cared. Rats jumpin', I mean rats up on the windowsill and on the flats. They got flying mice!

Charles: And water bugs, three inches long, that flew right in your cell. Literally.

John: Plus it was no-man's-land. You wouldn't know how much danger you'd be in until they locked you up and you found out who was on your right and left. They'd do little evil things like saying "I know these guys don't get along, let's put one of them here, the other next to him, and see how they handle it." And you'd hear a voice from the next cell, "Yo, *I got you* when you come out the door."

Charles: If they knew you had a beef with a guy, they'd move you right on the tier with him to see who'd win and who'd get stabbed.

Drew: It was a place for punishment, and it sounds like the punishment involved taking away everything that goes with having a home: peace, privacy, protection. If you're in a home that is not a home, but the opposite, is there anything you can do to maintain your sanity?

Tony: Pray.

John: Constantly keep your mind active. You got to constantly read, constantly exercise, constantly talk to a friend. If you sit back and start daydreaming, the next thing you know, the sound of the place starts coming into your mind, the things that are going on eat you up, and a lot of guys lose it—they go over there for thirty days and come out *crazy.*

Drew: So when there's no outer dwelling to live in, you have to create a kind of inner dwelling, like Tray was saying, where your own mind, your own body, becomes your only home.

Donald: I think that is the ultimate temple.

That Neighborhood Feeling

> When I leave the protection of my house, I do not immediately step into a hostile world. I remain at first in a protective neighborhood, an area of trusted relationships, of vocation, friendships, etc. Around the individual house is the broader area of that which we call home (*Heimat*). It thins out slowly from the relatively known through the comparatively unknown, into the completely unknown. (Bollnow, "Lived-Space," 35)

Drew: Let's not talk about the prison setting for the moment, but the communities in which you grew up. I'm an upper middle-class white person wondering what it's like growing up in the inner city. Did your community really meet Bollnow's description of a protective neighborhood, trusted relationships, security, peace?

Tray: I would say yeah, because I grew up in East Baltimore, and even when I left my home, within a few blocks' radius I'd always feel comfortable. When I liked to start some trouble I never felt safe until I crossed Jefferson Street and I was home.

And you know, that might even explain a lot of black-on-black crime, 'cause you feel this inner peace, like I can do whatever I want here. I didn't feel free to steal stuff from a store downtown. I just felt uneasy. Whereas when I was in my community I'd steal, or sell dope, because I felt that sense of security. [*laughter*]

Drew: There's a sort of paradox there—the feeling of comfort and security actually opened up a space for criminal behavior!

Tray: It didn't have to be criminal behavior. I was even more comfortable approaching women in my neighborhood.

John: In most inner-city neighborhoods people know who's from there and who's not. They also know what's going on, and pass that information through the grapevine. "Stay away from that place, there's guys selling dope or getting in a beef. At this other place they got a recreational center where you might get help finding a job." So in your neighborhood you were home. Outside of that was *unknown.*

Tony: But I think neighborhoods, especially in the inner city, are not quite what they used to be. When I was growing up, you really had the feel of home and protection because you had not only Mom and Dad taking care of you, but everybody in the neighborhood. If your parents weren't home and you were hungry, there was always somebody there to take care of you.

Same thing if you did something wrong. When I was growing up, we was just the opposite of what Tray said. You did your dirt everywhere else *but home.* I could go into somebody else's neighborhood and do whatever I wanted, but you didn't do no stealing, you didn't do no dope, you didn't do *nothing* in your neighborhood. I might get four whuppings, and then I'd get home and get another one, 'cause everybody that done whupped my behind called home to tell why they whupped my behind.

John: I left Baltimore and went and lived in New York for a while in a transient hotel on Eightieth and Broadway. It had Latinos, Haitians, Puerto Ricans, white folks, everybody, and I got along there but, you know, I felt a little out of place. But I remember one day I took the walk up to Harlem and started to feel like I was in West Baltimore again. All the black folks standing out there, familiar faces, it means I'm *more at home.*

Drew: I hear you saying there's a racial dimension to the sense of home. Maybe for the African American there's a feeling of "not-at-homeness" in the largely white world outside. Is that true?

Mike: It works both ways. If *you* went by yourself in an all-black neighborhood you would feel out of place, as well as *be* out of place.

Drew: I would. I do. [*laughter*]

Mike: And when we're in a predominant white neighborhood, we're out of place. If I go in a store, the salesman's going to follow me: "Can I help you? Can I help you?" Every step I take. Whereas when *you* go in a store you're not bothered.

John: Also, in certain environments you just feel more mentally relaxed. I grew up where people would sit out on the front steps, wash their cars, listen to music, walk around. But when I moved to an apartment complex out in the suburbs, nobody's doing that stuff. They're riding in their cars.

Tony: It still could be a black neighborhood but it wouldn't feel right.

Gary: It's more of a class thing, really, than racial. Although I'm white I was brought up in a black neighborhood. I can fit in in the suburbs, but I get along better in a neighborhood like the one where I grew up.

Selvyn: Growing up in another country, it wasn't until I came here to America that I was in a whole different environment. Culture shock. One day I got lost in a white neighborhood. There was a white woman sitting in a car and I asked her which direction I should go. She immediately locked the door. Blip! And that made me so pissed off that I wanted to rob her. It hadn't been my intention.

Later when I'd go in stores and feel like they're watching me excessively like I'm going to steal something, I'd make a point to steal something. Sometimes it'd be the smallest piece of candy. I'd just walk out and throw it in the trash.

[Name withheld]: I've had the same kind of experience with a shoe store. They treated me as though I didn't have any money, like I came there to just look around or rob them. I knew they had the shoes I wanted to purchase, but they acted as though they didn't. Unconsciously I made a mental note. Later, even though I was selling drugs and didn't need the money, I robbed these people.

And I didn't put on a mask. I let the man know it was me.

CHAPTER NINE

Homecoming

The Maryland Penitentiary reminds me, in certain ways, of the New York City apartment building that formed my childhood home. Both are massive structures (especially, in the latter case, to a young child's vision). Both are well-guarded citadels. The correctional officers echoed the uniformed doormen of my youth.

But the prison reverses all the meanings of home. The guards are there to keep you in against your will, not protect you from intruders. And whereas the boundaries of the home establish a zone of privacy, prison walls do the opposite: they compress you together inescapably with hundreds of unsavory characters. A somewhat shy and solitary person myself, I couldn't imagine a worse punishment.

When the prisoners describe the cell, that little region of their own, I was no less struck by the Alice in Wonderland reversals. There's a door to your "home" but you alone don't have the key. You're not free to go in and out as you please, but your enemies, the guards, can. You have a big picture window, but it faces inward where there's no view. Nor can you find much domestic privacy. Cells designed to hold one inmate are now often inhabited by two. In this, the Maryland Penitentiary is not anomalous: as I write, statistics show state prisons operating between 13 and 22 percent above capacity, with federal prisons 27 percent above capacity.

After class, it was always a relief to return to my tree-dappled street and spacious house with its high ceilings, abundant windows, and generous yard. I would dread the thought of a two-person nine-by-twelve cell. Who wouldn't?

Yet, un-homelike as the prison was, many inmates found a way to make it one. Selvyn paints up his cell real nice. Charles lays down Oriental rugs. Then too, the prison reminds John of the projects he'd grown up in. This strikes me as quite an indictment of inner-city life. Yet it may have also smoothed his adaptation to prison, along with the "homies" he met in there.

So circumstances, and the efforts of prisoners, accomplished what seemed an impossible magic: prison, that very opposite of domesticity, nevertheless transformed into a kind of home. And to a degree the authorities cooperated with this alchemy. I was told by one, "This isn't like some other jails where people come and go. Most of our guys are in for a long, long time. So you have to let them have a life"—that is, provide exercise, TV, yard time, and the like, keeping things reasonably loose. This went against my preconceptions of a maximum security prison. But once he said it, it made perfect sense to me, and not only from the prisoners' standpoints but the authorities' as well: the more content the inmates, the less trouble they would cause. A prison is finally a home not just for the incarcerated, but also for the guards, clerks, teachers, and administrators who spend so much time within its walls. Like grumpy siblings, everyone has to find some way to live together in peace.

But if there was a common interest in making a home out of prison, there was also a shared rejection of taking this too far. For one thing, the administration didn't want the inmates to get real comfortable. In your home you start to feel like "This place is mine and I'll do what I damn please." "No it ain't, no you won't!" announced the authorities, using tickets, procedures, delays, prison shutdowns, to ceaselessly remind everyone just who was in charge. The transfer, I was told, also played a role. Over time, inmates form friendships and develop power blocks. The authorities can periodically transfer individuals or larger populations in order to break this up. I don't know how much that is done. But as I write this, two of my students have already gone to Jessup and I've heard that several others will be transferred soon. Even when you've painstakingly built a home, it can be whipped away in a jiffy.

But it wasn't only the authorities who were wary of inmates becoming too secure; I heard that among the prisoners as well. "You want to keep a mindset that this is not some place for me to get comfortable." Otherwise you might lose the determination to get out. And they wanted not only to get out, but *stay out.* A force-field radiates around almost any home drawing us back toward its center. There may also be repellent vectors ("They drive me crazy. I'm *not* going home for Thanksgiving"), but the pull of the past, the strength of family ties, can bring one back despite every intention. Then too, it's a harsh world the prisoners encounter on release. The temptation is, as for a jobless graduate, to trundle right back home.

For as Robert Frost writes: "Home is the place where, when you have to go there, They have to take you in." So, too, with prison: commit the right crime and they can't turn you away. Maybe then, this *is* a kind of "maximum security" for certain inmates. Growing up in rejecting, chaotic, or broken homes, prison may provide exactly what was missing—security, predictability, structure—albeit in distorted form. And such men may just do better in prison, as some men do better in the military.

But as Tray says, "I always pray to God that won't be my fate." He and others were adamant about *not* making prison too comfortable. In a strange ways, this attitude partly mirrors a view often expressed outside: "Prison isn't supposed to be nice. They make it too cushy for men in there." This notion has helped lead to a movement to make prison conditions harsher. In recent years, more than half the states have eliminated one or more privileges previously accorded inmates (like TV, or leaves to attend family funerals).

Part of this logic focuses on what men have done in the past, and it embodies a theory of retributive justice. "They made their victims suffer. Now *they* should suffer." But another element is the concern with future deterrence. "If prison's bad enough, they'll from here on stay straight!" I used to think this logic was thoroughly mistaken. That's not how a criminal's mind works. But I was taken aback when I heard an inmate unknowingly concur. Pissed off at current trends, he complained to me, "Man, it's not like the old days—prison's getting worse and worse. If I ever get out of here I'm going to be damn sure not to come back."

So I see the point. But I still, for the most part, disagree. I don't think most recidivism is rooted in the joys and comforts of a prison home. As Tray says, "We're always subject to violence. . . . We're like in some kind of forest where everybody's a predator." No, the issue is that the streets can be even less of a home, more of a jungle, for one unprepared for its demands.

And prison can either hinder or further this preparation. Both possibilities are clear in the dialogue. First, the hindrance. You take men who, by virtue of color and class, are not that much at home in the "successful" world to begin with. Then put them in jail for twenty years, and "Everybody you know is gone . . . whatever job you're capable of doing is gone." It's like waking up from a Rip van Winkle sleep. Prison thus displaces an individual twice: in space, but also in time. It seems that the indefinite "warehousing" of people, as with any inventory, does not leave things unchanged, but creates decay.

Yet the men also speak of using prison as a place of preparation and advancement. Tray mentions a few of his strategies: "communicating with children, learning about computers, always reading. . . ." My class, itself, seemed another example. Impractical as philosophy appears, my students were using it to become more at home within themselves—"that is the ultimate temple"—and in the outside world where knowledge counts.

According to the logic of harsh deterrence, such classes should probably be taken away (and for most part already have, thanks to the 1994 crime act). People think free education will only make a prison a more inviting home. But statistics suggest otherwise. Educating inmates dramatically reduces subsequent crime and recidivism. They gain tools to build a home *other* than prison.

I find myself thinking of an image from Plato. To illustrate the state of the unenlightened he used the metaphor of prisoners chained within a cave.

Their necks are fastened so they cannot even turn to see the light at the mouth of the cave. All that's visible to them are dark shadows cast on the wall. These they take to be all of reality, having no object of comparison.

Though metaphorical, it seems an apt image of some contemporary prisons. If recreation is banned and professors are asked to leave, the inmates are left with only each other's often dubious society, and the reflections of their previous crimes. Light from outside is hardly allowed to filter in. From one perspective, I suppose, this gloomy environment serves the ends of both punishment and deterrence.

But I prefer Charley's vision. "When you read the Koran and the Bible you'll see that different prophets went to the *cave* for comfort and isolation." This is a cave where light can flood in, "a place for growth and development." Charley suggests that a prison can be such a place, if opportunities are provided and seized on by the inmate.

But why, I wonder, am I so adamant about this? Why be so concerned with the plight of these men? Maybe the truth is that I identified with the prisoners. If they had lost their home, so had I.

I think back to that building on Park Avenue where I grew up. I remember sitting, one day, mid-afternoon, all alone in my family's eighth-floor apartment. My father's funeral had just taken place. He had jumped from the bedroom window in a plunge I still hate to contemplate. A year earlier my brother had taken an overdose, and a year before that my mother died of cancer. That day I sat on the living room floor and surveyed the scene. Everything around me was white—the carpets, sofas, everything—reflecting my mother's love of order. Never had it looked so white. A blank world. Perched on different surfaces were a lamp, an ashtray, candlesticks. They sat as still as objects do when all the people are finally gone. Silence.

I had my father's black cracked-leather medicine bag, and I took out a vial of Demerol and a needle. I had no idea how much drug that was, or how or where to shoot it. Do you go for a vein? Avoid the vein? I could not remember, or more likely never knew. Perhaps I might screw it up and die. That wasn't my intention. But at the moment I was flirting: with suicide, like my father and brother; with sleep, with the numbing of consciousness; with admitting my pain, and my need to make it go away.

I shot up. A prick, and I drifted into the floaty zone.

I came down, but never came *home.* Couldn't. Though I lived in that apartment for two more months clearing up Dad's estate, there was no more home to return to. "Everybody you know is gone. . . ." And as in the prisoners' case, I somehow felt this was the result of my own violent crimes. Subconsciously, I placed myself on trial. Hadn't I hated my mother, even wished her gone? Hadn't I contested with Scott for our parents' love, apparently a duel to the death from which *I had emerged victorious?* And why did I go away at just the wrong times? Shouldn't I have seen what was coming with my brother, my father, and done something to prevent it? Unless it was really what I wished for. . . .

Subconsciously, I received a life sentence for my crimes. An inaudible voice remanding me to an invisible jail. Not like the sturdy fortress of the Maryland Pen. No, this was more like Plato's cave of the mind, a place of illusion and inner suffering. Admittedly, it was self-imposed suffering, but nonetheless it proved enduring. Obsessive guilt led me to torture myself over each day's minor failings. I'd be terrified my mistakes would bring on a repetition of the past. Inner rages would leave me filled with self-hate. I couldn't permit myself pleasure without shooting it to bits. Faced with this pain, and the futility of my struggles toward freedom, I sank into a deepening depression. A prisoner gets tired of rattling his chains.

Perhaps the unconscious logic of my imprisonment was no different from that discussed above. I was submitting myself to retributive justice. Having murdered, now I must pay the price. Am I to be allowed joy while my family lie in their graves? Then too, there was the strategy of deterrence. If I punished myself over the smallest misdeeds, surely, it seemed, I could prevent future crimes. In the dark caves of my mind I felt like a serial killer who might strike again if not constrained.

This inner prison, then, became my home. But as with Charley's cave, it was also a place from which I could struggle toward the light. Each Monday when I left the Maryland Penitentiary, I went half a mile west to a therapist's office. It was located at 829 Park Avenue (Baltimore). I had grown up at 850 Park Avenue (New York). In that office I visited and revisited the past, deciphering the mute symptoms that dominated my life.

Mike spoke of a guy who was in jail for upwards of twenty years until he dug his way out with a spoon. I just observed the twentieth anniversary of my brother's death. The past few years have involved a lot of digging; awfully slow, but even with a spoon you make progress. Maybe the hole never looks any bigger than it did yesterday. But then, one day, unexpectedly, your head pops into the light.

And then a tension ensues. Have I finally come home? Or have I foolishly left the only home I know? Everything depends on your answer.

PART THREE

Space and Time

CHAPTER TEN

A Space Odyssey

Martin Heidegger (1889–1976) is considered one of the most significant philosophers of the twentieth century. He is certainly one of its most ambitious, seeking to criticize the entire trajectory of Western thought, as well as the spirit of technology that dominates the modern era. However, his own life has hardly been immune to critique. Elected rector at the University of Freiburg in 1933, Heidegger for a time was disturbingly cooperative with the Nazi agenda.

Here, we are working with an excerpt from Heidegger's 1927 masterwork of phenomenology, Being and Time. *I hesitated to use it. Heidegger's work, filled with neologisms and technical terms, is notoriously hard to read, but I couldn't resist. His insights into lived-space gave us a way to talk about the experience of confinement within prison walls, and the forms of connection and freedom that yet remain possible.*

Bringing Others Close

"De-severing" amounts to making the farness vanish—that is, making the remoteness of something disappear, bringing it close. . . . *In Dasein there lies an essential tendency towards closeness.* . . . With the "radio," for example, Dasein has so expanded its everyday environment that it has accomplished a de-severance of the "world.". . . That which is presumably "closest" is by no means that which is at the smallest distance "from us.". . . Whatever . . . concern dwells alongside beforehand is what is closest, and this is what regulates our de-severances. (Martin Heidegger, *Being and Time*, 139–42)

Drew: Heidegger here is talking about what he calls "spatiality"—not so much the space that you measure off with a ruler, but our *experiential* sense of space. He uses a German term that the translators render as "*de-severance.*" For "Dasein" (his term roughly for human beings), de-severing amounts to making the experienced remoteness of something disappear, bringing it close. Something very near physically, for example my watch, may be experientially very far off if I'm not thinking about it. Even though it's on my wrist all day I have no awareness of it. It's not yet "desevered." Whereas there could be someone physically far off, like a friend in California, whom I do "de-sever"—bring close experientially. I'm thinking of them, concerned with them. Heidegger says it's the character of human beings to continually be taking things that are remote and bringing them close by virtue of our concern.

John: I wanted to ask you about the reverse of that. When you sleep in the West Wing of this prison you're no more than twenty feet from the street. You can look out your tier window and see people walking, but in my thinking they're a lot farther. We say, "Man, so close, but *so far away.*"

Tony: I have to agree with John on that one. You can see over the wall— it's like you can just reach out and touch it—but it might as well be a thousand miles away. If I'm out in the middle of nowhere, like Texas where I grew up, that's one thing. But I'm able to see the city every day, and at nighttime you can hear "free world" sounds, but you can't *participate* in them. When you're not very strong mentally, it'll whack you out real fast. Some of these guys around here, zap-outs, might be the reason some of them went whack.

Selvyn: I just experienced that going back and forth between the institution and the hospital. One guy with me said he liked to get out of the jail. I was telling him I really don't. Coming back from the hospital, the van stopped at the light and we observed this girl running. She had a long overcoat on and the wind was blowing, and underneath, all she had on was a skimpy outfit. The only thing it did for me was made me *mad.* Like John said, so close yet so far away.

Q: I see it a little differently. To me, de-severance is a mechanism for survival. I believe my upbringing was very beautiful; there's nothing I can find there to regret. When I look at the misery that surrounds me here, the way everything (except a class like this) reduces me to an animal, I think it's very important to hold on to the past. Most of the time I think about my family. Not so much the superficial things, you know, girlfriends and cars, but the things that are most beautiful to me—my brothers and sisters, my father and mother. That's who I try to bring close to me at all times and that is what really gives me hope. It's the only thing that keeps me sane.

Drew: I'm hearing two different sides. Selvyn said that for his peace of mind he has to keep the outer world distant. But Q says the prison environment is so unnatural, the only way to regain his humanity is to pull in pieces of the outside world, like his family, and make a home from those memories.

John: In prison I don't think you can lock yourself into one ideology. You can't say, "Well, this is going to hold me." You have to use a variety. There's times when I don't want to sneak up on the third floor and look out because it can be so frustrating. But then there's times that I need to bring the thought of people close to escape this misery.

For example, we have relationships with young ladies while we're in prison, not always the ones we knew before we went in. I was talking with one over the phone and I told her, "Before I can go to sleep at night I have to hold you in my mind, see you laying in bed with me." I'm not talking about sex or anything [*laughter*]—keep the class clean—but as I curl over, I imagine she's there with me.

Charles: When my wife leaves after a visit, I still hold it real close. And when I get on the phone I may say, "Hey, I'll be over there in about an hour." I know I'm not going to be. But we hold each other close and dear.

Q: And bringing my family close means I still have things to offer. Just because I'm locked up, my responsibility doesn't disappear. I can offer advice to my younger brothers and sisters; I have parents I have to reassure I'm alright. I worry about them.

Gary: Me, I don't want anything to do with the street. I'd rather keep it away, 'cause I feel too less a man. Whatever happens out there, I don't have any *control*. If I call somebody it's got to be collect, and I'm always asking for something. And visits hurt. I'll be in pain for a week.

Donald: If I write my son and give him some advice, and he uses it and it helps him, then I feel like I'm "de-severing." I have some power. But if I offer him advice and he don't take it, it just causes me pain.

John: Donald talking about his son made me think about my children. Since I've been incarcerated I've always had a good rapport with my son, but with my daughters it was different. My oldest daughter didn't find out I was incarcerated until she was ten years old. (My youngest daughter still doesn't know.) With my oldest, we came to that point where we had to inform her. She was getting tired of all these letters and pictures and no physical contact. When we first met in the visiting room, she knew I was her father but she was *hurt.*

But now I give her a phone call every weekend—she *demands* that. I can prepare myself for what I want to say 'cause her mother tells me little things: she stopped taking karate class, her self-esteem's going down. So I sit here in my cell and imagine what I want to get across. That's what I think de-severance is.

Then, a lot of us *dream* about being outside. And I mean these dreams are so real that when it ends you're going through a battle with yourself—"They're going to be looking for me, so how am I going to get back *in* the penitentiary? I can't remember how I got out. And I can't just walk up to the door and say, 'let me back!'" [*laughter*] You have that dream all the time.

Charles: All the time.

John: Then you wake up and say, "Whew, I ain't got to worry, 'cause I'm already here." And it's real, I mean it's real, Drew, it's real.

Tony: Then you feel even worse 'cause you say, "Why the *hell* was I trying to think of a way to get back in here?"

Drew: We've been focusing on you all in here, and your relation to the outside world. But how do people *out there* relate to what goes on in the prison? Is the Maryland Penitentiary very distant from their concern? Or do people bring you close, think and care about you, even though you're incarcerated?

John: I believe they do because there's times when I get on the phone and the first thing they say is "We must have talked you up." That's a colloquialism among African Americans that shows they were thinking about you. Or I call my aunt and she says, "Little devil, *where've you been?* You were supposed to call!" This being a hostile, violent situation, a lot of my family members are *concerned.* I know when something has flashed about the penitentiary—inmate dead, fire in the penitentiary, whatever—'cause, bam!, as soon as I get on the phone, that's all everybody's talking about. "We were worried!"

Selvyn: Yeah, I recently discovered how much my family had me on their minds. When I ended up in the hospital [for knee surgery], I got visits from people I hadn't seen in thirteen years. I didn't want to be sick in the hospital, but it took that to find out how many people really have positive thoughts towards me.

Donald: To me it's important to know people care. It helps me place value on them and know they place value on me as a human being. It gives me humanity.

Tray: I agree with what Donald said. But it's not important that *everybody* care because with the new political climate, people are caring about us that we really don't want to. Their concerns are malicious, like the Roper Committee [a Maryland-based victims-rights and get-tough-on-crime group].

I can remember times when I got on the phone with this girl, and one of her aunts said, "That goddamn Tray, I can see him right now." And all they talking about was bringing harm to me.

So some people it's not important that they concern themselves with you. With the political climate, I wish that some people would just stop being so concerned. [*laughter*]

Prison Journeys

Drew: We've been talking about spatiality and closeness, for better or worse, with people in the outside world. But you're all living together in a very confined space. Another challenge is to somehow expand the space you're in. What are ways people have of doing that?

Tray: Overturning their conviction. [*laughter*]

Wayne: When I'm in the kitchen I'll stand up there at the top of the stairs and look over the wall and to me that's like freedom. It seems like all that space outside these walls comes inside of me. But the minute I take my sights off, I'm back in the kitchen again.

And, you know what, Drew? I love rainy days. When I come outside, the rain's like a protective cover, like being in bed with a blanket over you. A sunshiny day, people are out and I feel crowded. But on a rainy day I feel all alone. It changes me on the inside.

Charles: I think also you can have expanded space when you're involved in organizations. Like in Project Turnaround counseling the kids, you're giving a presentation but your mind travels back to your childhood, and you talk about the things that you're presently doing, and try to give them some hope about the future. There's a lot of expansion there.

Tray: My space ain't too restricted because I think of myself as on an *odyssey*. Even in here. I don't look at this as my home; it's just an experience that's necessary in order for me to get where I'm going. I believe I'm here because I lost my road. That's what I'm searching around for, the road to the larger society. In the meanwhile I'm supposed to be restricted in space. I take the stoic outlook—my space is supposed to be restricted but my ideas don't have to be, and that's where I find all my freedom.

A lot of great men were born from these environments, Don King, Gandhi, Malcolm X. Just about all the great men I can think of have been to prison and they learned and expanded.

When I was on the street, I had *less* space than I do in prison. I would only associate with the criminal elements. People like you—"*Dr. Square*"— I would feel real uncomfortable around. It'd be like wearing a turtleneck. All I dealt with was young inner-city black folks, and you know that's real narrow.

Since I've been in prison, I've met people with sophistication, people from different races. I know a couple of Indian guys. You're the second Jewish guy I've met. And Wayne, I don't know, he's from Mars or wherever. My horizons have expanded.

This is not a homogeneous society in here. In spite of what a lot of people believe, only about ten percent of the inmates here are your hardened criminal like me. I used to steal from Rite Aid when I was six years old, I mean I came through the ranks. I got my space here deservedly so. But most of the people here bought a gun and made a mistake. They wanted to try it out, or got some emotional problem—grabbed a lady and she only had two dollars and their emotions went off and they beat her down. I don't have any emotional problems; I was just motivated by *greed*. But not everybody here is your inner-city criminal; you have college graduates and people from different parts of the world. We meet here, and get a chance to rest and get out of our immediate world, and we can think about things we couldn't on the street.

Drew: You talked about being on an odyssey. Odysseus leaves home and undergoes all kinds of adventures that help him grow as a human being until he finally returns home. What would be the home you imagine coming to at the end of the journey?

Tony: Tray had the blinders on when he left. When he goes back, he's not going to have them on. So even though he may go back to the same area, he's going to perceive things in an entirely different way. And if you think differently, your actions will be different.

Used properly, an environment like this can't do anything but help you. It's going to do one of two things; either tear you down or make you grow.

Drew: The usual image and physical reality of prison is that you're not going anywhere. It's interesting that some of you had the experience that being out on the streets was somehow more fixed, more static, whereas being in prison becomes a *journey*.

Tony: It's 'cause you're stuck here physically and the only place you can grow and move is *mentally*. So we do. If a man goes to jail for five years, he'll read more books in that time than the average person will in twenty years. And reading itself can expand the mind. Books can take you anywhere, across the water, into space.

I had a very narrow view before I came to jail. Take Mark Medley. Before I came to jail and was in this class, there was no way in the world that you could have told me that the fact that a fat, white Jew died, it would bother me. I'd have laughed in your face. "So what? It's just another white man gone. That's the same way they think about us." Now I think differently. It hurt me when that man died at my feet because he was someone I had come to respect and like and call a friend. And the fact that he was white and a Jew didn't make any difference. But had that happened on the streets, "another whitey dead" probably would have been the first thing out of my mouth.

Mark Medley was only age 39 when he died. We have no photo of him. He was in the penitentiary for a double murder. I believe he had a history of mental illness, and certainly looked the part. He was disheveled, overweight, and often appeared distracted. As Tony wrote in his eulogy, he seemed like a "zap-out" and that was all many prisoners knew of him. But beneath that he was a friendly, intelligent man, an avid reader, and a learned scholar, specializing in the interrelation of ancient cultures. He knew, to varying degrees, some 10 to 15 languages, and loved to pore over esoteric texts. I experienced him almost as a strange doppelganger of myself: we were both white, both Jewish, both the same age, both in our souls Talmudic-style scholars. He had even been in New Haven, kibitzing at the Yale Library around the time I was attending school there.

On August 7, 1993, after watching a video with Tony and some others, Mark collapsed and died of a heart attack. Earlier in the day he'd sought help at the prison hospital and been turned away, told to go on sick call. But I could almost imagine Mark, always playful, taking glee in having cheated the state by virtue of his premature demise. He was, as he informed me, in for "life without parole, plus life without parole, plus 5 years and 18 months, consecutive."

Tray: Before I came to prison, my entire lifestyle was selling drugs in a single neighborhood. All I knew on the street was other dope fiends and dealers who went to discos and stuff like that. All we talked about was who *had it* and who didn't, and who was *the Man* this week. That was the extent of my life. Every experience was the same experience.

Whereas in here, my journeys are different. Like, remember when you brought in your pictures from Montana? At one time I wouldn't have cared where Montana was. Is the keys [kilos] cheaper in Montana than they are in Florida? That's the only way my interest would have been excited. But when you brought the pictures of Montana it seemed real exciting. And I read up a little about it, not a whole lot. That's the Big Sky State. I never knew that.

Donald: Yeah, on the street, the only thing that meant anything there was how many bags of heroin or cocaine could we sell today, how much money are we going to make, who's going to pay this person for this package, who needs to be shot today, or who's going to do the stickup. If you brought up something about what's going on in the Senate, ain't nobody want to hear about the Senate. The deficit, what? That don't mean nothing.

Tray: And you know what's ironic? The new being tough-on-crime policies, right? We already got our sentences and chances are it won't be retroactive—so it's only going to affect the dudes that's out there. But they ain't even listening to it. The death sentence and stuff like that . . . those dudes ain't listening, they don't hear.

Drew: It sounds like the lifestyle on the street can be very obsessed. You're kind of a rat in a cage running as fast as you can and don't have time or energy to think.

Donald: That's it—obsessive, no time, and nerves.

Tray: The first recorded philosophers in, what's the place—Miletus—the reason they could sit back and ponder those issues is them not having to worry about eating or nothing—they was wealthy. They had it made. And being in prison opens up a little bit of space and security, and a lot of time.

Donald: And once you get some intellectual food in here, then you got to have something to sustain that. If you don't, then you're subject to slip back into that world. Like a lot of guys who go home and restrict themselves to the same kind of people they were with before—they can't feed that higher consciousness they developed in prison and they fall back into the same trap.

Tony: I think knowledge is just like heroin. It's addictive. And in order to get off heroin, you use methadone. Well, if you run out of the knowledge—when your jones [addictive craving] come down for knowledge and you can't get the fix—then you'll go for something else. And all your buddies are gonna be there trying to give it to you. You might be able to put it off for a while. But if you can't fill that knowledge jones, eventually you go back.

Making Space

In the beginning, God made space. Or so it says in Genesis 1. Before God could fill things up with sun and moon, plants, animals, and humans, He first had to make a place to put them all. So "In the beginning God created the heavens and the earth. . . . And God said, 'Let there be light'; and there was light." This, too, was a space-making, for light opens up a distance across which we can see and act. Shrouded in darkness, our horizons are limited. We move gingerly, relying on the proximate sense of touch to feel our way around. But turn on a light and a vast world leaps into being. It's such an ordinary magic that we forget to marvel. Not so, the author of Genesis who imagined the first time someone switched on the light.

As Donald and Tray discuss their former life, I hear an opposite cosmogony. They came from the narrow world of the street. "Every experience was the same experience." It's a world that never gets *started* really, run by an addict god in search of a fix. Nothing new, nothing that initiates light or expansion. Tray is excited to learn of Montana: the "Big Sky State." But his streets were bounded by a narrow sky winding above tenement buildings.

Selling drugs must have seemed a way to expand space. In our society, money provides the big bang that opens a whole universe of possibilities. With money appears to come power, status, and freedom. You're no longer confined to the street; you *own* the street and the shiny cars to cruise it, with a woman perched in the passenger seat.

But this attempt to open up space led only to its further constriction. The inmates describe the dealer's lifestyle closing in, obliterating every other concern. To me, dealer and addict began to sound almost indistinguishable—both trapped in obsessive worlds where thrills masked over endless repetition.

And this life finally led straight to jail (do not pass Go, do not collect $200). The street may be narrow, but it does stretch long. You come from somewhere and at least have the illusion you're on the way to somewhere new; prison's pinch is even tighter. The Maryland Penitentiary is a closed box housing almost nine hundred men within one city block. If Genesis 1 tells of a sentence that initiates creation, this seemed to me a *de-creation*: the judge pronounces a sentence and your world implodes.

That's why I was so surprised to hear the men's account of their prison experience. I expected to be told about the tortures of confinement. But they also spoke of an odyssey, a journey through an expanded world. I was taken aback. The liberal within me is even afraid to focus on this point for fear it will be used to glorify prison. In fact, prison often is a soul-killing hell. But human beings also have the power to transform and transcend their environs. Genesis does say, after all, "So God created man in his own image." And if we are created in God's image, it means we too must be *creators*, capable of making space. What else can you do in a nine-by-twelve cell? Necessity is the mother of invention. Maybe God was feeling claustrophobic, imprisoned, that day He/She created the universe.

But how does a human being make space? Our Heidegger text suggests that we live in a world proportionate to our concern. Experientially, we open to those things and people we care about. And the inmates spoke about a heart connection that expanded their world beyond prison walls.

In an earlier dialogue, Selvyn tells how his desolation was relieved by a loving letter from his sister. "That was like a light at the end of the tunnel." And when Selvyn would talk of such things his face would brighten. Maybe it's not only God who said, "Let there be light." Maybe we do it for one another.

Here I also get an image of Michelangelo's Sistine Chapel ceiling; God reaches out across space to touch Adam into life. Their contact is so tangential, and yet enough for the spark to be transmitted. So, too, when Charles meets Betty for thirty minutes across a hard table. "When my wife leaves after a visit, I still hold it real close. And when I get on the phone I may say, 'Hey, I'll be over there in about an hour.'" It's a lie, we know, but in service to deeper truth. The man who talks with Betty is no longer in prison.

But I wonder: from whence comes this space that can re-create a man and tear down prison walls? Perhaps a metaphoric clue is found in Genesis 2. In this second creation account, God "caused a deep sleep to fall upon [Adam], and while he slept took one of his ribs and closed up its place with flesh; and the rib which the Lord God had taken from the man he made into a woman." Sexist implications aside, I hear a hidden message. To have loving relation, you not only need the other person, but *space within your heart* to respond. By taking a rib, God creates both. A hole is carved in Adam's chest, which only Eve can fill. That, we might conjecture, is the true nature of the human heart: not some thick, fleshly organ, but a space within, receptive. But this heart-space also opens up room to suffer. If Charles feels comfort from his visits, for Gary, "visits hurt. I'll be in pain for a week." I see this also in John's relationship with his kids. In an essay he gave me, "A Father's Chance," he writes of the joy he takes in his football-playing son, his oldest daughter, an orange belt in karate, and his youngest daughter on the swim team. But "The most difficult part of my incarceration, aside from all the nonsense that occurs in prisons, is not being able to meet my responsibility as a father. I often wonder how long I can hold on to these fragile relationships and how long my children will recognize me as a father."

This is the pain of a man barred from the outer world. "Man, so close but *so far away*." But I think every parent knows something of this feeling. There are things you want to say, but can't quite; times you wish you were patient and you're simply not; harms from which you can't protect your child.

My wife and I are adopting a baby girl from China, and already I'm anticipating this. Having watched an entire family die, I'm scared to start another. No, terrified. What if I'm a lousy father, what if I can't keep my daughter safe, what if she dies too? I know that when we go to the Chinese orphanage and first pick up Sarah, a space will open in my heart that simply wasn't there before. Love will flow as from an open wound.

In a way, my coming to prison opened up such a space. I don't consider myself the most compassionate of men. White and well-to-do, I can be quite oblivious to those less advantaged. And to a degree this is purposeful. I remember when Rwanda hit the front pages, and then Bosnia, and I decided *I just don't want to know*. Why open myself to a suffering that I can do so little to fix? But entering prison, I realized that the sphere of pain seemed more limited, the possibilities of helping clearer. And I found my heart opening up to the men.

And then the suffering. This morning I called to make sure the count-out was prepared for today's class (fat chance, I thought). The guard said it was. But another teacher informed me that a sizable part of the prison population was being transferred this week to the new prison in Jessup. The Maryland Penitentiary is being downgraded to a medium security facility. Since my students are the hard-core lifers, most of them have gone, or would be soon. [Note: The subsequent dialogues in this book were chronologically recorded earlier, before these transfers.]

Watching my family die made me an expert in shutting down unwanted feelings. This mechanism clicked into place the moment I heard the news. Okay, I thought, we'll carry on. I went down to the prison as on any other day. Let's see who's still there. Tray was, at least for the moment: he surmises that, as the head of the sewing shop, his services are still required. Tony was there, presumably for similar reasons. Wayne too. The others— all gone. For three years I've worked closely with some of these men and we didn't even have a chance to say goodbye. The prisoners themselves don't know who's leaving until the guard stops by and tells them to pack up. I suppose it's for security reasons, but what an abrupt way to shatter a man's world. I remember Mark's words about the panopticon: "They have to liquidate their inventory. It's a matter of storage space." That's all.

I spent a few minutes discussing the situation with the men who remained. They didn't seem to want to delve too deeply. They had well-functioning shock absorbers that I wasn't going to tamper with. We decided to continue, reduced as we were. But ten minutes later class was shut down and I was ordered from the prison. A problem with the count-out.

My shock absorbers work pretty well too. But after denial, finally comes rage: at the prison authorities, at the men all leaving, at my brother whose birthday would have been the day before. And the rage masks over an even deeper sadness. Seeking words to capture the pain of loss, all I can think of is that moment in the *Wizard of Oz* when the Scarecrow says goodbye to Dorothy: "Now I *know* I have a heart, 'cause it's breaking." Terrible cliché, I say to myself. Can't possibly use it in the book. Jessup isn't Kansas, and John Woodland sure isn't Dorothy on her way home. But there's a truth there. Hearts do come to be in the breaking. Adam's heart was born when God ripped into his chest. At least Adam was under general anesthesia.

Then there was Mark Medley's heart attack. I had come in for my class, a day like any other, and was told he had died over the weekend. It was the third prison fatality that month. In one, the cause of demise was clear—a man was stabbed thirty-seven times in a personal vendetta the day after he had arrived. But why had Mark died? Was it his love of junk food, in fact, any kind of food, leading to a rather substantial belly and clogged arteries? Was it negligence on the part of the prison hospital? Certain inmates thought his death might have been prevented if his complaints had been treated seriously. Was it the grinding stress of prison, shooting blood pressure through the roof? Or the loss of that elusive "will to live" when you're looking at a sentence of double life? I even wondered if it had something to do with being white. The first white man who joined our class died of a stroke, though relatively young. Mark was the second to go. The third, Gary Huffman, was taken to the hospital with failing kidneys midway through this project. His wife's voice came over the phone one day from California asking for advice about medical parole. She told me his condition was considered terminal. What is this, I wondered? Should I put a sign over my classroom door: "White guys, beware!"?

For whatever reason, Mark's heart broke and he died. But this led Tony to notice how his own heart had come alive. "It hurt me when that man died at my feet." Tony asked, and the class agreed, that this book be dedicated to Mark Medley. It seems that when we make space in our heart, caring and pain come in the same door.

But if one could say anything about Mark, it's that he illustrated a different way of making space—one that employed the *head.* It's not that his heart was inactive. Though few people took the trouble to know him,

Mark would give apples to his friends and help them write papers; he exuded a kind of funny warmth. But what set him apart was his prodigious knowledge, especially of arcane details from the distant past. Classmates called him "the human computer." He could tell you about the burial customs of ancient Sumeria or trace the etymology of a given word through a number of Near Eastern languages prior to the third century B.C. Sometimes I had my doubts about his facts. After all, in my handout sheet asking for "Other information you'd use to describe yourself" he wrote, "A disorganized, schizophrenic idiot savant." True, no doubt, and probably connected with the double murder he'd committed. But Mark usually knew what he was talking about, the result of his intensive reading program.

This strikes me as a prime example of making space in, and with, your head. He lived as much in ancient Egypt as in the Maryland Penitentiary. We often think of education as a kind of filling up of space: the teacher stuffs facts into students' weary brains. But the times when I most felt like an educator, my experience was the opposite: teacher and student were together creating space. Each idea opened an avenue of new possibilities that in turn branched into other thoroughfares. Soon you're exploring a novel world.

This happened for me when I entered the prison. The thoughts and experience of these men took me on an odyssey not unlike the one Tray describes. If part of Odysseus's journey involved a descent to Hades, so too for me: I was leaving life in the ivory tower to confront a criminal underworld. But I was surprised to hear that for some of the inmates their imprisonment meant just the opposite: it was the closest approximation they knew to the ivory tower I was leaving behind. "Since I've been in prison, I've met people with sophistication . . . you have college graduates and people from different parts of the world. We meet here, and get a chance to rest and get out of our immediate world, and we can think about things we couldn't on the street." It's what every university would wish to be: a cosmopolitan atmosphere, a diverse student body, the leisure for study and free exchange of ideas.

If this is what a few men found in prison, I think it's because they sought it out. My students were atypical in using the prison as university. Many others look and see a cage, or a basketball court, or a place to kill time while it's killing you. That some could make the state Pen into a kind of Penn State shows our capacity to make space with our heads.

But if, in the biblical account, heart-space is created when God takes Adam's rib, how is the origin of this *mind-space* represented? Maybe it's in Genesis 3 when, against God's direction, Adam and Eve eat from the tree of the knowledge of good and evil. It "was to be desired to make one wise. Then the eyes of both were opened." Whereas we imprison our felons, God exiled them, casting Adam and Eve from the Garden.

The story has yielded many interpretations. Does "knowledge of good and evil" refer to illicit sexual knowledge? Is the story about the roots of sin in human pride and defiance? Is it an allegory of the rupture with nature brought about as human consciousness develops? Sure, why not. But something else catches my eye. The story links wisdom both with God-like vision, and the most sordid crap of human life. As part of exile, God pronounces upon Adam and Eve the pain of childbirth, the toil of seeking food, enmity between husband and wife, all culminating in ignominious death: "you are dust, and to dust you shall return." Sounds like God's a pretty tough-on-crime judge. Knowledge is punished by suffering.

But what if we reverse the equation? What if suffering is not construed as the *punishment* for knowledge, but the very path by which knowledge is secured? That seems to fit my experience. Much of what I know about life came from the pains and problems I've suffered through. Losing your whole family is not a pleasant way to learn. But it also turned me into a philosopher, questing for answers, digging into the self's dark recesses, reaching upward for the Spirit's call. Like a balloon, I expanded with each breath of pain.

And so, too, it seemed, had these prisoners. If to some degree their eyes "were opened, and they knew that they were naked," this was the result of much suffering. It had beaten space into their minds when nothing else worked. Maybe that's, after all, why God threw us out of the Garden. He knew that to grow we needed more struggle, more space. Stealing fruit was the easy part; the real tree of knowledge was rooted in all that followed.

CHAPTER TWELVE

Doing Time

Eugene Minkowski (1885–1972) was a French psychiatrist whose research and writing were influenced by the philosophical school of phenomenology. Early on, Minkowski's close contact with a melancholic patient convinced him that the central difference in this man's world was his sense of time, and the tools of phenomenology were necessary to understand this. That case study later became part of the book quoted from below, Lived Time, *published in 1933.*

We used excerpts of this work to open up the question of time as experienced in a prison setting. The prisoners found Minkowski's writing dense, but the topics he treats were central to their lives.

Redeeming Time

When we are concerned with time in our daily lives, we take out our watch instinctively or look at the calendar, as if everything concerning time were reduced to assigning a fixed point to each event and then explaining the distance that separates one from another in terms of years, months, and hours. . . . We put this aspect of time aside. It constitutes too narrow a base for a general study of the phenomenon of time. . . . What we must do above all is to seize the phenomenon of time at its roots, in all its richness and in all of its original specificity. (Eugene Minkowski, *Lived Time: Phenomenological and Psychopathological Studies*, 13, 14, 16)

Drew: According to scientific time, you're always in the present, right? The past is gone and the future hasn't come. But *experientially*, you're not necessarily there. You could be living in your past memories, and going over things that could have happened but didn't. Or you could be living in the future, building dreams and hopes. Where do prisoners usually live? In the present, the past, or future?

Charles: I think I live in all three. I live in the present by my participation now in the class. I prepare myself for the future, for the parole hearings and graduating from college. And I go back to the past when I rem-

85

inisce. For example, I got a shirt in my cell, twenty years old, you know, but it's good quality, one of the best I got. . . .

Drew: Like my pants. [*laughter*]

Charles: Yeah, like your pants, as a matter of fact it's the same material, Italian knit! I bought it from Hamburgers in 1974 for about fifty-five dollars, but it's worth a hundred and ten today. I had it on Saturday night and dudes say, "You look pretty good, Charles," and I say, "Yeah, this is my old favorite shirt." The dudes were laughing, like Charley got his '74 outfit on again. By the way, where *did* you get those pants, Doc?

Donald: I think the problem is that guys in here spend most of the time just discussing the good ole days, the glory days, "When I had my car, these two jobs, or those five girls." Or "When prison was better" or "Instead of knives and machine guns we had forty-five magnums." If you try to talk about the future it's just not acceptable.

Selvyn: I've seen guys with a couple life sentences plus some numbers behind it, saying "Yeah, my wife will be waiting for me like the old days." I be thinking, "Are you out of your mind?" I wouldn't say it 'cause they'd be ready to fight, but they're trapped in *that past.*

John: Quite a few guys try to live in the past. I like living in the future, thinking about what my life is going to be. But I think one thing most of us try to avoid is the *present.* Because the present here is the most painful.

Q: I see it a little differently. To me, time is like a dragon I have to slay. If I can master the present, I will have used my time to *redeem* time. Then I can go back and offer something to people who never had to be in that situation.

Drew: Can you give an example of redeeming time?

Q: I get up in the morning at eight thirty and I don't get back to my cell until about ten p.m. Between those times I'm constantly involved in activities that are beneficial and what I want to do. I'm reading materials I intend to use in the future for political work, and philosophical literature, concentrating heavily. The time flies for me, you know? Sometimes I can't even find enough hours to complete what I wanted.

Wayne: I call this "*doing time*"—when you use every available moment for your benefit. When you have time to sit back and mope and worry, is when *time begins to do you.*

Tray: Q probably has a different perspective on time 'cause he has one of those sentences where he's going home. He got a date so he knows what he has to do to get it all in, like the information he needs for politics.

But I think dudes like me, with life sentences, are able to be the *most creative* with time. We can enjoy every moment of it and get all we can without being restricted. Time doesn't rush me along. It's not like I got some expected date where I got to hurry up and slay this dragon. I'm living in the best of all possible worlds, and when I do get out it'll be the best time.

John: Tray talking about lifers being on this indefinite time, I don't think so. Whatever we plan on doing, we have a limited time to do it in. I mean, if I want to have a family I have to get out by the time I'm forty. Let's say I want to start my own business, then save enough money to retire—that puts you on a clock. If you want to meet hopes and desires, there's no indefinite time for anybody.

Tray: Hey, we have to figure in that you asked a young buck about time. Ask an old person, their perception is going to be a lot different.

Charles: It is!

Tray: John mentioned something about retirement. That ain't never in my concept. I ain't even going to die from where I'm looking at right now. I mean I'm vital. Maybe when I hit thirty, thirty-five, forty, the grim reaper. . . .

Charles: Closing in!

Tray: But right now I'm not concerned. If I make a mistake, so what? Whereas I guess when you get to a certain point in time, you're like "Hold up, I can't make any mistakes, I done made too many!" But I don't think I made too many yet. That may be just the naïveté that comes with—

Charles: Youth!

Tray: Youth. But right now I can enjoy everything, get the full experience out of everything, even my mistakes, because I'm living with a pure future.

John: I don't think it has anything to do with age. I think it has to do with maturity. A young child can have a concept of things he wants to do, set down chronologically. "If I want to be a doctor, I have X amount of years of school so I have to focus in." And it shows maturity because you're *thinking*, whereas immaturity is about emotions. Just do what you want to do this moment.

A lot of times you see that in the yard here—I'm not talking about young or old, but about *immature* and *mature* convicts. 'Cause a lot of young guys come in here and go right to hit the laws, right up in that law library. Then you have another group that all they do is shoot basketball for ten years. The immature one says, "I got forever."

Tray: You're missing the whole point. And I can understand this because not everybody thinks as *deep* as me.

You know this dude you describe as mature, the one who dedicates himself to studies and casework, expecting a break in the courtroom, hopeful they'll get out of prison soon—when things don't happen they usually the ones to go crazy. They become frustrated grouches. Whereas the dude he was describing as immature—like me—*I enjoy the moment*. My case went just as far, I'm having fun designing this great future too. But my present is so enjoyable because I'm not expecting and hoping.

Mike: You sure can't count the amount of time you got to do. Not when the majority of people here have life plus sixty-five, life plus twenty. You don't actually put the sentence out of your mind, because it is always there, impossible to forget. But it's a war you fight battle by battle. You got to go with an innate belief that some way you're going to elude that length of time.

Q: I don't dwell on the sentence because it can overwhelm you—you can actually go insane. You get caught up in this *time zone*.

Charles: You can get tripping, Doc.

Gary: It's where your mind jumps time.

Donald: Sometimes you come back, sometimes you don't.

Gary: But as far as hope, there's only one person I know of in the Maryland correctional system that doesn't have any, and that's that kid sitting over in Supermax who keeps trying to die—John Thanos [subsequently executed]. There are people who flip back and forth, lose hope and then regain it, but it's part of everybody's sanity that one day they'll get out. "Man, I got life without parole, but I still have a governor that can give me a pardon."

John: I disagree. I think there's a lot of guys in here who *don't* have hope. I've seen guys who as soon as they get their sentence from the judge, they take it as a literal meaning. They don't have enough insight to know that when the judge says "life," he's not talking about your natural life. A lot of them just give up.

And I don't think their lack of hope started here. In the black community, any community where you find a lot of criminal activity, you've got people saying, "There's no value to life, no hope in life, I have no meaning, I can't change anything, I'm *powerless*."

Charles: A lot of those individuals was locked up before they actually got locked up in prison.

Drew: They had already lost the future.

Regrets

But evil cannot disappear without leaving traces in the past. . . . The phenomenon of remorse occurs. . . . [R]egret shares in the essential characteristics of remorse. Like it, it has to do with a precise fact of the past and, at the same time, projects a ray toward the future. Certainly we can regret only what has happened; but all regret, if it is not to become completely sterile, contains an "It would have been better if," which is either to influence our future behavior or produces in us the hope that things will be different another time. (Minkowski, *Lived Time*, 159–60)

Donald: Initially I looked at the past with remorse, shame, regret, pain, however you want to define it. But from this class, I don't judge the past as harshly. Because only the future can tell me what effects it will have. Maybe coming to prison made me something more unique than if I were out there in a nine-to-five job turning forty. I might have a big ole gut and a fat ole wife, *miserable*. Ready to go commit a crime. But because of what I went through, when the time arrives and I'm out there, maybe it'll be different because I experienced my pain. From suffering in my youth, hopefully I will bypass that in middle age and old age. I would hate for it to have been reversed—it was all a party up to forty and from there it went downhill!

Tray: But sometimes memories can become real depressing. Me and John'll be talking and I'll tell him the first time I ever wanted to sell drugs. I was going into the seventh grade and I'd gotten fashion conscious. A dude gave me a job holding narcotics. I can remember sitting back there in the alley holding the stash for fifty dollars a night so I could save up for a slick wardrobe to start junior high. When I think about how bright my future is still going to be, that past experience doesn't seem as bad. But when I'm dealing with the present, and how that led me to the hardships of being incarcerated, it's an *awful* memory.

Mike: It's funny we should touch on this because I think about a young lady all the time. She got pregnant when she was going to Columbia University, getting her second master's. She's real smart, a Phi Beta Kappa and all that, and I had just come out of prison, right? And I was going to settle down when she had her baby. But she said she had to get rid of it because it was going to interfere with her completing her master's. I didn't really put up much of an argument, but after that happened it changed the whole course of our relationship. And I'm thinking now, if she had had the baby I wouldn't have continued running around. I really cared a lot about her. I view that as a major turning point.

Q: What I think about most in my past is the opportunities and privileges I had. When I look at the circumstances most of the guys here came from, I can see why they're here. But I went to all private Catholic institutions. After graduating from high school in Nigeria I automatically got admission to college over here, all expenses paid by my parents. When I came to this country I was seventeen years old. I had my B.S. when I was twenty, and stayed in graduate school from 1983 until I got locked up. So

I think about a missed opportunity. I could have become a Ph.D. by the time I was twenty-seven.

But I had to prove something to my dad. He's one of those traditionalists—if he gives you ten thousand dollars you have to account for every cent. After a while I didn't want to subject myself to that. I started saying "Man, I don't need your money, I can take care of myself." That was the mistake. That was the turning point.

Drew: I hear people talking about their turning points. It can be something you did, like in Tray's case, or something you didn't do that might have changed the course of your life. If Michael's girlfriend had her baby, or Q finished graduate school. So we not only live in the actual past, but in the *virtual* past that *could have been.*

Tray: I really think my whole life would have went different if I wouldn't have got as much praise for negative things. I can remember the very first time I ever stole something. I went into a Cut-Rate and stole a whole case of Now-and-Laters, the taffy. I was about six, and all my friends praised me for getting us the candy. I was filled with so much pride. And from that point on I always sought that gratification. It's like when I turned over that first key, shot my first victim and got away with it . . . that same pride. I think that very first time if I'd been *punished* rather than praised, my whole life would've been different.

Drew: It's funny, because I remember that kind of gratification, but from getting straight A's in my courses and my parents making a big fuss. Maybe we were seeking the same kind of experience but found it in different directions.

Tray: It's like sex ain't it, that feeling of being praised?

Drew: Yeah! It feels great. You feel important, loved, secure.

Tray: And ever since then I just went with it.

Drug Time

John: Thinking about my past, it may have been in the late seventies that I got involved with cocaine. And if you've ever been to NA meetings, people will always tell you that once they start using cocaine, this is a major downfall. Life for me became very turbulent. I started basing, and ended up in a hospital in New Jersey for three days. Then to keep using, I got more heavily involved in dealing. I got started with the crime that has me incarcerated now.

Drew: For a number of people, drugs have played a big part in how their lives unfolded. Since we're talking about *time,* I'm wondering what drug activity and drug use do to one's sense of time.

Mike: You know how you see those movies where subways, trains, everything is passing *real fast.* That's the effect drugs had on me. It's like when they lock these people up for leaving their babies for days, and you wonder what's happening, right? I was talking to a guy the other day who told me his sister did that, just left her twins in the house two or three days. Because when you're so caught up in the drugs you've got *no concept of time.*

Tony: I knew a female like Mike was saying. She stayed gone for a week and they took her kids. When she came back, she said "What are you talking about? I just left!" She was free-basing for a week straight, had no concept of time. Because you're in that false world, *never-never land.* You're over there with Alice.

Charles: When I first got into the white powder drugs, I didn't use but I was the holding man. The day used to seem *real long,* man, because I would be in the hallway just holding the stash and it was cold. And the days was long, but once I started snorting, the days picked up. They went faster—I started losing track of time.

Drew: Is that part of the reason people use drugs? To make something *happen* and happen fast, instead of days that just stretch on?

Tray: The way drugs distorts time is part of the benefit. Let's say I have a lot of pressing bills and the deadline's two hours from now. Once I start getting high, the two hours is gone. You defy all time. In this prison, time is constantly rushing and moving—we got to get out of here at two forty-five for count-out. But if I had a blast right now, two forty-five wouldn't mean anything. If I was bipping (or so you better understand me, "inhaling it in my nostril"), then time would be completely defied.

Drew: So this might be the reason a lot of people try to use drugs in prison—they're "serving time" and have time constraints, but that all gets wiped out.

Tray: Nobody philosophizes before they start getting high, "Oh if I sniff, I can fool time." But once you start, that's the *beauty* of it.

John: I think people use drugs to change their perception of reality. The world can be stressful, with a lot of guidelines and deadlines. When you start using, they become insignificant. "Not to worry. I can handle it." But eventually, you're perceiving the world one way when everybody else is seeing it as it actually is. So when you come back to reality, people say, "What the hell is wrong with you? You were supposed to be here, do this, take care of that!"

Tony: And when you realize all those responsibilities you forgot in never-never land, by then they've probably doubled. So you're even more depressed when you come down. Only one thing to do. "Let's go get high some more!"

Gary: And anybody that's involved in the narcotics trade, using, selling, whatever, they're subject to lose their life at any minute, go to jail at any minute. Very stressful. Taking the drugs relieves that stress. It puts you in the state of mind where *you just don't care.*

Drew: It sounds like a vicious cycle: doing drugs puts you in danger, so you do drugs to deal with the feeling of threat.

Gary: That's how it is.

Charles: But another aspect we have to look at, is that these users are *responsible.* There's still a time frame, because they know they have to get up that morning—most of them flatfoot hustle—go downtown, shoplift, boost, do whatever thieving they have to do to get that drug, and catch the man before he leaves. These are the people that buy the dealer his home, his five-carat flawless diamond ring. It's the drug *users* that get these people these items, not the drug *dealer.* He needs someone to sell to, someone who takes on the responsibility to get out there and hustle.

Drew: It's the same way that money being made by a big entrepreneur is coming from his thousand workers. The users have to be good employ-ees and bring in the money before the factory whistle blows. It's a para-dox—they have to organize time very well to get the drug that frees them up from time.

Tray: Whatever way you look at time, whether it's in the drug world or not, time is real cruel. It moves us all and never gives us enough. Like the Hindus, I believe if given enough time, people that do negative things will eventually get tired of them and go to something positive. Everything I've ever done I got tired of and proceeded on. Like in the beginning when I was stealing candy, I moved to robbing, then selling drugs, and on and on I kept progressing. Without the limits time places, we would all get to something positive. But in this short amount of time we're given, you got to do all your mistakes, then make your life right, and then find room in there to purify your soul so you have a good afterlife. Everybody spends more time in the ground than they do on earth. So I'm trying to dedicate myself to getting rid of time. Because when I think about the future, that traps me, and my past traps me. The only thing I can do good with is this moment *right now.*

CHAPTER THIRTEEN

Redeeming Time

A friend of mine described a TV news feature he had watched concerning inner-city violence. The interviewer asked a black child, maybe eight years old, what his hopes and ambitions for the future were. The child gave the question deep consideration. He replied, "I'd like to make it to ten."

It's a funny thing to lose the future. How can you lose something that hasn't yet arrived? Yet this child's future lay buried in a small coffin, apparently like some of his friends.

It takes hope to keep a future alive. John talks about the loss of hope endemic not only in the African American community, but "any community where you find a lot of criminal activity." What is the connection with criminality, I wonder? One answer that occurs: if you've already lost your future, you've little more to lose. As a dealer, a burglar, a hustler, you could get killed or hustled right off to jail. For a person with a future, the potential losses might be unacceptable. This certainly seems true for me. What of those years I have to look forward to of happy marriage, of seeing my daughter grow and flourish, of joining friends for wine and conversation over a good meal? What about this book I am driving to complete, and the two others on the drawing board; what of the workshop I'm giving in November, then the trip to China to pick up Sarah, then Thanksgiving with my old college buddies, then. . . . There's far too much future for me to place it at risk. But what if I gazed in a crystal ball and saw nothing? Then crime's high-stakes gamble might seem worth the odds.

But the inmates also told me of another connection between time and crime. In chapter 18, we talk about youthful impatience. John speaks of his uncle, a successful dentist, who tried to interest him in the practice. Patience is the path, he was informed; plow through school, slowly build a clientele, put a little money away each month, and one day you wake up a success. John (and others) wanted success, but they wanted it *now*. In the old *Star Trek*, the starship Enterprise could switch into warp drive and leap over light-years in an instant. It was a wonderful sight: the ship suddenly shooting forward, leaving light-trails and disappearing, only to resurface in another galaxy. And the men seemed to harbor a similar dream. (Isn't it the quintessential *American* dream?) Dealing or hustling might fire those jets, the punk transformed into the Man in a moment. Through crime, they were trying to master time.

But instead they ended up *serving* time. These men who had been so impatient were now forced to patiently endure the years. Nothing like double life in the hoosegow to bring your rushing life to a halt. It was the mirror opposite of the *Star Trek* fantasy, as when Sulu would say, "Captain, we've lost power!" and the ship would come to a dead stop in space.

But where? In Einstein's theory of relativity, objects can only be localized through reference to a four-dimensional space–time continuum. So too, in human experience, are space and time interwoven. Nowhere is this clearer than in the case of a prisoner. When the judge pronounces sentence: "So-and-so shall be confined to the penitentiary for the term of forty years" he throws a man into an alien space–time framework. It's not just the extremity of the physical confinement, but that it will go on for so very long. And it's not just the length of time, but that it must be endured in such limited surroundings. Space and time form the crisscrossed bars that a prisoner stares through toward the outer world.

We've talked about making space. But how about killing time, I wondered? Q says, "Time is like a dragon I have to slay in order to survive in here." I imagine this like one of those three-headed dragons you see in medieval illustrations. One dragon's head is the *disappearing future.* If a person can be left futureless by life on the street, how much more so when he faces life in prison. Then there is the dragon's head of the *empty, endless present.* It reminds me of one of my favorite movies, *Groundhog Day,* where Bill Murray finds himself trapped in time: each morning he wakes up and it's still February 2 in Punxsutawney, Pennsylvania, with the same song on the radio in the same boardinghouse. He starts to go nuts. So too, I think, would the prisoner waking up for his three-thousandth day in the same damn cell. Even if it's a different cell, it's the same damn cell. And finally, there's the dragon's head of the *screwed-up past.* Late at night it breathes the hot fire of "If only I had but now it's too late." Future, present, and past all attacking. That's the thing about three-headed dragons: cut off one head and another may strike, even while the first has time to regenerate.

Whether you're in jail or on the street, drugs provide one way to battle the dragon. "If I was bipping then time would be completely defied." No future to worry about. Pressing bills and obligations—they've all disappeared in white powder up your nose. Then too, forgotten are biting regrets of the past. Even the duration of the present is obliterated.

So these men had tried to escape time, jump time, bend time to their will. It hasn't worked. But Q talks about a new project he developed in prison: that of "redeeming" time. Perhaps no one is as conscious of sheer temporality as an inmate serving an extended sentence. He must work the fabric of time each day as a tailor works and reworks his cloth.

If I'm intrigued by this notion of redeeming time, maybe it's because time has been such an issue in my life. For one thing, I've spent years in a doctor's office rehashing the past in minute detail: the shouting that echoed from behind closed doors as I'd huddle with a book, purposefully oblivious; the last time I saw Scott alive, and what I said to him, and failed to say. The past, I've come to realize, is ingredient in my present, often twisting it into distorted patterns. To redeem time I've had to go backwards in time. It has proved an arduous and perilous journey.

Then too, there's the pressure of present and future. Today, for example, I am determined to finish this section on "time" on time. I'm keeping to a self-imposed schedule designed to make sure the book is completed before Sarah arrives. But when I turned on my home computer this morning nothing happened. Broke again! And when I picked up my phone to call the repair shop, nothing happened again—no dial tone, *nada*. The phone's out. I want to scream. Too many distractions, each wasting precious minutes. I feel the day closing down around me like a shrinking prison cell.

Several years ago, this experience of time pressure was so powerful and recurrent that I had to work the Twelve Step program on "time obsession." I was addicted to rushing, like a gambler to a bet. If it took fifteen minutes to get to my therapist's office, hitting the lights right, that's how much time I'd leave, cursing myself all the way for cutting it so close and swearing to never do it again. Sure, I'd get high from the adrenaline of being tightly scheduled. I've calmed down a lot since then, but still the question remains: just what is it to "redeem" time?

The prisoners, it seemed, usually began with the future. One key was to keep hope alive. Most were facing the kind of prison time that threatened to consign them to the scrapheap of failure. When Mark died at age thirty-nine, it shook Tray up. "I'm not so much afraid of dying," he said, "but of dying a *failure*." Most of them equated that with dying in jail, and focused on what they'd do when they got out. John looked forward to a clean start in New York State, maybe with help from a supportive relative. For Charles the goal was to own a small business, as he had before incarceration. Tray was less modest: he planned on being a big-time entrepreneur able to buy and sell former enemies, and distribute largesse to a community in need. Was any of this realistic, I wondered? After all, these men had *long* sentences—but, then again, with possibility of parole; if they got out they'd still be ex-cons—but weren't they also intelligent, highly motivated men? Finally, I simply don't know where optimism ended and sheer fantasy began. Maybe they didn't either. Their hope was the bread that kept a hungry soul alive, and they weren't examining it too closely for mold.

A salvaged future can thus redeem present and past. It gave Q the schedule of a man on the move. It gifted Tray with a way to accept his ill-fated entry into drug dealing: "When I think about how bright my future is still going to be, that past experience doesn't seem as bad." It's just a temporary setback, or even a learning experience preparing one's life for something better. We're used to the notion of time flowing forward, such that the past sets up what is to come. But such examples suggest it is often the reverse. Our future goals seize priority and reorganize our understanding of what came before.

So here, I think, is one strategy for redeeming time: focusing on a hoped-for future. It seems especially useful in dire circumstances. But Tray also points out some of its problems. Our hopes and expectations are like a castle built on air, ready to collapse if the wind changes. Focusing on the future can also bring worry, pressure, and distraction. We miss out on the present moment. Times slip away that might have been worthwhile.

I know this. I spend too much time living in the future. I have discovered, for example, that if the coward dies a thousand deaths in anticipation, so does the expectant author. Will this book find a publisher and a readership? Hell, will it even find an agent? Will the inmates and I be able to work through the complex editorial, legal, and financial arrangement of the project? For that matter, will I ever get the damn thing written? I suppose if you're reading this, such questions have been resolved. But not from where I'm sitting now. The future gnaws at me with the teeth of a hundred small demons.

Come to think of it, that's not a bad description for the past as well. The prisoners brood on turning points in their life: Michael's girlfriend having an abortion; Q's refusal to account to his father; Tray getting praise for stealing a case of (the aptly named) Now-and-Laters. I also brood on the moments when my life turned a corner and suddenly changed direction. Like the last time I saw Scott.

It was a night where we shared love and yet everything went wrong. We were supposed to go to a Mets baseball game together. I was to meet him at the subway station, but for some reason fell asleep and missed the appointment. I never do that. He came round and roused me, a little angry but ready to let it pass. We took a long walk from Manhattan's Upper East Side down to his apartment in the Village, intoxicated as always by the city's night-energy formed of neon, honking taxis, fruit and vegetable bodegas, and a hundred beautiful women we would never know. As we walked, we argued about music. Scott maintained it was clearly the paramount art form of Western culture. What painting or poem could approach Bach's B Minor Mass? I retorted that one couldn't possibly make such comparisons, that each art had its own excellences. Now, I marvel at my deafness. In his suicide letter, Scott wrote me, "If all of life were music, I would gladly partake." That night he was speaking to me from his heart and soul, and I replied with intellectual pedantry.

When we arrived at his apartment we watched *Anchors Aweigh* with Gene Kelly and Frank Sinatra. It was great. The high point was definitely Gene's hallucinatory dance duet with an animated mouse. But as I was going, Scott took out a bottle of bourbon and poured himself a stiff one. He announced that he hoped to become an alcoholic—he had been trying for a while, he told me, but so far it hadn't worked. I didn't like this idea at all. I became glum and punishing. To cheer me up, he raised high his glass of bourbon and exclaimed "Old Heaven Hill!" with the appropriate drawl. I wouldn't laugh. I simply said goodbye and closed the door for what shortly turned out to be forever.

It's a funny thing about those moments. When it's the last time you see someone before they die, it feels as if the two events must be magically connected. If only I had woken up for the Mets game, or listened more sensitively to Scott's love of music, or laughed when he raised high his glass, accepting him in all his frailty. . . . But I know it's an illusion. And it's probably an illusion that if only Tray hadn't been praised for stealing those Now-and-Laters, if only Michael's girlfriend had had the baby, if only. . . . But, of course, you never know for sure. What happened, happened. What didn't, didn't. The past is so damned irrevocable. If the future is a castle hanging in the air, the past can be a dungeon made of unalterable stone and filled with instruments of torture.

Then there's that midway house called the present. That must be the key, I think, and Q's words bear me out: "If I can master the present, I will have used my time to *redeem* time." But in what does this mastery reside? For Q, it is keeping busy with desired and beneficial activities. For Tray, it is enjoying the moment. But finally, I can only speak for myself.

I have spent a lot of time trying to control the future, using worry like a magic talisman. If only I can foresee every danger, somehow, I imagine, they will all be averted. Then too, I have spent much time trying to undo the past, or atone for its sins, or prevent its recurrence. I don't ever want to see someone die again like Scott. It all reminds me of the joke about a man walking down Main Street waving his arms wildly. "Why are you doing that?" a passerby inquires. "To keep away the tigers!" the man replies. "But there are no tigers in this area," the passerby patiently points out. "SEE!" the man says.

Dare he abandon his magic when it seems to be working? All he knows is that as long as he waves, the tigers seem to stay safely at bay. For me, the preferred method for scaring off tigers of past and future tragedy was vicious self-attack. If I felt guilty enough, if I constantly examined my faults and deprived myself of pleasure, then no one else would die on my watch. And it's true that nobody has lately. SEE!

But the problem is, I was becoming the tiger. With claws I would lacerate my own flesh. No matter how I tried to cage myself up, there I was inside, trapped with me. And the sufferings of the past, the fears of the future, were the bars making each day into that cage.

I have experienced some of that during the past week. When I went in last Tuesday to find that most of "my" prisoners were already gone to Jessup, the past was suddenly present again. Having worked with these guys for years, I had come to feel them as a sort of family. And, again, I was witnessing a family wiped out. Again, it came without warning, no chance to say goodbye, the result of uncontrollable forces that rendered me powerless. Sadness being a hard emotion for me, I have continued to feel an inchoate rage along with a vague but pervasive guilt. Deep in my heart, didn't I want them gone? Didn't I want to be released from our class-without-end? Just as in my heart of hearts, hadn't I wanted my own family gone? And had my dark wishes again magically caused this all to happen? Time to crawl back in my cage.

Yet I also know I am getting out of prison. Just being able to articulate all this and turn to God for help, and to other people, allows me to set foot out the door. It's scary there: I can identify with the released prisoners who scamper back for safety. But I know I will be protected. And bit by bit I'm absorbing the gifts of my freedom: the forgiveness of myself and others, and the sunlit joys of the everyday. To work on this chapter and appreciate the turns of phrase that come to me unbidden, or wrenched out with pliers like a rotten tooth; to accept that sometimes the computer doesn't work, and the phone doesn't work, and my brain doesn't work; to take a noon break on this hot summer day, and linger over lunch and the latest sports scores; to write again until it feels like time to stop, and head over to Loyola's pool in the late afternoon when there's no one splashing around but me; to list in my mind, as I swim, ten things I did right during the day, ten things other people did right, ten things God did right; to thus let the day be a temple unto itself, reflecting in its golden dome the image of days that were and are yet to come, but finally standing alone in its splendor. Time redeemed.

PART FOUR

Sex and Race

CHAPTER FOURTEEN

Sex Talk

Cornel West, trained as a philosopher, is one of the leading voices in contemporary debates on race, class, and culture. His work is influenced by traditions as diverse as the Baptist Church, American transcendentalism, the Black Panthers, and European intellectual history. He's the author of some nine books, ranging from rigorous academic discourse to the accessible (and best-selling) Race Matters.

Cornel himself has worked in prison settings, and he generously accepted an invitation to speak at the Maryland Penitentiary and to write the foreword for this book. His talk, as usual, was galvanizing and controversial. A few inmates didn't like his Christian orientation and his rejection of elements of Afrocentrism. However, most responded enthusiastically to his populist and prophetic call for the empowerment of "common folk" and, most particularly, of the African American community.

Before he visited, we read excerpts of Race Matters. *It helped to lay the groundwork for some of our most difficult discussions—those focusing on issues of sex and race, both in the context of prison life and in that of the larger society.*

Sex and Race

Black sexuality is a taboo subject in America principally because it is a form of black power over which whites have little control—yet its visible manifestations evoke the most visceral of white responses, be it one of seductive obsession or downright disgust. On the one hand, black sexuality among blacks simply does not include whites, nor does it make them a central point of reference. . . . This can be uncomfortable for white people accustomed to being the custodians of power. . . . In fact, the dominant sexual myths of black women and men portray whites as being "out of control"—seduced, tempted, overcome, overpowered by black bodies. This form of black sexuality makes white passivity the norm—hardly an acceptable self-image for a white-run society. . . .

For most black men, power is acquired by stylizing their bodies over space and time in such a way that their bodies reflect their uniqueness and provoke fear in others. To be "bad" is good not simply because it subverts the language of the dominant culture but also because it imposes a unique

kind of order for young black men on their own distinctive chaos and solic-
its an attention that makes others pull back with some trepidation. This
young black male style is a form of self-identification and resistance in a
hostile culture; it also is an instance of machismo identity ready for violent
encounters. (Cornel West, *Race Matters*, 86–87, 88–89)

Drew: Cornel West takes on what he says is often a taboo topic—black
sexuality. In racist culture, people tend to be taught that the black body is
somehow unattractive or inferior. But racial attitudes in this country also
associate African Americans with a kind of sexual power—like you got the
animal energy and the bigger pricks. [*laughter*]

Charles: The blacker the berry, the sweeter the juice!

Drew: There's something positive about it, because for once the African
American is envisioned as having a power unavailable to the European.
But it's not an exclusively positive vision. This stereotype ties African
Americans in with an animal nature as opposed to reason and intellect, a
kind of violent and potentially immoral power.

I wonder, did you grow up with some of this sense of black sexuality
and its power?

Tray: I was already twelve or thirteen before I started socializing with any
whites, and I noticed that a lot of white females were attracted to me. I
only had a sexual relationship with two. My first one was up in Hamp-
stead. And for some reason when I was with her I felt that I had to perform sexually more so than with black women. I mean I felt like I cold-
blooded *had to excel.* After the first ejaculation I had to keep going.
Whereas when I'm with a black woman, if I get tired, that's it. But with a
white woman there's an ego thing. Because I always heard, growing up,
white people think we *long.* [*laughter*]

Wayne: I first became conscious of how people felt when I started going
to integrated schools. In Glen Burnie I was caught on a baseball diamond
with this real good friend of mine, this European girl, Cindy. They put me
out of every school in Anne Arundel County—I really didn't understand
why. I had to go to a private school.

But to me those sexual myths apply more to the Europeans. Because
when my mother was going to work, they were always coming on, threatening you'd lose your job if you don't let them feel you up. So to me it
was the Europeans who were trying to be dominant sexually and always
misbehaving.

John: Cornel West talks about how black sexuality doesn't even include
whites. Sexuality for me was more or less dominated by just African
Americans. I guess I fall into the category like a lot of African American
men—three children, three different mothers. One is extremely light, one

is my complexion, and the other one is extremely dark. I'd hear dudes say things like "I don't even mess with light-skinned sisters," or vice versa. I used to try to do some type of introspection: Say, "well, what kind are you attracted to?" No specific kind.

But interacting with a European female is not common in Baltimore, having such a large African American population. Not common at all. And it is still often taken as something you just don't do. We see a betrayal to ourselves to date a white woman when we should be responsible to black women. And there's a lot of pressure from African American women not to do it. You kind of get ostracized and it might be hard to ever come back, unless you got some money.

Tray: If I ever became in love with a white woman, somehow it seems like I would be betraying my grandmother or mother. My father was shot thirteen times by the police and they happened to be white.

But I don't have no problem with anybody having an interracial relationship. What turns me off personally is the fear of being excluded from my people. You're seen as not being all-black anymore.

Drew: When Wayne had a relationship with a white woman, he was ostracized by the white community. And now I'm hearing you may be ostracized by the African American community. But can this turn into a new kind of racism? If somebody is attracted to a person of another race, why should they have to be punished and ostracized?

Donald: It depends on what the motive is for the relationship. Some are genuine. Others are just for status. Say you have an affair with a white woman—sometimes guys will act like you've gained a prize. Especially if it's a bourgeois woman with a little money and a middle-class job. If the man and woman genuinely cares, I think it may be acceptable. But the problem is when you want the status.

O'Donald: Personally, I don't think it could be a genuine love between interracial couples. Because if a black man gets together with a white woman I think it has a motive behind it. Either he's trying to change something—make a statement that "I'm not going to hold to the status quo"—or he's trying to build up his masculinity. I think the same regarding a white male who gets together with a black woman. I think it *never* could be genuine.

Wayne: I disagree. Because that girl from Glen Burnie was a real good friend. Some days she would pull up in the driveway with me sitting on the passenger side and I'd have a real fight to be true to myself. She's my buddy and if they don't like it, the hell with it!

Tray: You know, this is one of the only topics that I feel real uncomfortable about. I consider myself bold in conversation—I will say things that most people won't. But right now, with you being white and us talking about sexuality as it relates to race, it is very uncomfortable even to me.

But you being a white man, I want to know, do you feel uncomfortable? West says that one thing you all can't control is black sexuality. Not with legislation, not with economic restraint—black folks going be *working out!* [*laughter*] And I want to know, does that cause the power structure discomfort?

Drew: The power structure, or me personally?

Tray: With you being white, you're the closest to the power structure we get to.

Drew: I don't think that I feel threatened directly by black sexuality. I mean I don't lay awake at night and worry that my wife is going to leave me for one of her cute students at Morgan [State University] who gives her the ride of a lifetime. [*laughter*] That's not getting in the book!

But the other thing West talks about is the close association between black male sexuality and a kind of machismo violence. I do think white Americans feel threatened by that. The white nightmare is that gang of seventeen-year-olds who are swaggering down the street being really tough. They have this violent energy that's outside the bounds of control.

John: If white Americans see this as being threatening in African Americans, then how about the young white males who do the same thing? I don't care if it's the guy on the football team, or in a leather jacket, or the punk rockers. You're talking groups of people going through the same period in their lives. They're insecure about their manhood. They got to let other people see that they're men. With the white guys you say, "That's how they do it at that age, they pumped up, their hormones are running." But in our case we're "violent," two inches from doing a rape. I think that's very racist.

Charles: When I think about violence and sex, it don't come to a black man raping or beating a woman. I always think of a European. I think about how the white man raped our black sisters, our black foreparents.

And when I think about "Can the European control black sexuality?" I say *yes.* Because I look at it from a biblical point of view. Pharaoh slayed all the male children and let the females live. And when we, as African American men, are in prison we are enslaved, cut off. We can't interact with our sisters and make kids. I believe the white government promotes certain things that keep us as a black race from being fruitful and multiplying. They give us a lust desire after money, put drugs in our neighborhoods, all promoting violence.

And we fall into those traps.

On the Benefits of Not Getting Any

Drew: Let's focus on the issue of what happens to sexuality once you're in prison. How has being in an all-male environment, largely or totally without heterosexual opportunities, affected you? Your sense of masculinity, your self-image, your desires?

H.B.: Turned me into a eunuch. I'm sexless. Until I go home with women. I know that I'm trapped in here and I can't *afford* to let sex be a major concern to me because I've seen what happens to people who do. They end up in all kinds of things . . . peculiar. [*laughter*]

I feel very unnatural because I love women, I enjoy them tremendously, and I'm used to being around them. I have not done that for nine years. But I'm a eunuch until I go home and some sister will be happier than she's ever been in her life.

But you see, I got a double whammy because I got AIDS. And I'm *not* going to hurt anybody. So I got to find me a fine sister who perhaps also has AIDS.

Wayne: When I first was incarcerated I had a problem with the books [pornographic magazines]. But now I can honestly say that I don't masturbate. Like Shakespeare says, I'd like to stay dedicated to reason and not to passion, because having a rape charge is what got me here.

All those times I felt the need, I had to satisfy the need. You have a spouse but you want to wander around. Like a spider, you take a weave here and a weave there, and you get caught up in it, and the next thing you know you're *eaten* by a spider. So, I always want to have the power to stay with one woman.

But don't think temptation stops, because it just gets harder and harder as time goes on. The more I resist, the harder it gets.

Tray: Being deprived of sexual activity has made me one horny bastard, straight up. But in terms of my self-image, I think it has *improved*. Because when I look at a woman now, I feel like after nine years of no sex (other than, you know, a little dig in the visiting room and stuff like that), they *got* to want me. Because you know how all these STDs are on the increase and I haven't had any sex in nine years. . . . I mean, they *got* to want me.

And as a result of being deprived of women I have greater appreciation for them. Because prior to coming to prison all the relationships I ever had was purely sex. You come over—*let's do it*. But since I've been in prison I'm able to relate in more meaningful ways. My girlfriends on the street, by me knowing that I can't get no sex, I can enjoy their other dynamics, their sensuality, their intelligence, and stuff like that. Whereas when I was on the street, I don't care how smart you are, how warm a person you are, we're getting ready to *do it*.

John: I think not having sex has helped my self-image too, but it's somewhat different than Tray. A lot of times African American men—well, all men—think that their image of self is based on their partner. So, if you got a girl and she's kind of wild and loose, you subconsciously say "Damn, what's up with me? I must be a weak dude or a sucker." But being in prison I've been able to detach my self-image from female relationships. Only what *I do* is a reflection on me.

So my self-image has improved and my desires just get satisfied in a different direction. Like masturbation. They have a video downstairs and people can tell if it's got some sex in it because if so I'm sitting there. Dudes send us pictures of girls in G-strings from the clubs and maybe I'm in that clique. Or "I've got a couple to trade for a couple you got."

Drew: Sounds a lot like trading baseball cards.

John: But when guys try to give me personal pictures of their fiancée, I don't want to see your girl. I'm not doing that kind of time.

H.B.: My masculinity was *not* measured by my sexual prowess. It was my yardstick, I suppose, when I was about sixteen or seventeen, but I had a talk with a very wise older woman and I found out what *being a man* really is. It has so very little to do with how much sex you have. It has to do with your sense of responsibility, your self-respect, your independence, courage, willingness to sacrifice yourself for the benefit of other people. A genuine concern for the protection of children, the protection of women, loyalty to your friends. Paying your rent. Buying your own shoes and not stealing somebody else's. The sex is almost like a reward—not the thing itself, just something nice you get during the course of this human exchange.

Tony: I have to agree with most of the guys who said being away from females probably enhances their masculinity. Because one of the things about being in here, it makes you have to use your mind with women. You can't be yapping because there ain't too many women who will stay with you, especially in this institution—you figure most of the people here got more time than the world's probably going to be around. But when you do get that attention from a female, you know she's with you because she likes what you're saying. That's got to make you feel good about yourself. Guys have wives and girlfriends who have been with them nine and ten years. There ain't but one reason that woman could still be with them—got that *mind locked,* then the rest of it's easy.

Tray: Yeah. But we get a lot of rejects. Girls that done had problems with guys on the street. They be girls in dire need of communication, but when they find somebody on the street that gives them that, *and* long-legs them, they leave us. When they hurt again they come back. That's why we get a lot of the funny-looking girls and the fat girls, the girls you guys on the street reject.

But there's exceptions to the rules. Like me—I got a star. I got a real pretty girl, I do.

Donald: Tray made a good point. The reason we get a lot of them women is because they're wounded. Whatever relationship they were in was not offering them what they needed on an intellectual or spiritual level. But we have that to offer. And when a lot of these females get involved in a sex relationship, they still will come back to us most of the time, or find another guy in prison.

Charles: We got the *time* to give them, the time to communicate. That's what they need more than anything.

Sex behind Bars

Drew: Let's go on to some graphic stuff. Like exactly what does and doesn't happen sexually within the prison?

Donald: We kind of touched on it a little bit.

Drew: No pun intended?

Tray: The same sexual activity that's available to you out in free society is available to us. We can't have the romantic aura, like laying rosebuds on the bed and ordering champagne. But we have heterosexual relationships with women. Sometimes they out in society, sometimes they may be in here, like guards. Then we have a whole lot of homosexual affairs that go on, and a lot of masturbation and fantasies.

Drew: How is the heterosexual stuff available?

Tray: It's definitely unauthorized.

Charles: We don't have conjugal visits. But we have functions where police might turn their head. You and your wife may be sitting there. Just the way that she prop her leg, you might be able to get up in there.

Drew: Is this how Donald got thrown in lock-up?

Donald: I wasn't exactly doing anything. I was in the auditorium during a special event and we were up on the stage to take pictures. A female guest dropped one of her earrings. She was moving around, and during the course of looking she stole a kiss here, and started playing there, you understand? An officer jumped all over top thinking we were trying to have sex, which we weren't. But you know in situations like that, when for a long time you haven't been that close to full-body contact, the hormones start kicking. We weren't actually doing anything other than just fooling.

John: If the officers catch me sitting there with my son's mother at a function, the red flags go up. But the officers turn a blind eye to all the homosexual activities that go around this jail. In a sense they're condoning it. I think it has to do with their self-esteem. They feel good about themselves if they can look down at us, but if they see we're human beings too and have people who love us, they kind of feel threatened.

Tray: You have to realize most of the officers that work here grew up with us. And where they were the ones that were going to school, we were the ones with the big cars and jewels. Now's their opportunity to get us, and they do everything they can.

Drew: Are homosexual relations looked down on by them, by you?

Tray: Well, you got your homosexuals and then you got your fuck-boys, right. . . .

Drew: Can I get a definition?

Tray: A homosexual is one who really enjoys homosexual activities, probably due to some biological thing. They can receive respect from the population. Whereas your fuck-boy is somebody who's more or less forced into it for their personal safety—whoever is going up in them protects them. So this connotes weakness.

Donald: The F-boys—I don't like cussing so I won't say the word—a lot of times they're forced but sometimes it's a psychological thing. Them young guys, twenty or under, come into this prison and they really want fathers. So they'll gravitate towards older guys. Now if one gravitates towards me I'll push him away. I don't want that kind of bond because it's going to cause me problems. But another kind of guy might trick him into having sex. Then he would become one of the F-boys.

He trusted this older guy. He probably told him a lot of things that he wouldn't tell other people, about being afraid. Then the guy tricks him and gets tired of him—soon all the others who know about this relationship come along and go up in him. Now he's one of the F-boys.

Tony: And it always amazes me that the guy who forced him into it, because he's on the "male" end, thinks he's not gay.

Donald: But one thing has helped break down the problem of forcing guys into sexual relationships: AIDS. Guys would say, "Man, I ain't snatching nothing no more because this guy coming from the street will be bringing the virus." Starting in '85 and '86, you got the fear of catching HIV from the intravenous drug users coming in. So a lot of it stopped right about that time.

H.B.: I don't think there's that level of consciousness in this prison. It needs to be, but it's not. There's almost a suicidal . . . a kamikaze type . . . I can't find the right word. There's a sense of giving up and not caring. You can smell it. You can taste it. The danger of catching AIDS doesn't put a lid on homosexuality in here. It's just as prevalent as when I come here nine years ago.

But I think the thing that keeps homosexuality less a stampede than twenty-five years ago is not AIDS, but the access to the women you love at the functions. The telephones, so you're talking to a member of the opposite sex. Female guards, so you're concerned about your reputation. And pornography. Twenty-five years ago kids were getting raped left and right because all you did in the Maryland state correction system was eat, sleep, and work.

Drew: So now there are other sexual outlets. But I also want to raise the Freudian concept of sublimation. The idea that sexual, erotic energy is a big part of being a human being, and if it isn't allowed a natural outlet for expression, individuals redirect it into other activities. In that view, some of the highest forms of culture, like a composer writing a symphony or a philosopher trying to figure out the world, may be sexual energy getting sublimated and redirected. Do you think people do that here?

Donald: A couple of times when I was exercising out in the yard I got to a point where I felt the same thing as during orgasm. The apex of that feeling lasts for a minute maybe, then after that you just feel good. And I've experienced that reading books or solving a difficult problem. It happens when I've tried my hardest, exerted a lot of effort, I can't do anything else. Then this feeling come over me—I call it a "quality orgasm."

Tray: Last night I was sitting up reading physical science. And you know, when I was home and could get laid whenever I wanted, I would never be up trying to understand general relativity.

And I think about how talented a lot of guys get in here with their poetry. You got some of the best poets and musicians. Freud talked about Leonardo da Vinci and how good he got because of that repressed energy. And it could be, but my ego won't let me admit it—that I'm as *talented* as I am cause I ain't gettin' none! [*laughter*]

H.B.: The real artists in this prison . . . there's a word called endowment. They brought their talents here with them. But there *is* a euphoric thing that occurs during the creative process. In my case I find it to be something of a higher spiritual order than sexual energy. It's almost like the feeling that you get when you offer something to eat to a homeless person. Or you see somebody get hurt in the street and you run and save their life.

Donald: I think we're being the victim of semantics where we limit ourselves to saying it's a kind of a sexual energy. Because I've also experienced it when I make sincere prayer.

Drew: The Freudian perspective is from the bottom up: you start with sexual energy and can sublimate it higher. Maybe people are suggesting the reverse—there's a spiritual energy that can be brought down to the sexual level.

Charles: Yeah. There's a part in the Koran that says when man was formed and created, he's in his best state. But from that he descends to the lowest of beasts. . . .

CHAPTER FIFTEEN

Who Am I?

When I think about sexuality, several associations come to mind. First, pleasure. After all, sex feels good. Then there's intimacy. Sex can be, though isn't always, about giving bodily expression to emotional closeness. Then too, I think of babies. My wife and I were trying for years to have one, both in the traditional way and scientifically assisted. We had some fun and a lot of heartache, but without producing any progeny. But sex has certainly been known to make babies, or so I'm told.

Yet as I reflect on the dialogue in chapter 14, another point comes clear. Sex is not just about something you do or make, but something you *are*. It's one way we discover and declare our identity. Am I feminine or masculine, hetero or gay, powerful or submissive, traditional or adventurous, good or bad?

And also, as the dialogue suggests, am I black or white? If you're involved with a white woman, Tray says, "You're seen as not being all-black anymore." Blackness, in this sense, is not just a matter of a skin color. It's an identity you establish, or at least refuse to run away from, and the choice of a black partner is crucial in so doing.

It seems that whatever move you make, there's no escaping the game. Who you screw is who you are. According to O'Donald, a black man hanging with a white woman is either making a statement about the status quo or building up his masculinity. Something's going on. Donald suggests she may be the prize meant to prove he's a stud. And this game is enacted even in the privacy of the bedroom. Tray says that "I felt like I cold-blooded *had to excel*" to live up to a white woman's expectations.

Not everyone agrees that this game is all there is. Wayne, for example, simply likes Cindy. He's black, she's white, but it's not about all that. They're not trying to dismantle social categories, or prove a point, or preen their feathers with an exotic mate. Wayne just likes Cindy.

But no one seems to accept this. It made me mad to hear how Wayne was put out of every school in his (mainly white) county. And I was equally frustrated that his black friends rejected him, that O'Donald suspects wrong motives in all such relations. "Don't these guys see," I'd think, "that this is just like the racism they've been subjected to, just like white prejudice against interracial couples?"

Yet, on reflection, I can also understand a difference. The whites who don't want their daughter going out with one of "them" usually harbor a belief in black inferiority. The opposite seemed to motivate the black critics in my class. They saw racial self-hatred and betrayal in blacks who chose whites. After all, for so long, African Americans have been taught that they are not good enough, that it is those *other* people, with their blue eyes and blond straight hair, who are desirable and worthy. Choosing a white partner seems to confirm the racist hierarchy.

As a big-nosed Jewish boy who married a cute button-nosed WASP girl, I can relate to the issue. It's true I have been ashamed of my Jewish looks, labeled myself ugly, sought out the Aryan type. But it's also true that I love my wife passionately. Although vectors of racial and sexual identity may have influenced my choice, at some point my choice outran those categories and blossomed into something finer. Wayne, I suspect, really did like Cindy.

But this also goes to show how much questions of sexuality and identity become intertwined. Your partner, or lack thereof, is read as a proclamation not only of your race, but of your status, power, and value as a person. And such may have been particularly at play for these inmates. Growing up poor, black, badly educated, and marginally employed is not exactly conducive to feelings of self-worth. But sexuality can supply some of what's missing. If you're plenty macho, get a hot woman (or three), give her the ride of her life. . . . As Cornel West points out, sexuality is one of the few areas where African Americans are thought of as having power, *even over whites.*

But the prisoners also attacked the racism implicit in myths of black sexuality. As John says, it's not just the African American teenager who puts on the threatening macho act. What about the white football player or the leather-jacketed punk? Charles thinks "about how the white man raped our black sisters, our black foreparents," and Wayne suggests the violation is still going on: his working mother constantly had to fend off attacks.

As they spoke, I experienced a kind of gestalt reversal. Probably like many white Americans, I am used to associating violence with blacks. If the Baltimore local news features a solved rape or murder, I expect to see a black man led away by the cops. But now I was hearing things from the other side: to blacks it was the white world that had always been saturated with domination and violence. And this had been enacted sexually, as through other forms of power. Charles reads this even into the high numbers of African American men in jail, keeping his race "from being fruitful and multiplying."

I find my thoughts drifting to the different perceptions of the O. J. Simpson trial in 1994. Polls suggested that most whites thought him guilty, most blacks suspected him not. So it's not just about the evidence but the lens through which people view it. I suppose it isn't hard for whites to imagine a powerful black man murdering two whites in sexual vengeance. Conversely, it's not hard for blacks to imagine a white police force framing an "uppity nigger" who crosses racial/sexual lines.

I guess I'm white: I thought O.J. guilty. Despite Mark Fuhrman's malignity, I doubt the L.A. police force had quite the cunning, forethought, and sheer *competence* to arrange the frame-up and multiple evidence-plantings that O.J.'s defense suggested. For similar reasons, I doubt Charles's theory that black incarceration is the end result of a white plot to keep his race from multiplying. Where was I when we planned it all out?

On the other hand, I also see how the history and continued presence of white racism gives rise to these suspicions. If O.J.'s prosecutors had a hard time convincing black jurors of his guilt, it's only the mirror-image of a prior prejudice: many a black man was unjustly convicted by white jurors especially after messing with a white woman. I can also see how the high rate of inner-city black violence is one outcome of a history of white violence: the political, economic, and psychological consequences of racism have wreaked havoc in the black community.

Then too, I think Charles is right that African Americans are subject to discriminatory "racial profiling," prosecution, and tough sentencing that ensures the prison population be disproportionately black. To take but one local example I saw in the paper the other day: Interstate 95 in northeastern Maryland has 17 percent black motorists; yet fully 77 *percent* of the drivers stopped and searched on that road (1995–97) were minorities.

Whether or not it was the result of a conspiracy, the inmates I was conversing with were now in jail, their sexuality disrupted. And I wondered what that did to a person. I attended Yale in the mid-1970s when there weren't too many women around. A friend of mine had a solution for his plight. "For the next four years I'm putting my balls on the shelf." He never got them down: he was shot to death in a hold-up by some New Haven teenagers. But in the Pen I was dealing with guys on the other side, the shooters. And they too would be putting their balls on the shelf—for twenty, thirty, forty years. What does one *do* in such a situation, I wanted to know? But along with this, who does one *become*? If sexuality is so crucial to your sense of status, manhood, connectedness, power—in short, your identity—who are you after it's all torn apart?

As is often true, I was surprised by the answers I received. Especially those where the men celebrated their newfound celibacy. It left you free of communicable disease; better able to relate to women; in possession of greater self-control and self-esteem; with a mind freed up to explore general relativity. Was I hearing some Platonic or medieval discourse on the virtues of sublimating eros?

Again, these men had learned to play the hand they've been dealt. If incarceration has made them celibates (more or less), why not don the monk's cowl and realize the benefits of continence? It illustrates a principle I found recurring throughout our talks: in accepting a diminishment we can transform it into a grace.

But the trick for many of the men was to do this while still maintaining their identity *as men*. It didn't necessarily help that the Pen was an all-male institution. Such environments—the army barracks, football locker-room, boys boarding school—can teeter like a seesaw on a point of sexual ambiguity.

On the one hand, they may be seen as a place so rough-and-tough that women are excluded. This confers a macho honor on all its inhabitants. And I felt that atmosphere when I'd walk into the prison yard, surrounded by muscular toughs gathering in clusters. I'm hardly the Arnold Schwarzenegger type and it showed. I'd stride toward the school trying to assume an air of virile authority but I doubt the prisoners were impressed.

Yet if an all-male environment grants macho distinction, it also casts things in a suspicious light. All those men living, playing, *showering* together—exactly what are they up to? Why no women around? Strange images float before the mind, like that of a burly convict blowing a kiss to his cellmate. Our sexual categories are threatened with chaos.

This, I surmise, was the source of the 1993 political hubbub that followed the proposal to allow gays to serve openly in the military. I sensed that the stated objections (it would undermine fighting effectiveness, etc.) were a cover for other concerns only hinted at. The army, we're used to thinking, is, by God, *for men*. It's a place for those who embody the masculine virtues of courage, toughness, and aggression. But what happens when we let women in? When, even worse, soldiers come out as openly gay? Suddenly, everything become suspicious, topsy-turvy. Queer-bashing, personally or politically, becomes a way to counteract this threat.

And I could sense some of that in my discussions with the prisoners. Many of them seemed to look down on those who engaged in gay sex, and they wanted to be very clear that they sure as hell didn't. We're men here, not queers. It seemed a point of honor that female guards found them attractive and engaged in illicit liaisons with prisoners. And they also liked defending the traditional "man's role" in relationships, though I found some of their comments sexist and offensive. Maybe we just disagree. There are surely cultural differences at play, but maybe it's also a matter of their circumstances. Homophobia and sexism can serve to affirm their masculinity when everything conspires to strip it away, for in our society, masculinity is associated largely with power—earning power,

power to act in the world, sexual power—and it's hard to assert any of these in prison.

Of course, that didn't stop the inmates from trying. The saga of the fuck-boys is one sad example. It's clear that fuck-boys are made, not born, and that their genesis is not about sex as much as power. The fuck-boy is not really gay. But he's powerless and so has no choice. Nor does the abuser define himself as homosexual. Tony comments, "it always amazes me that the guy who forced him into it, because he's on the 'male' end, thinks he's not gay." This confusion is understandable in the light of our sexual categories. Gayness tends to be associated not only with engaging in homosexual acts, but with the "effeminate" position—weak, submissive, "womanly." But the abuser doesn't see himself this way. He has the power to dominate and assert his will. From this angle, having a fuck-boy doesn't call your manhood into question but confirms it.

And what of the fuck-boy, I wonder? He's committed the cardinal sin in prison: betraying weakness. But I feel touched by the plight of these young men. Maybe it's because I identify with them. Slender of build, not schooled in the ways of the street (unless you count Park Avenue), I can imagine being forced to be a fuck-boy myself. How else could I scrounge protection in the Pen? And what might come of this dismal fate—pain, humiliation, HIV—I'm not sure I want to think this all through.

But what saddens me the most is those young men who, as Donald suggested, went searching for a father. To seek a role model for growing into manhood; to reach out in intimacy and reveal secret fears; to dare to trust someone with that deep core of your self; and then to have them rip it out of you, penetrate you against your will, change you into just another fuck-boy.

It turns out that sex is not just about proclaiming identity. It can also be used to destroy it.

CHAPTER SIXTEEN

Black, White, Jew

In this dialogue, as the one that preceded it, we are discussing material in Cornel West's Race Matters. *The issue of nihilism and self-hatred in the black community is a poignant one for the men in my class, so many of whom were African American. Since I am Jewish, Cornel's essay on blacks and Jews allowed us to reflect on our relationship. Cornel subsequently co-authored, with Michael Lerner, a book on the topic,* Jews and Blacks: A Dialogue on Race, Religion, and Culture in America *(1995).*

Building a Self

The eclipse of hope and collapse of meaning in much of black America is linked to the structural dynamics of corporate market institutions that affect all Americans. Under these circumstances black existential angst derives from the lived experience of ontological wounds and emotional scars inflicted by white supremacist beliefs and images permeating U.S. society and culture. These beliefs and images attack black intelligence, black ability, black beauty, and black character daily in subtle and not so subtle ways. Toni Morrison's novel, *The Bluest Eye*, for example, reveals the devastating effect of pervasive European ideals of beauty on the self-image of young black women. Morrison's exposure of the harmful extent to which these white ideas affect the black self-image is a first step toward rejecting these ideals and overcoming the nihilistic self-loathing they engender in blacks. (Cornel West, *Race Matters*, 17–18)

Drew: How we come to view ourselves is based a lot on the ways we experience others viewing us. We internalize their gaze. As a Jew in our society I have been subjected to certain kinds of racism, although I don't think it's as extreme as you have experienced as African Americans. Very few people have called me a "Jew-boy" or made fun of me or beat me up. But if I pick up a magazine I see pictures of handsome men and beautiful women, but they have blond hair and blue eyes and cute little noses. So when I look at those pictures and I look in the mirror, I say to myself, "I'm ugly. I'm weird looking. I'm different." When I was growing up, I was very self-conscious about my big Jewish nose. I would literally cover it up with my hands and hope the rest of my head would grow bigger and catch up. My whole life, there has been some way in which I have been ashamed of being and looking Jewish. And I wanted to ask you about your experience as African Americans in our culture.

Tray: I started equating beauty with what I saw in the magazines. I couldn't do anything with my blackness, so I put all my energies into what suits I looked nice in. Where everybody else was concentrating on the math, science, and reading, I was concentrating on how to get the dollars to get new outfits so I could be equal to the white guy in my class. If I could come in with my big gold chain and the right clothes, it kind of balanced things out.

Tony: By the time I was sixteen I had to have my hair processed. (Those older of us remember that.) If you looked at a magazine, you seen all the people that even if they were black they were so light and bright and close to white it didn't make no difference. And they had nice hair, *straight* hair. So I used that gunk, and I just knew I was *it.*

And remember when waistline leather jackets were the thing? I was sitting in the park in Los Angeles and I watched two dudes beat someone to death for a leather jacket. Then you wake up, you realize exactly what's going on and learn to decode a lot of this. White corporations making all this money, but they don't gear the ads to the people who can afford them. I remember seeing kids beat up, shot up, and killed for tennis shoes and a leather jacket. We as black folks have to realize that it's what's *in here* that's important, not the clothes you put on.

O'Donald: I grew up in South Baltimore, so I was around a lot of white people. And it influenced the way I thought and acted. In my dress, everything had to be white, white shirt, white anything. Even my females had to be light-skinned or close to that. I was about eight or nine when this was going on.

But in the part of South Baltimore where I lived we had a project side that was predominately black. In order to be accepted with them I couldn't wear all that white stuff. But to be accepted it was more than the dress—I started doing what they did. I didn't really want to. There was no longer *me.* I was made up of two different societies, two different worlds. So I started doing these things like breaking the law, selling drugs, beating.

And when I turned ten they had a test-trial thing and my test was to throw a log off a bridge. So I threw a log off a bridge and smashed the front of a car window and the person got put into a coma. I was arrested and charged with it. The guys tricked me into taking the charge. So at age ten I was given *juvenile life.* I was placed in a state training school and all the psychologists were white. So I equated being somebody important with being white. I didn't know what it meant to be black.

But being in prison has really changed my mind. I no longer want to have any white things.

Drew: I hear people saying that it was hard to have a sense of pride coming from within. One of the problems with racism is that it makes you look outside yourself to build self-esteem.

But racism can also be used as a tactic to try to feel better about yourself and *get* self-esteem. A cheap and quick fix is to say "Well, I'm sure as hell better than that dude over there. He's the scum of the earth." I wonder if within the African American community there is much of an attempt, consciously or subconsciously, to use racism as a way to feel better about who you are. Could be racism against whites, or against Jews. . . .

Donald: I think in our community there are a lot of people who don't deal with racism. They teach *race pride*, for example about the great achievements of ancient Africa, and you feel good about it. But they don't think there's a problem with white people feeling good about their race if they don't have to do it by stepping on someone else.

But we also have people in our community—Elijah Muhammad's probably an example—he galvanized people by saying that the black people are greater, the white people are *devils.*

Drew: Which method do you think works better to promote a sense of self-esteem?

Donald: The first, the one that is not based on superiority and discrimination. Because that's real. The other one is based on a falsehood. You find out you're not superior to others and revert back to that state of mind you were in before.

Wayne: Also African Americans are kept in such close community that when you instill hate inside of individuals, ultimately that hate will spread out on each other. There's no European within your grasp, so you vent that anger inside the community.

Tray: I don't believe teaching a racist doctrine to a group of people can build them up. In the African American community I think that we do need to embrace a doctrine that will elevate our self-esteem and let us know we can control our own economic, political, and educational situations. For a lot of years we always believed that we gotta go to white folks, and that's what's destroyed us.

But we can be pro-black without being anti-white. Black folks can't destroy America without destroying themselves, and the reverse is also true. We're intertwined. My destiny is yours. Yours is mine. And we can do like the Jewish people do, how they took care of educating their own kids and built a power base within their own culture.

John: A problem, though, is when the dominant culture that is white owns most things, we feel that ownership equals power. In the African American community if you got a car, people think you have money and must know certain things. Somewhere along the line we have to start redefining stuff. Because a man has wealth it doesn't mean anything. It doesn't mean he's intelligent or a good person. It doesn't mean he adds anything to society. All it means is that he has some money.

I can think back to times when I didn't need drugs and money to make myself happy, when I could be by myself and laugh. But I lost it somewhere. I remember when I went to Morgan State, just going to college wasn't satisfactory enough. I had to be in college and driving. I had to be in college and driving with a wardrobe. I had to be in college driving with a wardrobe and with girls. Where was it going to stop? That kind of pressure made me decide I got to get some money, and that led me into the criminal thing. Where do you get a bankroll when you're a black man and your family ain't got no money? You break the law. And before you know it, those good intentions sure enough paved the road to hell for me because the arrests just started to pile on top of each other. And it all started with that thinking—that without material values my life has no meaning.

Tray: I just want to say something real quick. All the benevolent people throughout history needed wealth before they could be altruistic. Martin Luther King, the glorious things he did he was able to do because he had money to get his education. Gandhi was a lawyer, a good lawyer. He probably had a little money before he thought about helping the world. But you never saw a poor person do a damn thing for anybody.

Various voices: I disagree.

Tony: Look at Mother Teresa.

Tray: You can disagree all you want. Mother Teresa had the wealth of the Roman Catholic Church. And John says being rich don't make you intelligent. *Wrong.* You buy intelligence. The people around you become your brains.

John: This is the perfect example of what I'm saying. *You can't buy intelligence.* You buy an intelligent person to work for you. And that means you're really powerless. You're sitting here thinking you're calling the shots and he's snickering, "Tomorrow morning I'll take another $100,000 out and by the end of the year I'm going south and he'll be broke." I hate to say it, but so many African Americans always talking about "I had this, but they robbed me." No. Nobody robbed you. You robbed yourself. You never got an education, you never understood what was needed to compete in these environments. So don't get mad at the next man, get mad at yourself.

Tony: And Tray used the example of Gandhi. But once Gandhi got his movement started, he gave up everything, all his wealth. One of the reasons he wanted the British out is because their whole value system was destroying the Indian. And this lust for power, money, resources is what's corrupting our community too.

Tray: But Gandhi still needed money to facilitate his cause. Until we can build within the black community our own economic, political, and educational programs we will continue to be victims. We'll keep killing each other over tennis shoes.

Prisons

Nihilism is to be understood here . . . [as] the lived experience of coping with a life of horrifying meaninglessness, hopelessness, and (most important) lovelessness. The frightening result is a numbing detachment from others and a self-destructive disposition toward the world. . . . The genius of our black foremothers and forefathers was to create powerful buffers to ward off the nihilistic threat, to equip black folk with cultural armor to beat back the demons of hopeless ness, meaninglessness, and lovelessness. The recent market-driven shattering of black civil society—black families, neighborhoods, schools, churches, mosques—leaves more and more black people vulnerable to daily lives endured with little sense of self and fragile existential moorings. . . . Like all Americans, African Americans are influenced greatly by the images of comfort, convenience, machismo, femininity, violence, and sexual stimulation that bombard consumers. These seductive images contribute to the predominance of the market-inspired way of life over all others and thereby edge out nonmarket values—love, care, service to others—handed down by preceding generations. The predominance of this way of life among those living in poverty-ridden conditions, with a limited capacity to ward off self-contempt and self-hatred, results in the possible triumph of the nihilistic threat in black America. (Cornel West, *Race Matters,* 14–17)

Jack: Twenty or thirty years ago in the African American community, if all of us lived in the same neighborhood, I could go to anybody's house to eat. Even though my family might not have something Monday, his family might, so nobody went hungry. Clothes were passed down, people looked out for each other. But today it's a thing where every man's for himself. *Me, me, me.*

Drew: Do you think the church was more active thirty years ago in helping people?

Jack: Yeah. Now all the churches want is money to build a bigger church, to buy the Reverend a bigger house and planes. [*laughter*] And basically we're the ones that get beat because over the years we've been taught to be gullible, to rely on somebody else to take care of us.

H.B.: The problem is we lost some very significant values from our African heritage. In Africa there's a very, very strong sense of community: everyone's considered my aunt, my brother, my grandfather.

Tony: I also think that the more we "got rights," the more we tried to *assimilate.* Black families and neighborhoods were tighter back when we didn't have rights. You knew they didn't want those "niggers" around so you had to fight to get what you wanted. And you knew you had to do it *together* because one man couldn't do anything.

Tray: Also, before the civil rights movement we wasn't allowed to go downtown and see these big pretty things that white people had. When the barriers came down and we seen them, we wanted them *bad.* And we sacrificed what our grandparents taught us, like how to love each other.

But we can't really make it. They don't want us there. When you try and get a job in a law firm, they'll tell you to get out because you're black. When you go to Howard Beach you get beat upside the head. When you live in a city in which fifty-six percent of the males are in prison or on the run, it lets you know that society is rejecting you. It got so bad for me, when I go to court I don't want a black lawyer. I want a white lawyer and a white judge. Is that self-hate or is that self-hate?

Drew: We've been talking about self-hate and nihilism within the African American community. But what happens when people go to prison? I can see people becoming more hopeless. Or I could see people who have been wandering aimless, use prison to start to look within for a different set of values, for something that helps you put yourself back together in a more positive way. Which tends to be true?

H.B.: I think the first is more common in this particular prison. In fact, in *any* prison I have ever been in, the first is more common. But there's always a small handful of people who fit the profile of the second. Personally, I see myself as one. I see this man here. And that man there. [*pointing at people in the room*]

See, you have to grab yourself by the ear and set yourself down and say, "Forget about this 'system' stuff. It's time for *me* to have a talk with *me.*" And you decide, what are you going to let them do to you? You're not letting them lock you up. You did that to yourself. You knew that armed robbery meant twenty years in prison if you get caught. It's that simple. So forget about that. That mistake is done. But now what are you going to do?

In my case I decided that for me to hate myself, not believe in myself and feel like I'm this awful thing, would be like committing a robbery again. I'm no longer a human being who made a mistake. My whole life becomes a crime.

After a certain period of time in a place like this you reach a point of no return—it's about seven years—and if your heart ain't pumping the right amount of blood through your soul and not just your veins, you're in trouble. Because you're going to turn into a madman then. This place is going to consume you, and you can't let that happen.

John: The penitentiary has always been known to make you or break you. You're not just going to float around in here. The nihilism that brings you in here, either you're going to get rid of it or it's going to engulf you and eventually destroy you.

Drew: But getting back to the race issue, what are things like in prison in terms of black-white relations?

H.B.: I think sometimes we confuse racism with our sense of cultural norms. For example, I met a guy in this prison, a white guy. We was on the same softball team so we got to be buddy-buddy. Then one day I was walking across the yard and almost got hit in the eye by a pebble. I say, "What the hell?!" I turns around and he's got a fist full of pebbles and this damn crazy-ass look on his face. I walked up to him and I say, "Hey man, let me tell you something, don't be throwing no damn stones at me. You could put somebody's eye out like that." He says, "Oh man, I was just playing." It was a cultural thing. You see a lot of white guys playing with each other that way. We don't get it!

Drew: It's a secret white ritual. [*laughter*]

H.B: I do know a lot of black guys in here who despise white people simply because they're white. I've also walked up on white guys with pictures all over their bodies who look like they sharpen their teeth—motorcycle types, Pagans—and they were in a discussion about "that nigger" and then suddenly everything got quiet till I walk past. So racism here is *not subtle.* It's open. But as a matter of fact, it's so damn open that it's almost invisible. The white guys stay in their little area, black guys stay in their big area (because the majority of us in here are black), and as long as you do that everybody gets along fine.

I've seen a Pagan who I know is a racist give a black guy who despises white people some tobacco to smoke. It was a penitentiary thing. But that's the kind of racism in here. It's peculiar. So bold that it's almost nonexistent.

Selvyn: Sometimes you get more respect or cooperation from those guys like the Pagans who don't like black people. It's a Mexican standoff: You don't like me. I don't like you either. Now, are we going to cooperate? It's the ones that start patting me on the back I have more problems with.

Donald: A lot of the racism is covert because we're in a majority here. I personally believe if the whites were in a majority some of the things they would do would be much worse.

John: And there's another kind of racism in here. Say you have some white guy from a good home and he's committed a crime that will bring him into the prison system with predominately black men—they try to work something out for him. Regardless of how vicious the crime may be, he'll bypass coming to the Maryland Penitentiary. But the judge will say to a black man, "Handle it the best way you can. That's *your* problem." You commit the same crime, but don't go to the same prison, and then they beat us home!

H.B.: Yeah, when I got arrested they had a young white man in the same county in the same court system before the same judges and prosecutors. And this young man killed his parents in their sleep, chopped them up and put them in trash bags, and set them out on the curb for the garbage man. His mother and his father. They gave him twelve years and suspended all but eight. He's home now. I'm sure of it. I shot somebody by accident in a robbery and I came out of the courtroom with twenty-five years, no parole, plus ten. When they pull a stunt like this they say, "*He* never had a record." What's that got to do with anything? I never killed my mother and father, chopped them up, and put them in no trash bag!

Blacks and Jews

Black anti-Semitism and Jewish antiblack racism are real, and both are as profoundly American as cherry pie. There was no *golden age* in which blacks and Jews were free of tension and friction. Yet there was a *better* age when the common histories of oppression and degradation of both groups served as a springboard for genuine empathy and principled alliances. Since the late sixties, black-Jewish relations have reached a nadir. Why is this so? (West, *Race Matters*, 71)

Drew: In a lot of ways I haven't wanted to get into this issue. I'm Jewish, you're African American. I feel we have a good relationship and I didn't want to spoil it by raising a topic where you might start yelling at me, I might start yelling at you. But at the same time it's not honest to sidestep the issue and pretend it isn't there.

Growing up I had very little contact with African Americans. I've been thinking about what kind of stereotypes did I have, what things were said in my family. I remember my parents talking about "schwartzes," a Yiddish word for "blacks." It doesn't mean "nigger" or something like that, but I think there's a bit of racist overtone, "us" versus "them" superiority. At the same time Jews have often had a tradition of social liberalism, and I was brought up to care about the underdog, about justice, about equality. So maybe the fact that I'm here volunteering in prison also came out of my Jewish background.

I wanted to ask if, when you were growing up, you had contact with Jews or were taught anything about them?

Charles: The first Jew I ever met was a dude named Abe. He owned a corner grocery store in South Baltimore on Paca and Warner Street. And I'd go to my man Mr. Abe, I'd say, "Look, Mr. Abe, I want to buy some candy from you and I want you to give me some candy." He'd give it to me and I'd go out and set up *my* rack, I wasn't more than eight or nine, and I'd sell the candy. When his store closed, I opened up mine.

The only conception I had of Jews was they were strictly business. That was the only dealings I had with them.

Tray: I never distinguished between Jewish people and white people until I got in the court system. My father was killed by the police when I was about eighteen months old. So I was always taught that you could be friends with one white person but if there's a group of them, they're wicked. But when I was about thirteen, if I came before a Jewish magistrate I'd always expect lenience. I don't know why, but I just expected it. I specifically remember Magistrate Goldstein. It was a charge I was guilty of, some kind of drug beef, but I just knew I was going to go home, he sent *everybody* home. He sent me back to training school for thirty days. I just felt so hurt. If it had been a black judge I don't think it would have hurt as bad. I hated that magistrate more than any other because the betrayal was much more deep.

Drew: West writes that one cause of black anti-Semitism is "higher expectations some black folk have of Jews. This perspective holds Jews to a moral standard different from that extended to other white ethnic groups. . . . Such double standards assume that Jews and blacks are 'natural' allies, since both groups have suffered chronic degradation and oppression at the hands of racial and ethnic majorities. So when Jewish neoconservatism gains a high public profile at a time when black people are more and more vulnerable, the charge of 'betrayal' surfaces among black folk who feel let down" (pp. 76–77).

Tray: He sent me up for thirty days.

John: And someone my age can remember a time when whites wouldn't do any kind of business with blacks, but Jews would. We were represented by Jewish lawyers when many whites wouldn't take our cases. But then if anything went awry it sours things. Like Tray was saying, you think, "I can expect a double cross from the other guy, but from you, there's a problem."

Drew: I've wondered why anti-Semitic language has been increasing in the African American community. I grew up fairly insulated from thousands of years of anti-Jewish sentiment, but I've felt more of that from the African American community and certain of its spokespeople than anywhere else in the past few years. It's been stunning.

Mike: Allan Bakke. That's what I think really started it all. That was a major situation where Jews kind of knifed us in the back. African Americans were trying to make entrance into professional jobs, schools, what not, and up popped Allan Bakke and killed affirmative action.

[Mike refers to the landmark 1978 decision wherein the Supreme Court struck down the University of California's "special admissions program" for minority groups.]

Drew: Now why would you consider that Jewish? Is *he* Jewish?

Mike: Yes.

Tray: Another part is religious. Historically Islam and Judaism always conflict, and in the last fifteen years Islam has had a greater influence in our community.

Charles: I think Louis Farrakhan is also looking at how much money the Jewish race makes from the black community. I remember when I was about nineteen I used to paint houses for Jews. Out there in Green Gate Valley they got houses on slopes, man, pull-in driveways with curves and water fountains, big ole houses.

Drew: Are you saying that wealth was pulled out of the black community in some way?

Charles: Yeah, Farrakhan believes some of those funds should be put back.

Tony: On the other hand you do have some people who are just plain envious. The Jewish community as a whole tends to be rather wealthy, and it doesn't matter what race you are, those that *don't have* tend to be a little envious of those that *do.*

Charles: Quite a few of the aunts in my family did domestic work in Jewish houses. And a lot of times they came home and brought clothes and stuff and I'd say, "Where'd you get this from?" and they'd say, "the people we work for." Those relationships were there between the Jewish and the blacks.

Drew: Well, I have to admit when we were growing up we had a maid who was African American. Her name was Sally. And she was, I mean this sounds kind of clichéd, but she was like a second mother to me.

Charles: That's right, Doc. She was your nanny.

Drew: Yeah, she was my nanny. She's in her seventies and we're still friends. She refers to me as her Jewish son. But also, looking back on it, I know the exploitation that was involved in that relationship. She had her own kids and yet she had to live in our house and take care of us. And she had ambitions to move on and become a nurse, and my mother did certain things to block that from happening because Sally was so valuable to our family. So I feel close to her and also some guilt about the past.

But I want to go back to this sense of betrayal you've talked about. If there's somebody blocking affirmative action, taking money out of the community, or a judge giving a tough sentence, you might feel more anger because they're Jewish and say, "Well, this person *should* have understood, *should* be my ally." But I feel some of that in the other direction. If I hear somebody from the Aryan Nation talking about Jewish conspiracies, or how Jews are money-grubbing, exploitative people, I'd probably say, "Oh, another fascist. I'm not going to worry about people like that." But when I hear those racist stereotypes coming from the African American community, from people who are leaders in the battle for rights, justice, and to overcome racism, I say, "How can they be spewing this hate? Don't they know this is the same kind of rhetoric that's been used against African Americans?" So I feel a sense of betrayal and anger.

Q: I believe it's become more prevalent now because of the poverty and the frustration in the African American community. It's a fact that Jews do control some of the financial institutions, and do have a say-so in the media that controls the images you see. And they should be very careful to take into consideration how African Americans are suffering very deeply. They should understand the plight of the oppressed because they suffered a Holocaust just like we suffered a Holocaust. And if they want to be this ally that they have been over the years, don't desert the African American community now. Men are starving out there on the streets.

Drew: I hear the anger about racism and ghetto conditions. I agree it's terrible. But I think the notion that it's the Jews who are behind this, taking money out of the African American community, running the financial power structure, is wrong. The Jewish population may have some power and wealth, but it's really very small—two, three percent. But as a small ethnic group that's also been subject to discrimination, it becomes a convenient target to fight against, as opposed to the people who have most of the power.

I do think Jews are supposed to care about all who are oppressed. So I think what you're saying pulls us back to our ethical center. But Cornel West says that African Americans also have to rediscover the moral center of the civil rights and the black freedom movements. If the movement is racist toward groups like Jews, doesn't it abandon its ethical center?

Tony: If you become racist you become what you've been fighting against.

John: Our Muslim community once was Nation of Islam, but we broke away because of that blaming the white man. We came to a decision that our biggest battle is to correct ourselves as human beings. Racism has to be attacked whenever it comes up. No double standards.

Q: But it's difficult to put together what West is saying with the history of Jews participating in the slave trade.

Drew: West said the breakdown in black–Jewish dialogue is partially from ignorance about each other's history. Most African Americans I don't think have much awareness of the two-thousand-year history of anti-Semitic persecution. On the other side too, we may be ignorant about Jewish complicity in slavery, and insensitive to the history of the African American.

John: But there's also a problem of African Americans knowing their own history. Because then we would know that some of the "facts" that Farrakhan is spouting about Jewish slave traders aren't true.

Donald: I think that most blacks know more about the Jewish Holocaust than they do about their own history. And a lot of Jews don't know about the black Holocaust, or even recognize there was one.

Tray: That Middle Passage, where millions died before coming over here.

Drew: What is the Middle Passage?

Various voices: The slave ships. People killed themselves, jumped in the sea. People thrown over, heads cut off. . . .

Donald: You don't know what the Middle Passage is?

John: We're gonna have to get you some African history!

CHAPTER SEVENTEEN

Welcoming the Stranger

"You shall not oppress a stranger, for you know the feelings of the stranger, having yourselves been strangers in the land of Egypt." So God addressed Moses in Exodus 23.

But who is the "stranger," I wonder? My Torah says that the Hebrew word *ger* "was the term applied to the resident non-Israelite who could no longer count on the protection of his erstwhile tribe or society." So the stranger was not simply geographically displaced. This person was also socially displaced, no longer considered part of the tribe from which he or she came. The temptation for the Israelites to oppress such a person living among them must have been great. But God enjoins otherwise repeatedly (the "stranger" is referred to thirty-three times in the Torah). The Jew's own suffering opens up the possibility of *compassion*, of "experiencing with" the other. The Jew knows what it's like to live in exile, subject to cruelty and humiliation. And the Jew knows the value of all that restores humanity: a moment of kindness, a gesture of respect, of little cost to the giver, but to the receiver, of momentous import. Don't forget, God says. Like a Jewish mother, he's a bit of a nudge about this subject.

When I wandered into the prison setting, who was the stranger and who the Israelite? On one level, the answer seems obvious. I, after all, was the prosperous Jew dwelling in America as a comfortable homeland, whereas the men I worked with were outcasts several times over. First, they were estranged by virtue of their blackness. Their ancestors had been brought over by force and enslaved. They, themselves, had grown up in ghetto areas, as my ancestors once had in Eastern Europe. A further ghettoization came about with their prison exile, not only geographic but moral in nature. By virtue of their crimes they were to be set off, confined, deprived of rights, liberties, and protections I take for granted. Any penitentiary creates strangers within our midst.

But once inside the prison, I also felt the stranger. Having grown up in white and exclusive environs, I had wandered into a different world. The Baltimore prison, like the city itself, had an African American majority, including most of the inmates, guards, staff, and administration. By virtue of my skin, I seemed the foreigner here. And race aside, this remained an alien world. I knew how to deal with a college dean, but not a chief of security. I knew something of the life of a Loyola student, but not that of a seventeen-year-old incarcerated for double murder. I was as much a stranger in this Kafkaesque universe as the prisoners might have been visiting Loyola's pristine campus.

Who is the stranger then? Suffice it to say the prisoners and I met as strangers to each other. Black and white, Muslim, Christian, and Jew, poor and rich, prisoner and free man, we gazed at each other across multiple chasms. But we also extended a hand of greeting. As I've mentioned, from the moment I entered the prison the inmates assisted me to feel at home. Maybe it was the self-selected nature of the class. Those men who would rebel against a white or Jewish teacher simply didn't show up. But maybe it was also that the prisoners knew the "feelings of the stranger": what it was like to be a different color, to stand alone before a hostile crowd. Such affliction can either embitter a person's heart or soften it with compassion. And my own compassion may also have been rooted in strangerhood. From the loss of my family and the weight of guilt and despair, I too felt like an inmate and exile.

All strangers, we were somewhat at home with each other. The race thing didn't seem a big deal. Only once did I sense a violation of that principle. Having started a section on African thought, we threw the class open to new participants. Some young men joined who had studied this subject, taking an Afrocentric perspective. I offered them and others an opportunity to lead the class. We decided to have two speakers on Egyptian philosophy, the first man black, the next Mark Medley, a Jew.

Well, that first guy really pissed me off. I don't like to admit it, but he did. He talked about the great contributions of Egyptian culture that had been stolen without attribution by the West. Well, okay. I think his position involved some serious exaggerations, but at least it had some scholarly basis; works such as Martin Bernal's controversial, but respectable, *Black Athena* take something of this line. But what pissed me off was the young man's racial dogmatism. He wasn't just extolling Egypt, but attacking in veiled manner other cultures. The Jewish biblical account had reversed the truth. Moses was a second-rate and corrupt figure. Egypt, in his view, embodied the good, and other societies (Jewish, Greek, European) brought darkness and distortion. I tried to argue back, but wasn't too effective. For one thing, I felt a little intimidated. I just wasn't used to his dogmatic and hostile style. Second, I wasn't sure of the appropriate response. Admittedly, I did see things from my white and Jewish perspective and he had the right to disagree. I didn't want to shut up opinions other than my own. That would only reinforce this student's distrust. However, I also felt the need to forcefully oppose what I believed to be racist comments. But how to do so without myself being, or appearing, racist? I seethed and vacillated, finally calling an African American philosopher friend. Help! What's going on here?

He saw it as something of a power game. This student was going to challenge my white authority with street-style tactics to see if I backed down. Do the opposite, my friend exhorted. Stand tough, confront every false move with evidence and argument, counter any jive with some slick moves of my own. Then, only then, would I win respect.

Sounds good. The problem is, it's just not my style. I could imagine my voice cracking at the crucial moment, and my tough phrases coming out in a high-pitched whine. So I was relieved when next week I found myself off the hook. The young man didn't show up for Mark's presentation or any more of the classes. Having made his points, he and his followers vanished. My long-standing students were not surprised. He had come to teach, they told me, not to learn. They sagely shook their heads and (mostly in their thirties) muttered about the arrogance of youth. I was grateful for their support—they chose me!—and for being able to resume our more polite discourse. But I also felt some sense of loss. In a desert oasis Jew and Egyptian had briefly met, then wandered apart still strangers.

In the larger society, that seemed the norm. One of Louis Farrakhan's lieutenants, Khalid Muhammed, had just delivered a virulent attack on Jewish power and conspiracy at Kean College in New Jersey. Leonard Jeffries, a professor of African American studies at City College of New York, had been removed as department chair after delivering a speech with anti-Semitic overtones. All this was starting to infiltrate our class. Though I like to think of myself as a fervent defender of academic freedom, I felt little sympathy for Jeffries. But I found that my students had a different point of view. The tension crackled in our discussion. It started to feel *personal.*

Then my wife, a professor at the historically black Morgan State University, went to a talk there by a local black politician who included a backhanded reference to Jews. She was upset. As a feminist philosopher concerned with multiculturalism, her work focused on understanding and countering oppression. This was one reason she was hired at Morgan. But now she felt prejudice from the other side. The situation intensified when she taught a class on anti-Semitism during her Power and Gender course and one of her students proclaimed, "I don't care what anybody says, I hate Jews!" Others ran out the familiar stereotypes: Jews were rich and powerful unlike blacks, so they couldn't be the victims of racism. Students who disagreed kept silent.

My wife came home that evening furious. We talked late into the night about how best to respond. But when she went in to teach her next class, she found herself unable to, except through a single spontaneous gesture: she walked out. These students to whom she had felt so close were now strangers to her and she to them. Better to express it directly than pretend otherwise.

And I also felt the need to let estrangement emerge. The prisoners and I had discussed race relations several months previously. At the time we'd used the occasion to affirm the common humanity that lay beneath our differently colored skins. If we had a statement to make about black-Jewish relations, it was embedded in the very work we were doing together. And I still believe in that statement. But the growing tensions in the broader society also led me to feel all we'd sidestepped back then. It was a little too nicey-nice, like a Coke commercial in which a carefully selected multiracial chorus links arms and sings about world harmony. It doesn't feel real. And if anything meaningful is to be resolved between blacks and whites, blacks and Jews, it has to be real and include the anger.

But anger made me uncomfortable. Growing up, I had little experience with such feelings worked through and successfully resolved. If people were pissed, they stayed pissed until death did them part, and the rage often played a part in that death. My brother and father were angry men when they committed suicide: angry at self, others, and the world. I remember the day it hit me: they were *murderers*. In anger, they had killed themselves. So anger scares me. I didn't want to face any anger the inmates might have toward me as Jew, or that I might have toward them. Anger was too closely associated with death. That many of the men were, in fact, murderers probably didn't help me.

Still, we seemed to have survived our anger, once it was openly expressed. I could hear the men's sense of betrayal as they talked about Jews, who *should* have been their allies, abandoning them in time of need. I understood. But I also got pissed off in return. Racism, poverty, injustice, all terrible, but why scapegoat the Jews? I felt betrayed by men I had counted as friends. If that were all our talk amounted to, it would have but added its small drop to the growing sea of animosity. But more important, I think, was the way we challenged each other in a positive way to live up to black and Jewish ideals.

Our conversation forced me to think more deeply about Torah. I've come to believe, with Q, that Jews having been "strangers in the land of Egypt," must concern themselves deeply with the African American's plight. (Surely, this is also embodied in Jesus' life and teachings. He was, after all, a Torah-taught Jew.) There was a time when this concern was more clearly manifested, for example, by Jewish-black linkages during the civil rights era. It hasn't totally disappeared, but seems to be fading.

And what does this mean to me personally? My great grandparents came over from Russia, the land of shtetls and pogroms. My grandfather built something better here. Although gradually losing his sight to diabetes, he still managed to run a successful drugstore in the Bronx. He and a helpful uncle were able to support my father through medical training at New York University where he was one of the first Jews admitted. And through my father's hard labors we ended up on Park Avenue. Thus did we escape Pharaoh's hand. In America, we no longer had to live as strangers under religious, political, and economic privation. Here was a land of milk and honey, luxury cruises, and private schools.

But had we obeyed the commandment to not oppress the stranger? Yes and no. Contra the scenario of Jewish wealth extracted from African Americans, I couldn't see how my father's medical practice had done any such thing. He was simply a good doctor helping grateful patients. But once well-to-do, hadn't we exploited Sally, our live-in black maid? I've given her financial assistance over the years to help clean up family karma. Maybe my prison work was, as well, a way of making amends and seeking to help the stranger.

But this seems awfully presumptuous. The enlightened Jew helping the poor black. No real racial equality can be built on such grounds. And perhaps this was a problem with the black–Jewish coalition of the civil rights era. Jews, after all, played the part of helpers, but unidirectional help comes perilously close to oppression. It can reinforce the lesser status of the "helped."

So, equal relations demand that these roles also be reversed, placing center stage the agency and conscience of the African American. The civil rights movement, according to Cornel West, occupied a high moral ground because it addressed something more than narrow self-interest. In the quiet courage of a Rosa Parks, the nobility of a Martin Luther King Jr., the steadfastness of students who, under attack by firehoses, dogs, and dead-of-night bombers, would neither retreat nor pick up weapons: in all this, there was a moral call that transcended the conditions that provoked it. Blacks were speaking to issues of freedom and equality, the eradication of injustice and racial hatred. Blacks, then, were implicitly working on behalf of Jews.

The poet Mark Nepo writes, "Whether conscious of it or not, we are all engaged in the search for the unknown other who might complete us and join us to the whole. . . . This, then, is the purpose of the stranger: to enliven what is dormant within us." From this perspective, Q was needed to call me to my Torah obligations. Conversely, Jews are needed to challenge racism among blacks. We can summon each other back to our highest ideals and become partners to make them real.

A year previous, we had a holiday party in class—Christmas, Hanukkah, Kwanzaa, who knows what. I gave the men silly pop-up cards. I was allowed to bring these paper products into jail, and I thought they might brighten up a cell. The men surprised me with a gift in return: a personally inscribed gilt-edged Koran. And the day of the above dialogue I lugged into class a heavy and annotated Torah to read them the "stranger" passage from Exodus. Charles and John surprised me again; they asked me to get them each a copy. I thought they were joking, but they were dead serious—these biblical books are holy texts of Islam.

At first, I hesitated: the Torah I had was expensive. But finally I knew I had to come through. Farrakhan wants Jewish wealth returned to the African American community? What better way than through the donation of Torahs?

Curious, I thought, very curious. Me, a nice Jewish boy, perusing his Koran, while Charles, the Muslim imam, studies his Torah. Sometimes when welcoming the stranger, you discover you're not such strangers after all. That's when things can really turn strange.

PART FIVE

Journeys

CHAPTER EIGHTEEN

Heroes and Hoodlums

Joseph Campbell (1904–1987) is the best-known contemporary interpreter of comparative mythology, folklore, and religion. First drawn to the field by a youthful interest in American Indians, he went on to produce a series of important studies including The Hero with a Thousand Faces, *and the four-volume* The Masks of God, *among many others. Campbell saw the world's myths both as attempted explanations for the mystery of creation and as psychospiritual guidelines for how best to live. He was struck by the universality of the answers given; for example, he argued that the same "monomyth" of the hero is found across cultures divergent in space and time.*

In addition to reading an excerpt from The Hero with a Thousand Faces, *the prisoners and I focused on* The Power of Myth. *This book was drawn from a series of PBS interviews with Bill Moyers broadcast after Campbell's death. The interviews proved an accessible route into Campbell's thought, enabling a discussion of the myths that, for better or worse, had helped guide the prisoners' lives.*

Youthful Dreams

> The usual hero adventure begins with someone from whom something has been taken, or who feels there's something lacking in the normal experiences available or permitted to the members of his society. This person then takes off on a series of adventures beyond the ordinary, either to recover what has been lost or to discover some life-giving elixir. . . . That's the basic motif of the universal hero's journey—leaving one condition and finding the source of life to bring you forth into a richer or mature condition. (Joseph Campbell [with Bill Moyers], *The Power of Myth*, 123–24)

John: When you look at who's a hero for African American women, you think of Maya Angelou. She comes from one of those southern rural areas. She went through the sexual abuse, all the discrimination toward women, and she grew from that and became something great.

And for us, we look at Malcolm X. He came to prison and went through an initiation where he had to struggle to develop himself and conquer certain things. And the way he returned made him a hero, because he came to the common people and taught about his experience; prison, drugs, getting his life together. A lot of African American men identify with Malcolm X more from the experiences than his particular doctrines.

Drew: Maybe in terms of a certain mythic structure, African American youth can't identify with Martin Luther King's life journey as much as with Malcolm X's.

Mike: Yeah, King came out of a middle-class background. His father was the pastor of one of the largest black churches in the country, and King went to the best of schools. I don't think he suffered a day in his life, you understand? That's why fewer people identify. It's also his politics—you know, the nonviolence thing is very hard to sell.

Charles: I think Malcolm X and Martin Luther King was both heroes. For each, their whole thing was to uplift the black race, right? They just had different methods. It's like two people climbing a mountain. One person goes right and the other person left, but they both struggle to get to the top of the same mountain.

Tray: Campbell says the hero gains the power to bestow things on his fellow man. In my community, a hero was the man who went to prison but came home, got a whole lot of money, had a big Cadillac, and gave us big dollars. He had the essential thing to bestow. Malcolm and King didn't bestow anything I could really recognize. I mean okay, we can eat wherever we want to now, the restaurants are desegregated, but I never thought about that because I took it for granted. They were just people to read about in school.

Mike: But Martin and Malcolm did bring something back to the black community. Up to that time we never saw a black man on stage articulating how they felt regardless of what the larger community felt about what they said. That's what they bestowed.

Charles: When I was young my heroes were guys that could pick-pocket the best and the guys that could creep the best and steal diamonds.

Drew: What's creeping?

Charles: Creeping is like if you go in the store and beat it without them knowing. You go into the employee-only room, get the money bag, and roll out. And they don't know that they've actually been beat until they close their business. I mean a creeper was a great hustler because you didn't carry no gun. There was never no risk involved. Even if you got caught smack in the room you tell the people you was looking for the bathroom. You had to go so bad! [*laughter*]

Drew: Why were those people your heroes?

Charles: Because those was the things I wanted to do at that time and *they knew how.* Plus these guys was clean-cut dudes. They wore nice suede and patent leather shoes with double knit slacks and polo shirts. These dudes would have on a gray shirt, gray pants, gray shoes, gray socks, gray silk underwear. It was the style. It made you feel that you *belonged.*

Wayne: When I was out living in Glen Burnie my uncle became my first hero because he was a solid, consistent, hard-working person. And I honestly look at my mother as being a hero. Because with my seven brothers and four sisters she had to always work to bring food in. And she would never let us see when she was down. If things were getting the best of her she would go somewhere and hide.

But another hero of mine was a Jehovah's Witness, a guy name of L—. This guy used to go to school and everybody would try to rattle him but he would hold firm. He wasn't an aggressive type of person, but he could maintain who he was no matter what people said against him. I used to try to knock him off that edge, get him to resort to violence. But he would never be moved. So one day when we got to be friends I asked him, "Why won't you be violent?" He said, "Because I'm a Jehovah's Witness and my mother brought me up this way." We were down there by the river, fishing, and he said, "You know I would just sit back and study and do what my parents tell me, and as a result of that it became a habit. And when something becomes a habit, a habit is hard to break." He couldn't hardly move from what he believed in.

In my heart of hearts I envied him because I couldn't be like that. I was always dictated to by people and situations. All that taunting. You know, "Get him, Wayne, get him, Wayne!" I wanted to quiet that noisy voice, and the turmoil on the inside that says "You're a scaredy cat," and repeats it over and over. So I was manipulated by the crowd on the outside. Not this guy.

Tray: Whew! I wish I could have seen that kind of intangibles in people. I always chose people by tangible things. My heroes was the guys who had the prettiest girls, the prettiest cars, and dressed like Brother Charley was talking about. I wanted that. I strove for that. I always admired people who had *things.* The million-dollar-a-year athletes, or the criminals in my neighborhood—the flim-flam artists, and mainly the drug dealers, because they had things that I could see and what was devastating me most was the *poverty.*

Mike: I want to disagree with Tray. When I was growing up, dope dealers wasn't glorified. I aspired to be like the guys who did the bank robberies, because even the dope dealers were afraid of them. I can remember the guys that would rob banks and then came back and give a little kid a stuffed animal. The dope dealer, he just didn't have that kind of respect . . . especially if he was selling heroin, because everyone saw it for what it was.

Gary: My view is similar. When I grew up anybody could sell dope. It was just something a bum did because he couldn't do nothing else. And it took advantage of people that were sick. Someone I aspired to be like was John Dillinger. [*laughter*] I'm serious! I liked him because he just said *the hell* with the whole corrupt system here in the United States. I'm not going for this taking people's farms, and stuff they worked for all their life, and foreclosing on them. I'll take money from your banks and hurt the status quo.

And I liked Ché and I liked Fidel, because they spit in the wind, said, "I'm not going to let you run my life. I'm not going to kiss your ass to get along with you! I'll get it my own way." I never did like the power structure in this country. I think you could share wealth a lot better than what's being done.

John: I agree with Gary. A lot of these heroes we're talking about is a person coming from an oppressed group. He's living in a society where authority and government is the oppressor and he fights back. It's not really ill-gotten gains because it's taking from someone that's taken from you.

I remember when we hit the street, African consciousness wasn't that high then and we didn't have too many black gangsters to look up to, so we just kept taking Italian gangsters' names. It was Joey this, Johnny that, Dutch this. It sounds crazy, but we identified with these guys who were fighting the system, making their lives pleasant, and taking some money back into the community to help those who were oppressed.

Tray: I had every gangster tape. There were seventy-two of them—the gangster chronicles! Al Capone on them, Dutch Schultz, Lucky Luciano. I had every last one of them because I wanted to be a big racketeer.

Drew: I'm hearing the pattern of what Campbell calls "the hero myth." He says the hero sets out from the common world, goes into a different realm with its own dangers and forces, where he pulls off something heroic using physical abilities and cunning. You see that in your descriptions of gangsters. He wins a great victory (through the heist or the deal) then returns to bestow boons on his fellows.

But now that you're looking back, would you still endorse this ideal or was it a false myth?

John: There are elements I would still accept and parts I wouldn't. I do accept the constant fight to get your way in an oppressive society. What I would disagree with is the means you use. Selling drugs, robbing banks, and murdering people is not anything to use as a means to an end. Starting your own business, becoming a journalist, whatever, that should be the correct means.

Donald: When I was around age nine or ten, I can remember people telling me that I was going to be a doctor. They brought me a tongue-depressor. But I never did get the opportunity to *see* any doctors. I didn't get any practical information to obtain the goal. No one told me that you would have to go to this school or study that to become a doctor. But somebody sittin' around told me this is how you burglarize a house. This is the kind of gun you use to stick somebody up. I was taught these things by people in the trade.

Drew: So even though you were offered a more positive possibility, that kind of hero wasn't present to see, and the practical guidance wasn't there.

Tony: There weren't no Ben Carsons around [the world-famous African American neurosurgeon who works here in Baltimore].

John: I don't know—I think we all had *both* kind of heroes. The hero that aspires to reach his goals by positive means, and the hero that strives to meet his goals by *any* means. But the first person, it seems his task is long-suffering. My uncle was a dentist, my father was a dentist. I saw how if you did right, you'd get things in life. I remember my uncle telling me, "Rome wasn't built in a day. Take your time and you'll get what you want."

But I saw those other guys too—everything for them was so *fast*. They didn't live on a budget. Working people have to say, "I can't buy this expensive piece of clothing" or "I'll wait and put it on layaway." Well, these other guys would walk right into the store, pull out the bucks, and say, "Give me two, and one for my man." That captured my attention.

A lot of African American youth are being pulled in two different directions. One set of heroes says, "Here's how you obtain the things you want, but it's going to take a while. It's going to take hard work. You have to be patient." The other guy says, "Come with me, you can get it next week!" That's the one we're attracted to. We shun the other people because "Man, even hearing you tell me about it is *exhausting!*" [*laughter*]

Group: Yeah! . . . That twenty-year-thing. . . .

John: I know this was definitely my personal downfall. I wanted everything right then. I couldn't wait. And because I couldn't wait I came in here. This is where you have all the guys who didn't want to wait.

Charles: John hit it on the mark. Because I can remember, growing up, there *was* doctors in my block. There was numbers runners, but there was doctors too. If someone got sick in the middle of the night, my mother would say I got to go see Dr. White or Dr. Knox, because they was right in the community.

But like John said, we wanted everything in an instant. We live in an instant world—instant lottery, instant potatoes, instant coffee. So when you see a kid, he want it *right now.*

I was working for one of my uncles at the shoe shop and he used to tell me, "Man, you're too fast!" Because I'm saying, "Look, man, I'm going to take the money and do what I want."

This man had his business for thirty years and still got it today. A shoe shop, a laundromat, and a cleaners in one building, and it came from just taking his time.

Tray: But you know something? In America, people like that don't get no attention. Just the criminals. The world is fascinated with a crook, whether the crook is a politician, a lawyer, or just a straight-up crook like myself. Take, for example, a guy who killed one person. He's called a murderer and sent away to be miserable the rest of his life. The person who killed thirty people, he's called a "serial killer." A group be following him, he gets visits in prison, a special cell with cable TV. Some humanitarian writes a book about him and his family gets wealthy off the book rights. Then you take a person who killed tens of thousands of people. They invite *him* to a state dinner to negotiate. [*laughter*]

Drew: But you can imagine people reading this book and saying, "That's exactly the problem with your project. You've got a bunch of murderers, rapists, who knows what, expostulating about their lives and ideas. But nobody would be making this book or buying it except for the crimes they did." So isn't this, again, making criminals into heroes?

Donald: There are some people out there that we're heroes to. But when they read the book they'll be able to discern that a transformation has taken place in each one of us.

My crime got a lot of publicity at the time. And when I came in here I got a letter from a kid, about twelve or thirteen, and I was shocked. I mean he had me up there like I was a *god.* I had a shootout with the police, downtown in the projects, and he thought that was great. And now he's somewhere serving ten years.

People can discern whether or not we made a transformation when they read the book. We're not saying that we're heroes, but maybe we'll save one person's life . . . instead of that child I helped turn to crime because he identified with me back then.

Death and Resurrection

There are both kinds of heroes, some that choose to undertake the journey and some that don't. In one kind of adventure, the hero sets out responsibly and intentionally to perform the deed. . . . Then there are adventures into which you are thrown—for example, being drafted into the army. You didn't intend it, but you're in now. You've undergone a death and resurrection, you've put on a uniform, and you're another creature. (Campbell, *The Power of Myth,* 123, 129)

Drew: Like being drafted into the army, prison's not something you chose. You were thrown into it. You probably haven't thought of it as an "adventure," but it is a new place, a new set of challenges, a kind of death and resurrection. So I wanted to ask, do you think there's a way in which people make their prison time into a kind of heroic journey? Have you experienced that?

Tray: A few weeks ago a dude shared at a meeting. He said that religions are for people who are scared to go to hell, but spirituality is for those who have already been there. I've experienced the hell, and today I'm very spiritual, dedicated to using my suffering to tell generations that'll follow, "Hey, this ain't the way to go!" I'm loud sometimes and I'm kind of obnoxious, but I have a genuine concern for people today.

And I got a thing about honesty and integrity. If I don't like a person I won't smile in his face. I won't pretend. Everything I do has to be honorable today. And now I don't find anything honorable in causing other people pain and destruction. That's what prison has done for me.

Tony: I hate it when people talk about "rehabilitate," because the word means "go back to a former self." Former self is what got me here. But let's just say I remade myself.

Gary: What woke me up was hearing this guy speak at graduation—Charles Dutton, the actor. He used to be here. And he gave a speech that was bitter, man, hard reality. He was talking to us. Because he had done time, had gone to school in prison, then went to Towson, then Yale, and now he's got his own TV show [*Roc*]. He made me stop and think: maybe I don't have a chance, but maybe I can stop someone else from being in my position.

Q: I read a book someone gave me as a gift. Tolstoy's *The Kingdom of God Is Within You.* And that book showed me there is a purpose for everything. My coming to prison wasn't just because I'm 197-XZ. There's a reason for my being here. In the hero's adventure, you go through a phase where you're forgotten, before you resurrect. After all, you have monasteries for monks. You read about Jesus Christ going into the desert for forty days. Of course, you have to prepare yourself to be able to do the things that God has made for you.

Once I began to see the position I occupied, I realized I just can't go through this experience without giving something back. We have experts in the community, you know, criminologists, but they haven't been through it physically. I know I have to tell someone about this experience. In here you're considered a dead person, but I'll have been able to die and come back to life. Maybe that will be an inspiration to someone else out there, someone caught in an overwhelming situation.

Drew: Well, I can imagine people saying "It's all very nice and fine to have these lofty sentiments and imagine you're going to make a better society, but what do you convicts really have to contribute?"

Tray: There's folks outside I know I can reach. I can tell them the way I went is *definitely* not the way to go. And because I've experienced all this drug abuse, dealing, coming to prison, and all the pain and misery that came out of it, the message would have a stronger impact.

Charles: If you're a drug dealer in my community, young'uns still come up and say, "Who was Charley? I heard about him." They got a myth about me. But when you go back, and you've transcended from caterpillar to butterfly, you can give them the correct information about life.

Q: The heroes out there are still the drug dealers and the people with material things. But now they'll have competition because there'll be a Charley.

Wayne: I'd just like to say that everybody I learn from is my hero in a sense. You know, sometimes I talk to Donald, and he'll say, "Oh man, it's gonna be alright." So he's a hero where hope is concerned. John's a reader, I'm always trying to keep up with him. Charley, when I go to ask for something I don't have no trepidation. He'll sit back and joke a while, but then say, "Go ahead, Wayne." He'll give it to me. And Tray is my man because he don't bite his tongue. Sometimes you have to say what you have to say. Now Selvyn lays back. He shows me that it's not necessary to talk all the time to get a point across.

To a degree, everything becomes a part of me. Everybody in here are the crumbs that make up this piece of cake. And so everybody's a hero to me.

CHAPTER NINETEEN

Gangster

I wondered about the role heroes had played, or perhaps the *lack of heroes*, in the earlier lives of the inmates. As we discussed Joseph Campbell, it became clear that there had been heroes galore, just the wrong kind. Dope dealers, bank robbers, gangsters. So alien from my experience, why did these gangster-tales sound so familiar? Then it came clear—this is none other than a version of the American Dream. Like Horatio Alger, the gangster used his wit and energy to climb the ladder from humble beginnings. He had become, like Lee Iaccoca or Bill Gates, a titan of industry, a thriving entrepreneur. Even his success was marked in the traditional American way: not by the achievement of wisdom or title, but of treasure available for display.

As Tray says, "I always admired people who had *things*." He's not alone. It's not simply the things themselves we're taught to admire, but what they signify. Like the warrior's spoils or the athlete's prize, wealth shows we're in the presence of a winner.

But this winner was a sleazy hood. Why was he so attractive to the men? One explanation I heard: you seize on whatever heroes are available. For example, my father was a doctor. I saw that I, too, could make it through medical school, prescribe drugs, earn a hefty fee, and gain status and respect for my efforts. Wasn't Tray seeking much the same things when he enrolled in Gangster 101? He too earned his "license" to sell drugs, make big money, gain the respect (or fear) of his peers. The fact that he had to use illegal methods merely reflected that other routes were effectively closed off.

This is surely true to a point. Spread before me were myriad opportunities that inner-city kids clearly don't have. But the discussion suggested there was also more to the story. The inmates did witness successful doctors, dentists, and shop owners. They just weren't attracted to them. Such men build patiently within the system, whereas the gangster dares to overthrow it. Seeing its corruptions, he refuses to play by its rules. If banks foreclose on hardworking farmers, then Dillinger's bank-robbing becomes an act of liberation. It's the Robin Hood tale, the myth of the outlaw-hero, played out in modern dress.

I can understand why inner-city black kids might be drawn to this myth. The "system" that preaches equal opportunity has unfairly shut them out. They want in on the goods of our affluent society. At the same time, they have an understandable desire to attack the world that has excluded them. The gangster seems to combine both moves with panache. With his right hand he lives out the American Dream; with his left he attacks the "whole corrupt system" that America has become.

But even this attack has a uniquely American flavor. I think of Mr. Smith going to Washington to confront corruption; the Rebel Without a Cause rejecting a fallen world; Marlon Brando in *On the Waterfront* refusing to play ball with the unions; even of countless gangster films themselves. Our country was founded on such an act of defiance, or so we are told. What schoolkid hasn't heard about colonists throwing English tea in the Boston harbor?

If particularly American in flavor, the gangster also fits many features of the hero-myth that are universal. The mythic hero, as Campbell describes, faces and overcomes a series of challenges. Similarly the gangster emerges unscathed from dangerous gunfights, outwits opponents, manipulates events with cunning. *Can the same be said of a dentist?*

Even the gangster's quick success had mythic overtones. By contrast, the dentist's slow progress is so mundane—"Man, just hearing you *tell* me about it is *exhausting!*" Magic lies in the instantaneous transformation. Fairy tales speak of the frog kissed into a prince, the poor orphan who finds an enchanted ring and suddenly commands great power. This is what the gangster myth promises. You can turn from a slum kid to a drug lord overnight.

And the hero wields this magic for others. As Campbell describes the recurring myth, something has been absent from, or oppressing, the kingdom, and the hero returns with the remedy. How did that relate to the gangster, I wondered? Tray supplied the answer. "What was devastating me most was the *poverty*," he said, and the gangster "had the essential thing to bestow." *Money.* Frankly, I doubt gangsters bestow a whole lot. But the men did tell of criminals (themselves or others) who bought presents for the neighborhood kids, paid off overdue rents, and in other ways shared their largesse. How much of this was fact, how much self-serving or mythic fantasy, I'm in no position to ascertain.

But I can say something about my own petty flirtation with the ideal of the outlaw-hero. It probably reached its peak while I was in college. I was a member of a seditious group that grew up in my freshman residence hall. We were demurely known as the Buttfucks. Trapped in the pressure-cooker world of Yale University, we wanted to let off some steam. For example, certain members made a practice of stealing parking meters from surrounding New Haven streets. Back then you could twist the heads right off. It wasn't the money we wanted, but the mayhem. We elected one particularly fine parking meter, in absentia, president of the Freshman Student Council. Pancho Valdez was his name and he officially reigned in student government until it was revealed Pancho wasn't actually a student.

Then there was Professor Garibaldi, an ancient anesthetic machine that we put to uses unforeseen by its builder. Its bellows would be filled with marijuana smoke by willing assistants. Then, when duly compressed by yet another aide, it delivered a powerful dose to the patient. But even stronger drugs were necessary the night we hosted a celebratory dinner for the Yale and New Haven communities. We had come together to honor our spiritual leader, YoMoDoBro, the Nineteen-Year-Old Perfect Asshole. I will never forget the sight as he was carried to the stage on a sacrificial toilet bowl, wielding a dildo and wearing proudly round his neck a decapitated Batman doll.

Nor will I forget the night my cohorts strategically hid in Yale's Sterling Memorial Library. After closing time, when all the lights were extinguished, they fanned out to carefully calculated locations and turned on the bulbs in appropriate rooms. That night New Haven was treated to a spectacle: spelled out in lights five stories tall was the word FUCK. A popular poster was made from the photograph but we have yet to see any royalties.

So we too played around with the trickster-outlaw. But "played" is the appropriate word. Enrolled in an elite college, we were ensconced in a protected world. We lived near the inner city, but were forever separated by walls and guards and a thousand marks of privilege. The "police" who patrolled the premises were campus cops largely there to protect the students. Actions seemed without lasting consequence. Perhaps this was illusory; after all, we could have been arrested for drugs or theft. But there was always a sense we'd get away with it. Surely the college would take care of its own, our parents would intervene, a friendly judge would let off the Yalies with a slap on the wrist.

Not so for inner-city kids. They're hardly sheltered by a zone of kindly authorities. Rather, they are victimized by discriminatory policies in law enforcement and sentencing. For example, the amount of drug use among blacks and whites is similar: over a given month, blacks constitute 13 percent of American drug users. But blacks are subject to 35 percent of the *arrests* for drug possession, 55 percent of the *convictions*, and an astronomical 74 percent of *prison sentences* meted out. (Blacks and Hispanics together constitute 90 percent!) No wonder our prisons are so filled with minorities.

Then too, the outlaw-hero play of the inner city can turn more lethal than the rarified Yale form. Gun homicide is the leading cause of death for black males aged fifteen to nineteen. And many who survive become victims and victimizers. Most of the inmates in my class were committing felonies by their teens, and look where they ended up.

John had thought of his drug money as a tool to help his family and others. Now he saw through the fantasy. The dealer doesn't bestow largesse on the community, but sucks it dry, stealing away money, energy, and children. Tray above all had wanted to be a success; becoming a big-time gangster had seemed the quickest route. But by the time he was seventeen the dream had destroyed all he had, leaving him an abject failure.

For H.B., growing up in a strict religious home, crime seemed a form of liberation. Fuck my father, the system, I'll seize my freedom. But the consequences were quite the opposite. He was now sick with AIDS and incarcerated. As for bucking the system, he couldn't even claim that, for the values of the gangster are just what the "system" professes: money, power, winning. They're not the *African* values that H.B. and other men bemoaned the loss of, values like community, cooperation, reverence for nature and spirit. These, in an American context, would have been genuinely nonconformist, unlike the gangster-myth.

And H.B. makes me think of my brother Scott. He too was the adolescent outlaw-rebel, though of middle-class variety. I remember those knock-down dragged-out late sixties battles between my parents and Scott about the length of his hair. I remember the drugs, the poor grades, the dropping out of college, anything to get back at Mom. Anything to not sell out to the hypocrisies of the adult world. And oh, how I, a mama's boy, admired his courage. How I longed to stand up and proclaim my freedom too. He was my outlaw-hero. But Scott saw through it. He left me a suicide note while he was getting high, "on a nice brew of tranxene, placidyl, Old Heaven Hill, and Miller Lite beer (got to keep in shape, right!)." In it, he writes, "Listen, I respect you more than me. I think I was smarter, more talented, more agile and intrinsically more charming than you, but you have developed into a fuller person, and have even exceeded my smarts and talents with your determination while I let my mind and body rot with drugs, depression, and inactivity." *No*, I want to call out, *please live*. A hero to me, but to himself, a failure.

And so the prisoners regarded themselves. A prison is a home for dead dreamers. But just as the inmates had died on a myth, so myth was a tool of resurrection. I heard that in the conversation. John still finds hope in the warrior-hero who pursues his goals more positively: starting a business or becoming a journalist. Q speaks of his own transformation as the precious gift he has to bestow: "Maybe that will be an inspiration to someone else out there, someone caught in an overwhelming situation." Charles wants to show kids you can transcend from caterpillar to butterfly. Donald heard from a boy who had idolized his violence. But that hero's power can be turned to the good, and maybe rescue some other kid.

The cynic within me remains skeptical about such declarations. After all, isn't this the kind of stuff you say to win your release? It reminds me of the pre-med candidates we interview each year at Loyola College. Why do you want to go into medicine, we ask, as I was asked so many years ago. "Because I want to help people, etc. . . ." Yeah, yeah, yeah. (I'm still waiting for the first candidate honest enough to proclaim, "Because I want to make the really big bucks!") And don't inmates practice the same shtick for judges and parole boards? "When I'm released I want to use my life-experience to help society, etc." Yeah, yeah, yeah.

But I don't think that's all there is. The men, for the most part, seemed deadly earnest, even passionate, about wanting to be of use. In prison they participated in organizations, wrote proposals, volunteered their time. It might, of course, be a self-delusion that they will stick to this ideal once on the streets, but it surely gives meaning to their prison years. Again, the power of the hero's myth. To journey into the underworld, to undergo trials and sufferings, to emerge transformed, and most important, to retrieve from that experience something precious for others—this is a theme that brings sustenance during hollow days and endless nights.

I can identify. With the death of my family I also embarked on an all-expenses-paid trip to the underworld. I had my own dark forces to battle, my own quest for a healing elixir. And I needed to know that this healing would be for others as well as myself. I experience that now when I sponsor people through the Twelve Step program. Having been to hell and back I can give valuable tips. (After all, you want a tour guide familiar with the scenery.) Then too, maybe this book will prove helpful to certain readers. And I know that whatever ground I have won in my struggles will make my daughter's job in life a little easier. My battle is for her too, and so well worth the fight.

This drive to *give* is powerful, perhaps as strong as any other drive in life that I know. It was there for Scott even as he prepared to die. Toward the end of his suicide note he writes, "I lied when I said I have no regrets. I regret missing all the great music I won't have a chance to wallow in and learn note by note, but perhaps, you will. After all, I'm leaving you a marvelous record collection, oh it is so wonderful, if life could only be reduced to music I would partake. . . . Who can I hope to live through but you, but you." Scott left me his soul when his body departed, and it was filled with Bach fugues, Monteverdi madrigals, and Mozart's soaring harmonies. He gave me the music of life.

And the inmates also want to live on, to give. I hear that music in their work with problem kids through Project Turnaround. Admittedly, it's filled with dissonant chords: they scare the pants off the kids, depress them with the horrors of prison life, then reach out in caring. Anything to get through. And so long as this music plays, the Maryland Penitentiary transforms from a place of punishment into a backdrop for helping others. Caterpillar to butterfly.

And recently, the Pen was so transfigured by a community forum hosted by the prisoners and televised by our PBS station. It was sponsored by PAC-VCR, the Prisoners Against Crime; Violence, Crime, and Recidivism Project. The inmates had detailed in a twenty-seven page document a series of programs to reduce violent crime that they could assist with and were now discussing with invited educators, politicians, and media figures. I turned on my TV and who did I see?—Tray, John, Q, and others. That must have been a hero's moment for them. And they rose to the occasion. Damn, I thought, they're better speakers than me.

The more they can realize the hero's dream in such ways, the less the gangster-myth holds sway. They can fight toward a college degree and hold it aloft like a holy grail. Or publish a short story, help a kid, appear on TV. But I also see how often, and how casually, these opportunities are ripped away. I just watched the penitentiary college programs all shut down. And with the transfers to Jessup, PAC-VCR was disrupted, Project Turnaround all but obliterated, my own class gutted. Who gives a damn, really? Prisons are for punishment.

Still, it leaves me sad. In a dark underworld a solitary ray of light takes on unusual value. A candle flicker that would be drowned by day shines bright as a diamond there. Its loss is all the more noticeable. It cannot, and must not, go unmourned.

CHAPTER TWENTY

Violence and the Soul

Thomas Moore is a contemporary lecturer and author who focuses on themes in archetypal psychology and mythology. He is the author of two recent (and somewhat surprisingly) best-sellers: Care of the Soul, *and* Soul Mates. *Moore's writings are informed by his diverse background. Having lived for twelve years as a monk in a Catholic religious order, he also has degrees in theology, musicology, and philosophy, and currently works as a Jungian psychotherapist.*

The brief excerpt we study here from Care of the Soul *provided a point of entry into an intriguing question: was "violence" wholly negative, or did it contain the hidden seed of something redemptive? If so, how might we best bring that forth, transmuting destructive energies into creative energies?*

Violent Life

The word *violence* comes from the Latin word *vis*, meaning "life force." Its very roots suggest that in violence the thrust of life is making itself visible. . . . It would be a mistake to approach violence with any simple idea of getting rid of it. Chances are, if we try to eradicate our violence, we will also cut ourselves off from the deep power that sustains creative life. (Thomas Moore, *Care of the Soul*, 126–27)

Donald: I agree with Moore that there's *constructive violence*. A good example could be the childbirth process. There's a lot of violence and pain associated with birth.

Charles: I think violence is in every form of life, everything. I have an uncle who's a shoe repair man and it takes violence to use the hammer and beat the shoe, take the knife and cut the leather. Once he puts the shoe on the finishing machine he has a beautiful pair of shoes, but it takes violence to make it.

John: In Project Turnaround when we're counseling kids, we talk very violent. Our tone of voice, our mannerisms, and our words are rough—but to get a message across that if you follow this path you'll end up *in here*.

Tray: And when one of them Project T kids gets me angry, that's when I give the best presentation. It's like the same intensity I have when I'm doing something *negative*—it's got to be there when I'm doing something *positive* or I won't do it right. I need that anger that makes me able to kick somebody else's butt. If you ever take that violent streak out of me it will reduce me to nothing.

John: But it's a force that has to have some degree of control. My bad temper was my downfall. I don't really think I'm a bad person, but I had the tendency to react when I would feel like I was being threatened. And I'm better at handling that reaction now than when I was out on the street. Because I didn't have any thought about how to control or direct it—just to react, and react as strongly as possible. That's the way I learned on the street. If you're going to be violent, you're going to be *all the way violent.* There's no "a little violent"—you go the whole nine yards or you're not going at all.

Wayne: I liked the reading [from Moore's work] because it helped me understand a particular scripture. In Matthew 11:12 it says that "From the days of John the Baptist until now the Kingdom of Heaven suffers violence, and the violent take it by force." I never really knew what that meant. Then I realized that when I come to the knowledge that what I did was wrong, it takes as much violence not to do it, an opposite violence going in the opposite direction. Now I use that same energy to redirect the anger. I come up with creative ideas to keep from doing a drastic thing I'll later regret. It's funny, really funny—the same energy that you use to do something, like commit a murder, you have to use to *not* commit a murder.

John: When I was thinking about rechanneling energy and violence, they had a special on TV last week about rap music; how the message is violent, and rappers are perceived as role models, and this might be creating more violence in the street. But in my opinion, this is an example of someone who has taken the potential for violence and channeled it into a constructive force. They could be guys like us sitting in the penitentiary. They could sell drugs, end up killing somebody, do stickups, car-jackings, whatever. Instead, they chose to *express* what they know. And they're not harming anyone—there's no causal relationship between what they say and violence on the street.

Tray: I beg to differ. Before any violence can be kicked off, somebody always writes something that's going to inflame people. In the nineteenth century, all you had to do was write that a black man raped a white girl and paint it up and glorify it, and you're going to have a black man lynched. And now the rappers get kids pulling out guns, shooting people for no apparent reason. That pen is real mighty but when it goes into a violent person's hand and he's real talented with it, a great many people get killed.

John: When they would lynch a black man, it had *nothing* to with writing. It was just something they were wanting to do anyway. And it's the same thing now with a lot of African Americans. Because our living conditions are so frustrating, and we have a lot of hostility, we just wait for a direction to express that. There wasn't no rap music when we committed crimes!

Tony: Yeah, but when we were growing up, most of the time if you had a beef with somebody, at the most you had a knife. Maybe a chain, a baseball bat. And if you got your butt whupped you accepted it.

John: Yeah, I think the difference now is the accessibility of guns, especially to younger kids. When I was growing up, say thirteen or fourteen, getting a gun was out of this world! Get a gun from where? Maybe if you beat somebody for one, but usually if you did, it was an old ragged revolver that had a rubber band on it and you had to tape it together. But now they're not pulling out old ragged guns, they're pulling out brand-new fresh pretty-looking big spanking-new guns. Where does a little boy like that get a gun from? And they got four or five of them! When I was growing up there might be one gun in the whole neighborhood. Say I had it. If you had a beef you had to come looking for me, and I had to duck past my mother and go up in the attic, and by the time I get it to you, you might have calmed down or the other guy might've left. Now everybody's got the gun right in hand. It doesn't give people the opportunity to think. Got a problem—go grab a gun and solve it.

Gun Power

> Guns are both banned and adored. A gun is one of the most numinous— mysteriously fascinating and disturbing—objects around us. Those who protest its banishment may be speaking for a rare idol of power that keeps the strength of life, *vis*, before our eyes. A gun is dangerous not only because it threatens our lives, but also because it concretizes and fetishizes our desire for power, keeping power both in sight and also removed from its soulful presence in our daily lives. (Moore, *Care of the Soul*, 134)

John: I think back to how I crossed the line and started dealing with a gun. My first reaction was fear. I remember someone telling me when I was younger, "Man, get away from it, because once you pick it up you can never put it down." And at the time I really didn't pay him much attention. But that gun became a crutch. I wouldn't go anywhere without it. It got so bad I'd forget I had it on my person. Once I was paying my rent downtown and the people said they got to take a money order. So I'm running across the street to the bank, and this twenty-five in my pocket hits the ground. I scooped it off the curb, tucked it back and run in the bank like it ain't nothing. Then I'm standing in this bank saying "Oh man, have you lost your mind?!"

But if I got dressed in the morning the gun was going with me. And once you're known for a gun, guys look at you different. Everybody gets into a frame of mind that when they come to deal with you, it's not going to be a fist fight—it's going to be shooting. So the fear reverses: you say, "I've got to keep it, 'cause *they're* coming toward *me!*"

Jack: When I was four or five, the main thing I wanted for Christmas was a gun. Just watching cowboys on TV, I wanted the two guns and holster and all that. As I got older I graduated from the cap pistol to a shoot gun, BB guns, pistols. . . .

Drew: Growing up, I had a toy gun that fired rubber pellets. But it would never have occurred to me to take the step to a real gun. I wonder, though, do kids and adults want guns for the same reason?

Jack: Basically the same. Power. If everybody's playing cowboys and Indians, and a kid can shoot longer and faster, he's going to win. Everybody looks up to him. Everybody wants to play with him.

Charles: I remember the first time I ever carried a gun, I wasn't more than thirteen. A dude—he was like seventeen or eighteen—said, "Shorty, hold a gun for me." I was scared, but I felt like I belonged. When I gave the gun back, it seemed like I went back to the little dude that I was.

Tony: I first started carrying a gun when I was in high school in L.A. I lived in what's known as Blood territory and I got banked one day in school—five of them jumped me. So I decided I wasn't going to get banked anymore. I bought me a thirty-eight and carried it until the day I got arrested right here. But there are times I've had fights and never pulled it. There's a person here, the first thing that comes out of his mouth is "Well, if I had my gun, you'd do what I want. I'd do some straightening." Which makes me think that if he ain't got his gun he must not be a man.

Drew: Sounds like you can almost become addicted to it, like a drug.

Tony: Yes. It's a hundred and five degrees outside and he's got a jacket on because he's been carrying a gun all his life and it's a habit. I said, "You're in jail, *you don't have a gun.*" He said, "It don't make no difference." It's ingrained on his brain.

O'Donald: The gun I had, I used to spend hours just cleaning it, looking at it, holding it. If I saw a gun that looked ugly I didn't want it. And I think when you're carrying it other people see some way a gun makes you light up. People don't mug you if you've got your gun on you; it seems like they can detect something that wasn't there before.

John: You can't just pack a gun and not have a gait or favor that side. There's a lot of little things that might let them know.

Tony: But I think it's psychological too. You feel secure. You know if I get in a beef today and I got a revolver, I got six buddies to help me. If it's an automatic, I got fifteen.

John: In my neighborhoods if you had a foe, the only way you could feel secure that he may not kill you is to go ahead and kill him. But I was also thinking in my cell about ways to get rid of someone without physically killing him: *kill his spirit.* Because if you kill his spirit you really won't have to worry about him anymore. He's just floating around, merely existing. He's no more a force ready to build up and come towards you. He's a person who's using all his energy trying to pull himself back together. Say you find out what's most precious to him. It could be some material thing, money, a lot of things. If you can hit him there you've eliminated him. Now he's confused, disoriented. The thing that made him what he was is gone.

Drew: Would you say that's what the prison system is trying to do to you? We talk about rehabilitation, but I wonder. Having been subject to violence, society may have decided that we'll kill some people through the death penalty, but with others we need to kill their spirit. Take away their manhood, freedom, power, whatever, so that when they come out they're not going to do any more of that shit.

Tray: The examples are all around. You see a guy get the letter that his court petition has been denied—it just takes so much out of him. And what gets us the most is that in America a man's supposed to take care of his family. You can't do that in the penitentiary and it kills you inside. Most of the older guys that have been here fifteen, twenty years have already submitted to homosexuality, turned informer, things that are just *taboo.* You have exceptions like Jack here, but most of them are broken. When they were young their backs used to be straight. Now they walk bent over or stay in the flats. They're flabby. Dead.

Drew: Moore writes, "The word *violence* comes from the Latin word *vis,* meaning 'life force.'" So the violence has gone out of those people, and society's happy with that. But the life force has gone too. And I hear you saying, I need to rechannel my violence in a more productive way, but I don't want to ever lose that life force.

The Soul's Voice

The soul is explosive and powerful. Through its medium of imagination, which is always a prerequisite for action and is the source of meaning, it can accomplish all things. In the strength of its emotions, the soul is a gun, full of potential power and effect. The pen, expressing the soul's passion, is mightier than the sword because the imagination can change the life of a people at their very roots. . . . If violence is the repressed life force showing itself symptomatically, then the cure for violence is care of the soul's power. It is foolish to deny signs of this power—individuality, eccentricity, self-expression, passion—because it cannot be truly repressed. If there is crime in our streets, it is due, from the viewpoint of soul, not just to poverty and difficult living conditions, but to the failure of the soul and its spirit to unveil themselves. (Moore, *Care of the Soul,* 135)

Drew: If the gun is a symbol of the potential for power and energy within the soul, to put down the gun there have to be other objects, other directions to seek that power.

Tony: A good example is going back to gangsta rap. The microphone's the power. They're saying "This is what's going on in the inner-city neighborhoods and you can't hide it any more. You may control the news, see what the mass media want, but you can't control my record."

John: For some African Americans, a camera's now a way of getting their power across. Look at Spike Lee, look at movies like *Boyz 'n the Hood.* They're getting their rage out, and saying "This is how it is. We don't like it. This is the way we think things should be." Or look at what H.B. did. His knowledge was on paper. With his writing skills, he could send out a product people would appreciate. Or this project we're working on right now—if it turns into a book, that's a sense of power. It's a way you can pass something on to others. To give an example, the little article we did, I never thought about really sending it to my family—maybe to my kids so they could see that I was doing something *other than time*—but then I sent one to my aunt and my uncle and they read it and were very impressed. A lot of times even getting a college diploma here, people in the street say, "Penitentiary college, yeah, what are you all teaching in there?—ha ha." So when they actually see these guys are articulate and they're saying something worthwhile, it puts another light on the situation. What we do every day behind this wall, people can't put it to a test. But the writing is something that's really out there. People can criticize it, make comments on it.

Tony: I remember when we got that check for our article. I could live to be a hundred and ninety years old and I'll never forget that. It's not the fifty dollars: it's the fact that somebody out there read what we were doing, listened, and wanted to share it with their readership. That's power.

Drew: When you're stuck inside the penitentiary it's harder to have power—to have an effect on the world out there, to have people listen. But it sounds like through these writing projects there's a way to get over the prison walls.

Tony: Yeah. You can have my body but you can't keep my words. My words are already out there. Hopefully.

CHAPTER TWENTY-ONE

Guns and Voices

I like to think I'm a nonviolent kind of guy. I greatly admire the teachings of Mohandas Gandhi and Jesus. I am a Quaker, thus tied to a long tradition of pacifism. The Quakers believe that since we are all linked by the Divine, to do violence to another is to violate yourself. It just makes no sense. Moreover, it doesn't accomplish the goal. Instead of stopping the enemy's destructive energy, one multiplies it by violent reaction. In the words of the Compassionate Buddha, "Hatred never ceases by hatred. Hatred only ceases by love. This is an unalterable law."

I can relate, having grown up in a war zone. The endless battles between my parents and Scott never seemed to find resolution. They were more like those in Bosnia and Kosovo: a conflict rooted in ancient grievances that go on and on and impose suffering on all, including civilians (like me) caught in the crossfire. There are no losers and winners in such a war, just losers. And along the way I lost all my family.

But reading Thomas Moore put a new slant on things. He associates violence not originally or primarily with destructive forces, but with creation. If we try to do away with all within us that is "violent"—unique, expressive, explosive—we threaten to do violence to ourselves. The task is to channel these forces, not obliterate them.

One night several years ago I was so filled with rage (at a now-forgotten provocation) that I started pounding my car's steering wheel and all but raced into a tree. It scared me and I discussed it with a Twelve Step friend. "You, angry?" she replied. "I can't imagine it, you *never* get angry." Part of me felt sickened by the dishonesty of the image I was projecting. Part of me was thrilled. I had *pulled it off.* I wanted to never get angry, or at least to convince the world this was so. Rage had seemed like a toxic waste pouring through the Love Canal of my childhood home. And I wanted to seal it in one of those toxic waste containers that have a half-life of, say, fifty million years. Bury it, no matter what the cost.

But the costs, as Moore said, are great. The more I tried to get rid of all anger, the angrier I seemed to get. Like a bevy of bats, self-accusations would swoop and echo through the caverns of my mind. "You're a bad, sick person. You're filled with hatred. You're not fit to live." Unbidden, I would start to have mental images of kicking myself or whomping myself with a baseball bat. Subconsciously, I believed this self-attack to be a perfect solution to the anger issue. I could unleash my anger and, at the same time, punish and control it. Talk about having your cake and eating it too! By turning my rage inward I thought I could protect others.

But I was a mess. Once into the angry cycle of self-attack, I couldn't climb out for days. I was the furious mother punishing the angry child, but of course this just makes the child madder, and then the mother ever more frustrated. Hatred never ceases from hatred.

And what I was doing to myself in my craziness, I sense in our society. Hatred is building on hatred. A history of white-on-black racism feeds poverty, unemployment, self-hatred, and rage. This can lead to drug addiction and rising rates of robbery and violent crime within the black community. This fuels an angry response. Cut off welfare for "them"!—though most goes to whites. End affirmative action!—though the notion that the social playing field is now level, the inequities of the past all cleaned up, is almost laughable. And then there's the violence of our legislative responses to violence. The 1994 Omnibus Violent Crime Control and Prevention Act expanded the death penalty, cut off funding for prison education, mandated life sentences for three-time felons; the list goes on and on. Will this lead to a safer and more congenial society? Not according to the Buddha: "Hatred only ceases by love."

Of course, the Buddha never got elected to public office. There's a satisfaction in vengeful rage that's quite popular, even intoxicating. Few are in the mood for that turn-the-other-cheek, love-thine-enemy crap. But Moore's message provides a place to start. If it's hard to love thine enemy, maybe we can begin by *listening* to him. Violence, Moore says, is the soul speaking. Like a colicky baby, even its most ear-shattering cries still have meaning: "Pay attention. Here I am. This hurts. Do something. No, I won't shut up."

And Moore suggests that even the gun is such a voice. Recognizing this in no way minimizes the horror of these weapons. I have heard no plea for gun control more persuasive than the inmates' own words. As John says of the increasing death rate, "Yeah, I think the difference now is the accessibility of guns, especially to younger kids." Statistics bear him out. In one city, over half the male eleventh graders surveyed said they could easily obtain a handgun. In the decade leading up to my prison work, the number of handgun homicides among juveniles increased 500 percent. In fact, 80 percent of all juvenile homicides are now committed with firearms. I know the NRA response: guns don't kill people, *people* do. Yeah, I think, people kill people, *when they have guns.* Adolescents are not known for their impulse control. But Moore also reminds us to focus on why guns are so attractive to kids, and to us all. "A gun is one of the most

numinous—mysteriously fascinating and disturbing—objects around us."
Like the outlaw-hero, it embodies an instantaneous magic. With a flick of
the trigger finger we kill. The power of the human body is multiplied a
thousandfold. Minimal movement. Maximal destruction. Magical.

But why, I wonder, the special allure of *destructive* magic to these men?
Why is the gun an idol of power, rather than technologies of creation? I
can imagine a number of reasons. Rage for one. When mad at the world
we want the power to destroy. Then too, there's fear. When you're frightened, a gun in the hand can symbolize absolute protection. This, I think,
is as true for some NRA types as a ghetto kid. If their rhetoric is to be
believed, criminals might sidle up, break in, or drop from the sky at any
time, to rape, violate, or murder innocent citizens who've egregiously left
themselves undefended.

I don't mean to make fun of such concerns—it's a distressingly violent
world we inhabit. But I doubt that more guns would provide the solution
to a fear that itself is propagated by the presence of guns.

But for the inmates it had been an avenue of power. Constructive
power can seem inaccessible when growing up in the inner city. Not so,
the effects of violence. For many of the men, squeezing a trigger was the
most influential thing they'd ever done. It forever ended some lives, filled
others with grief, and in certain ways, ruined their own. A terrible out
come. But in that moment something was also *affirmed*: my actions are
significant, their effects lasting. I count. I exist. More than you. And a gun
announces all of this quite loudly. The sheer noise forces you to hear. Just
as loud are its effects—gaping hole, blood, and shattered bone. If the gun
is a voice, that voice is screaming.

Upon receiving the Nobel Prize for Literature in 1980, Czeslaw Milosz
said, "In a room where people unanimously maintain a conspiracy of
silence, one word of truth sounds like a pistol shot." The opposite is true
as well, I think. In a society wrapped in silence, a pistol shot *can sound like
the truth.* It shouts out your rage, fear, power, to a world that seems oblivious. But what a horror this scream brings about. What a silence in its
aftermath. For the victim, buried in the grave. For the shooter, buried in
prison. We even speak of inmates as being "shut up" behind bars. Moore
suggests an alternative to shutting people up: provide them with another
way to talk. The inmates had come to this on their own. Their new voices,
John insists, can speak some of the messages the gun once had—anger,
power, demand—but it must do so in a way that could be accepted by the
listener and truly empower the speaker.

In a way, I was seeking this as well. I wanted to learn how to channel
my violence creatively, not just use it to beat myself up. Maybe that's one
reason I chose to work in a maximum security prison. If ever there were
men who knew about inner rage, and had thought long about its consequences and redirection, it would be such men. "Ten Steps to a Better

You!" taught by convicted felons? It sounds absurd. But the truth is, these men did have something to teach me here, as much as I did them.

And I heard some of these lessons emerge in our discussion. Like Wayne's comment: "It's funny, really funny—the same energy that you use to do something, like commit a murder, you have to use to *not* commit a murder." You can turn the violence constructively on the violence. That's different from turning it on yourself. My family had shown me the outcome of uncontrolled self-hate: suicide, self-murder. But Wayne is talking about fighting on behalf of himself. He struggles with the forces that would destroy his life, as well of those around him.

And I think I'm finally learning this art of self-defense. When I find myself getting angry, and then self-hating about the anger, thus guilty, depressed, and paralyzed, more and more I start to fight back. "Wait a second here! I'm not giving in to this crap. It may have killed Scott and Dad, but it's not getting me." My ex-sponsor taught me that one of the most powerful repetitive prayers is simply "*Fuck you*" directed toward the illness. That kind of rage can be healing. There's a song I think of here by two singers, "Justina and Joyce," that begins: "I will not lie down, I will not submit, I will not be quiet, I will resist." The chorus is simply "I sing no, no, no, no. No, no, no, no." The song is called "Affirmation." Sometimes "No!" is the strongest YES in the world.

Then too, I have a favorite psalm (35) for such occasions:

> Fight, O Lord, against those who fight me; war against those who
>   make war upon me.
> Take up the shield and buckler, and rise up in my defense.
> Brandish the lance, and block the way in the face of my pursuers;
> Say to my soul, "I am your salvation."
>
> Let those be put to shame and disgraced who seek my life.
> Let those be turned back and confounded who plot evil against me.
> Let them be like chaff before the wind, with the angel of the Lord
>   driving them on.
> Let their way be dark and slippery, with the angel of the Lord
>   pursuing them.

It feels so satisfying to read that aloud with hatred and glee as I battle inner demons. I like to imagine their slippery path as they scatter like cockroaches, the angel of the Lord in hot pursuit.

If this violence can be used to fight *for* yourself, so too, Tray suggests, can it be used for others. "And when one of them Project T kids gets me angry, that's when I give the best presentation." And I sometimes do the same when acting as a Twelve Step sponsor. I remember once standing in Baltimore's Penn Station frustrated with an early recoveree who (in my estimation) wouldn't admit where he was so *glaringly wrong*. I actually started banging in rage on a baggage locker. Then for some reason I was inspired to open that locker. Inside sat a copy of the book *Alcoholics Anonymous* with certain key passages highlighted. As comic writer Dave Barry likes to say, I am not making this up. A one-time sponsor of mine used to pray, "God, if you're going to give me any messages, don't be subtle, they won't get through. Hit me on the head with a two-by-four." That book sitting there, reminding me to work the Twelve Steps on my anger (including that stuff about admitting where *I* was wrong?!), was surely God's two-by-four. But when I told this sponsor about it, he added another twist. "Why not use that anger you were feeling to help somebody else? Take all that energy and find some drunk to fix."

Again, it's a sort of alchemy, harnessing rage for the purposes of love. I'm far from perfect at so doing. Compulsive people can be really aggravating to work with. (I should know, having burned out my share of sponsors.) But in working with ill people I don't have to rage against them, or against myself for feeling the rage. I can turn that power against the illness that has tortured us both.

While discussing the constructive use of violence, the inmates also brought up the violence of art. The rapper's message, the filmmaker's camera, the plays and poetry of an H.B. And H.B. is a good example. Coming into prison with a seventh-grade education, weighed down with fury and a drug habit, H.B. finally located his soul's truer voice. He read James Baldwin's *Notes of a Native Son*, Samuel Beckett's *Waiting for Godot*, and decided to become a writer. Told in street-jive poetry, his plays are eloquent with rage, hope, and humor. *Honey* is about a twelve-year-old girl beaten by her father in the name of God. *A Gift from the Hunters*, H.B's prizewinning effort, is about a ten-year-old swept up in youth gang violence. *To Hell with Dying* is the story of four black inmates doing endless time. H.B. thought it his best play. But it was *Smooth Disappointment* that won another prize—it's the saga of a junkie who loves his fix, but loves his family more.

Heroin, incarceration, gang violence, child abuse—these are the plagues that have all but destroyed H.B.'s life. But his scream of rage has been transfigured into the cries and laughter of a dark angel.

And he's not the only one. Tony talks about our first foray into publishing: "I could live to be a hundred and ninety years old and I'll never forget that. . . . That's power." The pen is mightier than the sword, they say. Tony was well acquainted with the sword (or its modern-day equivalent, the handgun), and it had gotten him nowhere but behind bars. Now he was gaining firsthand knowledge of the pen and it stood up well by comparison. It had a precision, grace, and complexity of expression lacking in the gun's big bang. The pen spoke of the power of his own mind, not some weapon he had grabbed. It added something to the world, rather than subtracting. Instead of condensing into a bullet that blows one man away, his words could multiply like loaves and fishes, feeding thousands he'd never met. And rather than landing him in prison, the pen got him out. "You can have my body but you can't keep my words. My words are already out there. Hopefully."

They dance on the page like free men.

PART SIX

Beginnings and Endings

CHAPTER TWENTY-TWO

The Turning

Martin Buber (1878–1965), author of I and Thou, *among other books, is one of the most significant Jewish theologians and philosophers of the twentieth century. Born in Vienna, he taught for many years at the University of Frankfurt before fleeing Germany in 1938 and taking up a professorship at the Hebrew University of Jerusalem. Buber's philosophy was influenced by his study of Hasidism, a mystically tinged Jewish movement emerging in the eighteenth century. Here I focus on the Jewish notion of the "turning" to explore the prisoners' experiences of self-transformation.*

Where Art Thou?

"How are we to understand that God, the all-knowing, said to Adam: 'Where art thou?'". . . Adam hides himself to avoid rendering accounts, to escape responsibility for his way of living. Every man hides for this purpose, for every man is Adam and finds himself in Adam's situation. To escape responsibility for his life, he turns existence into a system of hideouts. And in thus hiding again and again "from the face of God," he enmeshes himself more and more deeply in perversity. . . . This question ["Where art thou?"] is designed to awaken man and destroy his system of hideouts; it is to show man to what pass he has come and to awake in him the great will to get out of it. (Martin Buber, *The Way of Man According to the Teaching of Hasidism*, 9–12)

Charles: I think it's two moments in my life I can say that I have really asked myself where I'm at. The first time was in '79. I went into the city jail for assault. I had a lot of friends that was in there and I couldn't understand why the dudes was so *content* in jail. I thought, "Man, I don't want none of this shit. I want to go home, live my life."

When I got out I just wanted to get away from the hustling world because I'd actually seen what prison was like. I had a few dollars put away, and I started working in my uncle's shoe repair shop. But we got in an argument and I broke off. By a year and a half later, I found myself in a lot of illegal drug activities.

The next time I asked myself where I was, was Supermax. My mother visited me, she was jobless, and all three of her sons was in prison. She was going through some real emotional changes. She says, "What do y'all want out of life? You're the oldest, what do *you* want? How long are you going to continue drugs? Does that money mean that much to you? And do you realize what you be putting me through?"

When I went back to my cell, that's when I said, "Dang, Charley, where are you at in your life?" I was reading the Bible and the Koran and doing some real soul-searching: "What if a man gained the whole world and lose his soul, what can he give in exchange for it?" And I said, "Dang—*nothing.*" That's where I found myself. Right there.

Donald: I never asked myself "Where art thou?" from a religious perspective. But since I've been incarcerated, questions do come up all the time. Questions like "Are you being responsible? Why don't you want to be? How would that person feel? Is it worth doing?" I think that, for me, anytime a question is raised it helps me grow. Because when I just acted upon my feelings it caused a lot of devastation to family, friends, and myself. If I were to get in a fight and act on my feelings, more than likely somebody would get seriously hurt. But if I was to raise the question "Should I continue this thing or let it go?" usually I'll do the right thing.

But growing up in my neighborhood there weren't questions, there were *answers,* like "If that happens, then you got to do this." I wasn't raised to stop and think.

Tony: I find myself a lot of times asking "What the hell am I doing here?" When I answer that question, in comes responsibility. I have to realize, it's 'cause you did something you had no business doing, or if you did it, you had no business getting caught. Then I think, "Okay, that being the case, what am I going to do to get out of here?" I ask myself that, and that's why I try to surround myself as best I can with positive things—like going to this class, one of the highlights of my week.

John: When I started to do this soul-searching thing I noticed how I had a lot of wants that weren't really necessary. When I first came in here, every time there was a function I was supposed to be there. Every time there was a clothing package, I was supposed to get brand new clothes. Then one time I couldn't get a package, and I felt I'd been cheated until I started to think, "Man, get real with yourself. You're in the penitentiary, you've been here for a long time. You're a *burden* on a lot of people out there."

Drew: The term penitentiary has within it the term penitent. At least in theory, it's a time in which people look within, undergo rigorous self-examination, and come to a sense of penance for what they've done. But in actual fact, does prison serve as a time for this, or more of an occasion to focus on the faults of others?

John: I think when guys are in their cells at night everybody goes through their self-examination. But I don't think everybody comes out saying "There's a great number of things I did wrong that put me in this position." A lot of guys come out still trying to rationalize how they got here. "If I had did it *this* way, or if I had did it *that* way, it might have not been like this."

Tony: The first three to six months, especially for somebody who's never been in jail, is probably the most crucial time in saying how you're going to do your bit. You may not be able to handle that introspection. Some dudes zap out. They finally realize where they are and just about everybody in this jail, with a few exceptions, has all the time in the world, and they can't handle it mentally.

But if you can take it, and get away from the rationalization, you realize that no matter what the circumstances, at least seventy percent of my being here was *me*. You got to accept that. Then you can start to try and change it.

Tray: When I came to prison, the first three to five years, I didn't do a whole lot of self-examination. It was everybody else's fault that I was in prison. Being poverty-stricken made me break laws. But then I went over to Supermax for assaulting an officer. The officer went home for six-months paid and I stayed on lock-up two years. But I said, "Damn, if I'm so sharp, why do I always find myself in these messed-up situations?" And then I started thinking about every time I got in trouble. It was always because I wanted to be the center of attention and in doing that I acted impulsively. Accepting that first truth about myself was hard but then it gets easier and easier as you go.

But I think you can go a whole lifetime without looking at yourself, 'cause there's dudes in here that came in the same time I did, same charges, same conditions, and they haven't grown.

John: A lot of guys are into escapism. You'll be shocked how guys have all kind of schemes, work details, everything, not to go in their cell. Then if they do lock that door, they go to sleep or turn on the TV and radio so there's no self-examination.

And sometimes your loved ones can try to do things to make the situation comfortable. Everything you ask for they'll try to get, a radio, a TV, whatever's coming down the pipeline, food packages, clothing, money for commissary, anything. But in the long run they're not really helping you. You make the penitentiary a comfortable existence and it keeps you from doing the self-examination.

That looking at yourself can be a real gut-wrenching experience. Because some of us—not all—have done things to our family. "What loved ones? If you did something to them, man, there ain't no loved ones there for you." A lot of guys just want to keep from focusing on that because, as Tony was saying, they lose it. Their minds just snap and they're somewhere else now, in the Twilight Zone.

Tray: I sat on that South Wing for two years and over on Supermax for two more years, and I saw people messing with that self-examination and they went cold-blooded crazy. "Fourth floor, call Sigmund Freud in!" and then they were gone. The dude was gone.

Wayne: When I began to examine myself, I realized the reason I kept making the same mistakes over and over is 'cause I kept measuring myself by myself. So every time I did something wrong, I could justify it. But when I became a Christian I had a standard to go by—the Bible. I began to measure myself according to that, grow in accordance to my reading and learning.

Drew: What faults in yourself did you all find in most need of correction?

Tray: My greatest fault was I didn't value independent thought. Other people's thought became more important than my own—you know, the church's, the street institutions', the schools'. Hanging out with my homies, I would try to conform. That's where all my trouble came from.

Jack: One of my greatest shortcomings was a fear of failure.

Drew: Could you explain?

Jack: Okay. My family used to stay on me about going to school. And I kept throwing excuses back at them: "Why should I get a degree? I won't get a chance to use it. Look, I got life plus. I'm never going home." But they kept hammering away. And the bottom line, you know, was I was afraid of failing. It eventually came to a point where I had no more excuses to give. So in order to shut them up, get them off my back, I went to school. And as a result I graduated with honors. Two degrees. And I found out that the only way to combat that fear of failure is with knowledge. You've got to try.

Tray: Jack had the fear of failure, but I've always been afraid of success. You know, when I was on the street, in my line of work, success ended up with you getting two of them in the head, shot by your homie sitting in the back seat while you're driving. That's what success represented. So I always played it slow. I wanted to be *second* in command 'cause the first always got two in the back of the head.

If I wasn't afraid of success, I'd have competed in the educational arena and all that. You don't have to be no braniac to know that in America, in order to get ahead you have to play around in academia. But me being afraid of success, I said I'm going to hang around the hood and just be mediocre.

John: Shortcuts are my biggest problem. I always thought that I could figure a way around something. You know, society says you have to do it this way, but "Naw, not for me. I got another way." That was my downfall.

Tony: I have to go along with John on that one. My id was running wild when I was on the street. I want what I want and I want it now. If there's six steps, then I'm going to take it in three. 'Cause I want it yesterday.

There's one good thing about jail: the operative phrase is "hurry up and wait." You could be sending out to the street for something positive or negative—you still going to wait. So you've got no choice but to slow down. Hopefully, in the course of that slowing down you get back on the phone and say, "What I just told you to send, don't send it because that's going to get me into a world of trouble."

But out there on the streets you didn't take the time until you saw that red bubble gum machine in your rearview mirror. Then *it's too late.*

Drew: I'm wondering whether being in prison makes it easier or harder to go through this process of self-examination and self-mastery. I hear some people saying it's easier because you're forced into it by circumstances.

John: I think it's harder. You have thousands of nights of just sitting in here trying to figure out *what is your problem?* Thousands. And what makes it tougher is we have no way to say, "Am I actually figuring this thing out or am I night-tripping?" [*laughter*] Seriously. Because people in the street can think things out, try it the next day, get a response. For us, we don't have any way unless somebody like you comes in. The only thing we have to bounce it off is each other, and that's not bouncing anything. Because all of us are what the world calls "failures." So how are we going to bounce it off each other? You ask somebody if one and one is two, and he don't know either.

You can say, "Well I'm no longer a drug user or an alcoholic." But, why, 'cause there ain't none around? That's a big difference from being in an environment where it's damn near walking up to your door and trying to turn the key.

Tony: And even if you—that word that I hate so much—"rehabilitate" yourself, you can't prove it 'cause they ain't gonna let you go out there and try it. They keep you here forever and ever and ever.

Can You Turn?

Turning is capable of renewing a man from within and changing his position in God's world, so that he who turns is seen standing above the perfect zaddik, who does not know the abyss of sin. But turning means here something much greater than repentance and acts of penance; it means that by a reversal of his whole being, a man who had been lost in the maze of selfishness, where he had always set himself as his goal, finds a way to God, that is, a way to the fulfillment of the particular task for which he, this particular man, has been destined by God. (Buber, *The Way of Man According to the Teaching of Hasidism*, 32)

Drew: There's a big move in the country toward stiffer prison sentences, "three strikes and you're out." A discussion is going on, where one very powerful voice says, "People don't change, lock 'em up and throw away the key." The other voice says, "Wait a second. People *can* change if they have it within them and have a system that facilitates change."

Jack: I was reading an article in the paper last week by a senator about the crime bill. He was saying that before you do away with parole for three-time losers, you have to give the first- and second-time offenders an opportunity to rehabilitate themselves. Because now they sit around and vegetate. When you put them back on the street what can you expect them to do but the same thing they did before they came to jail? If you give them the opportunity to get an education, a skill or trade, and they still continue to mess up, *then* give them the no-parole. But you have to have that rehabilitation process working. Here in this state, they don't have it, don't have it at all.

Tray: I listen to how they're getting all tough on crime and I can really understand society's point of view. But a lot of that stuff is also starting to make me angry. I come up here when I was sixteen, and at twenty-seven I'm not the same person. But I know I'll never get the opportunity to practice that, to test that, as John was saying.

I look at the fifteen-year-old kids who're coming into prison now, paying a debt they never owed. The son inherits the sins of the father. They were born into poverty with no parents to teach them self-discipline and hard work, so then they do something real stupid, and hurt somebody. They get a lot of time. Then some philanthropist like yourself comes here and teaches them good things and they embrace them. It might take them nine or ten years but they embrace it. But they never get the chance to use it. It never gets beyond this perimeter. And then they turn cold again because people like you leave. His grandmother gets to dying, his sisters get to dying, and all the things that kept him warm for so long, they suddenly turn cold again. And once it's gone it ain't coming back.

Drew: I want to talk on behalf of "society." A lot of people are looking at the recidivism rate in prisons. They come to the conclusion: somebody in a prison environment can be clean from drugs, pursuing a degree, seem like a different person, but we don't always know. You can understand their suspicion. You've voiced it too.

But then, there's the possibility of the genuine "turning" that Buber describes. Can you accomplish this while you're still in prison?

H.B.: You better, 'cause there's a difference between *leaving* prison and *getting out* of prison. When you leave prison, you're subject to come back if you have all these imagined possibilities about what it's going to be like and discover that reality has stuck a pin in your balloon. The next thing you know you're going back to the same crowd, but still telling yourself bullshit about "I'm smarter than that, so it's not going to happen." It happens, and maybe worse than the time before. That's when you only *leave* prison.

But when you *get out* of prison, you get out before you leave. Prison really had nothing to do with your decision to change. You just happened to be there when you woke up one day and got sick and tired of what you saw in the mirror. You say, "Wait a minute, you ain't so hot, you ain't shit. You want to be nothing for the rest of your life?" And it helps to have a good upbringing, come from a solid family, because especially if there was a strong male figure you have a powerful sense of integrity, of what's right and what's wrong. Perhaps, at least, you've been in touch with your potential. Everybody's got potential to change for the better. You just happen to be in prison when you decide to change.

Sure you can con a parole board or other people—especially people who love you 'cause they want to believe you're going to succeed. But you can't con yourself. If you do you pay dearly for it. It ain't worth it 'cause it's bullshit.

One time P— said, "H.B., you finally got out of prison, didn't you?" And I'm saying to myself, "What the fuck she talking about?" But now I understand. If you can *get out*, you can stay out with no problem. But if you just *leave* prison, nine times out of ten your ass is coming back.

CHAPTER TWENTY-THREE

Getting Out of Prison

"There's a difference between *leaving* prison and *getting out* of prison." H.B.'s distinction stuck in my mind, and it began to organize my vision of this whole project. After all, many of the lifers I worked with might never leave prison. People asked me, "Why waste your time on this crowd?" But H.B. supplied the answer. Even if certain men weren't leaving, they could still *get out.* And this book would aid and abet that escape. As Tony said about our first article together: "You can have my body but you can't keep my words." Prisoners' words could circulate in the greater world where their speaker might never follow.

But it was not just the book itself that had liberatory power. Of equal concern to me was the process whereby it came into being. In our readings, discussions, friendships, the men were constructing their release from prison—that prison of mind and spirit that preceded any literal incarceration. Inner prison could be as impenetrable as any Alcatraz. You're poor, you're black. You've got a parent missing-in-action, and your school's a battle zone. Each one is a brick in the prison wall. So, too, the limiting messages that colonize the mind: "You're stupid, ugly, you'll never amount to nothing." Brick by brick. And some bricks the men had to take personal responsibility for laying. They had chosen to embrace criminality, hatred, self-pity, quick-fixes, and lies upon lies. For one man it was, "Hey, I'm not gonna wait for my crumb from the table. I'm gonna grab what I want now." For another, it was, "Fuck my parents. Fuck the Man. No one's telling me what to do." Each decision must have felt like a breaking free, yet each plastered into place another brick.

But if these men were locked in inner jail, they also sought release. Martin Buber writes about the continued possibility of the turning. No "three strikes and you're out" in the human soul. I was witnessing this in my class. Those who had once so rejected school (that had so failed them) were ravenous for knowledge. Denizens of a narrow street, they were now world travelers of the mind. Hated whitey?—let me now hear what he has to say. Despised my own black skin?—let me learn of its beauty. Talked

173

with my trigger finger?—let me educate my mouth. They were disman-tling, brick by brick, that inner prison.

And so was I. I have already described my sentence. The death of my mother, father, brother, I interpreted as the result of my crimes. Subcon-sciously, I housed a skillful inner prosecutor who set about establishing a motive. Hadn't I longed to beat out, no, obliterate, my brother; to be free of my smothering mother even through death; and to escape my father in his last, descending days?

Motive established, next came the modus operandi. In each case hadn't I abandoned those in need? When my mother lay sick with breast cancer I'd trooped off to start college. Upon graduating, oblivious to my father's deepening depression, I was off again to the West Coast. When he jumped from an eighth-story window, I was not there to catch him. But the worst betrayal, it felt to me, was of my brother. Shortly before his death I'd returned to Yale summer session to study organic chemistry in preparation for medical school. This was a step to fulfilling my parents' dream, to win-ning out once and for all against Scott. And win I did. That line in Scott's suicide note seemed to document my guilt—"I think I was smarter, more talented, more agile and intrinsically more charming than you, but you have developed into a fuller person, and have even exceeded my smarts and talents with your determination while I let my mind and body rot with drugs, depression, and inactivity." I heard my victory leaving Scott defeated, despairing—then dead.

So spoke the inner prosecutor, and the inner jury had little trouble reach-ing its verdict. Guilty. The sentence was embodied in my obsessive symp-toms. No death penalty here, but I would serve out my days in inner prison, without possibility of parole. No joy, no unconflicted success, no more dan-gerous leave-takings or happy beginnings. Wherever I went, I was to drag dead bodies behind me, like the chains weighing down Marley's ghost. I dared not attempt to break free: this might be punishable by death.

So I too became a lifer. But damn it, I too was determined to get out—that is, surmount my obsessive guilt. Like the convicts with whom I worked, I struggled assiduously to have my case reopened. They con-tacted legal experts; I prayed, reflected, talked with my shrink.

And it worked. I was granted retrial. I remember the day. I had been invited to speak on the mind-body relationship at Salisbury State College, on Maryland's Eastern Shore. Afterwards I was walking through a grassy meadow, the air redolent with the salt of the Chesapeake Bay. I found myself thinking about the past again, and an unaccustomed rage started growing within. "Wait a second," I thought. "That whole inner trial was a sham. False evidence was introduced. There was no competent defense. I didn't kill anybody, I was framed."

I found myself playing out an imagined retrial, this time with a good attorney—me again. Piece by piece, I dismantled the supposed "evidence" of murder I had subconsciously accepted. My mother had clearly died of cancer. No jury in its right mind could pin that one on me. Any "bad" thoughts and wishes I might have had were immaterial to her demise. My brother and father, now that might seem more problematic. They were clearly the victims of violent crime. But not mine. I had done my best to be loving and present to both of them and, frankly, I had done a pretty good job. Admittedly, I hadn't seen their suicides coming nor prevented them. But how could I have? I was neither omniscient nor omnipotent. I was just a kid at the time. Nor was my brother's last letter the accusation I had interpreted it to be. I asked the jury to listen again: "You have developed into a fuller person, and have even exceeded my smarts and talents with your determination while I let my mind and body rot with drugs, depression, and inactivity." Isn't this a testimony to Scott's respect for me? To his love for me, since he addressed his last words to me? And to the fact that he takes responsibility for his own death, releasing me from all blame? It's there in black and white.

I waited nervously to hear the jury's verdict in my mind. It came swift and certain: "We find the defendant, Drew Leder, *not guilty*." I was exultant. It might seem that the judgment would be no great surprise. After all, I was not only the defense lawyer, but every jury member as well. But in another way I *was* surprised. To win such a reversal after all these years was an exhilarating shock.

But I wanted more. Not just my exoneration, but the exposure and capture of the true murderer, for the new evidence introduced in court made his identity increasingly clear. It wasn't my mother, though I had often blamed family tragedy on her. Nor was it my brother or father, though they had committed violent acts. No, I thought, the true killer was . . . (Perry Mason pause)—none other than the *prosecutor*.

The obsessive illness that was prosecuting me had done the same to my family. It had filled my brother and father with self-loathing and soul-destroying guilt. It tortured them right into their graves. It was a serial killer, now hot on my trail. But I will not go gently, I will not die.

For the inmates, "getting out of prison" often began with acknowledging they did the crime, no one else to blame. For me, I had to realize the opposite. "*I didn't do it.*" But just as for the prisoners, writing this book is, for me, part of getting free. I am overleaping barbed-wired walls of secrecy and shame. And this writing has helped me understand some of what brought me to the Maryland Pen to begin with. I was exploring what I had in common with these lifers—rage, violence, death, guilt, and the potential for healing and transformation. But I was also exploring what set me off from the men. They did their crimes. I didn't. They lived in prison. I visited. At the end of each teaching day, I *was able to leave.* In that experience of leaving prison, time and again, I was physically rehearsing for that soul-act that H.B. calls "getting out of prison."

Then too, the fact that I am writing this at three o'clock Christmas morning reminds me that getting out of prison, at least for me, has required divine help. I think of Psalm 107:

> Some were living in gloom and darkness,
> fettered in misery and irons. . . .

> Then they called to Yahweh in their trouble
> and he rescued them from their sufferings;
> releasing them from gloom and darkness,
> shattering their chains.

> Let these thank Yahweh for his love,
> for his marvels on behalf of men;
> breaking bronze gates open,
> he smashes iron bars.

Three vignettes come to mind that have demonstrated to me God's power to free the prisoner. Number one: I was meeting my ex-girlfriend for the first time a year after our breakup. We had been together some seven years, so the split was still achingly raw, bringing up the feelings of all my other deaths. But when I saw her that day in New York's Washington Square Park, what struck me most was the new life in her. She seemed much happier, more confident, at ease. Was getting away from me such a wonderful tonic? No. She said it was all due to God. But, she wasn't into proselytizing. In fact, given that we had both been atheists, or at least agnostics, she was afraid I'd think her weird. But I didn't. I had already found myself drawn to spiritual matters and I could see how she had changed.

Then a strange thing happened. She was speaking of finding God through the Twelve Steps (the first I'd really heard of this approach), when suddenly a voice boomed out from the heavens: "THIS IS THE LORD. WAKE UP!" I kid you not. My friend heard it too. We looked around stunned, then realized what had happened. A drunk lay on the ground some twenty feet from us (this was, after all, Washington Square Park) and a patrol car had pulled alongside. The officer had delivered a jocular warning over the car's loudspeaker: "THIS IS THE LORD. WAKE UP!" And the drunk reluctantly struggled to do so.

We laughed. That's when I first learned God had a sense of humor. Yet how apt the message. The whole talk with my friend was like a wake-up call, punctuated by that divine announcement. I was learning for the first time about the Twelve Steps, and witnessing evidence of their power in my friend. It was me who was being shouted awake. I was like that drunk in the dirt. After all, my life-killing obsessions were just as intractable, as inebriating, as booze to a sot. But that's why the Twelve Step program could help me.

I'm reminded of the story where Jesus is brought to a young girl who he's told has died. He took her by the hand and said to her, "Talitha cumi," which means "Little girl, get up!" and she awakens (Mark 5:39–41). On that day I heard God say "Talitha cumi" to me through the mouth of the NYPD.

A year later I began to work the Steps, that ex-girlfriend as my sponsor. Which brings me to the second vignette. Soon thereafter, though spiritually but a babe in arms, I desperately needed help with a life decision. I was wavering (or more accurately, obsessing) between two different career paths. Should I be a doctor as my father, the internist, and my mother, the Jewish mother, had pushed me toward since I was a fetus? (Okay, maybe I'm exaggerating a little.) Or should I be a philosopher, the other career path I'd been pursuing? I was simultaneously finishing medical school and my philosophy Ph.D., and it was time to actually choose and get a job. (But I'm only thirty!) However, I'd found that I simply couldn't choose. I'd make lists of the attributes of one career path, then the other, and somehow the lists would exactly cancel out. Fellow obsessives will understand. In fact, either choice seemed equally bleak. I was paralyzed by fear, and even more so by the weight of ancient parental pressures. I knew I needed spiritual help to get free.

So, what would God have me choose? I asked. The answer didn't seem hard to infer. I should, of course, be a doctor. Philosophy was a fun mental game, but medicine was where you did the Lord's work—helping the sick and suffering, literally saving lives. No getting around it, medicine was my calling, reluctant though I was to embrace it.

I explained that to a good friend in New York. A fellow medical student, she had been a Classics professor before deciding at age forty to recommit her life. She surely would understand the power of medicine as a calling. But her response did not confirm my choice. Though herself agnostic, she asked, "Wouldn't God want you to do something that really makes you happy?" Having dissected a cadaver together, she also knew me inside-out. "There must be enough people around who really want to be doctors. God can use them."

Riding home that day on the Long Island Railroad I pondered her unsettling words. What, after all, did God want of me? Suddenly I was struck between the eyes by a powerful realization. My image of God was none other than that of my own parents, blown up big and projected on the heavens. My certainty that God wanted me to be a doctor—wasn't this just because my parents had wanted that? Sure, I had transposed some of the lyrics, but the music was the same. My parents had wanted medicine for me because, along with its altruistic goals, it represented the most prestige, most money, most security. The top of the top. Now I was reimaging that in spiritual terms—medicine as the most sacred calling, where you relieved the most suffering, saved the most lives. But it was just my mother's voice in Olympian disguise. I really had no idea what the real God wanted.

And this insight opened up what came next. A series of ideas hit me with a magnum force that forever changed my life. First—"God wants me to be a college teacher." In a moment, I felt this message surely true. And why that? Because, I suddenly understood, that was the true longing of my heart. I had a passion for ideas that doctoring would never satisfy. I wanted to read great works, teach students, write books. I realized in that instant, maybe for the first time, that "God's will" was not some iron band imposed from without (as my mother's will had so often seemed), but one and the same with my soul's deepest yearnings. This was a joyful surprise!

But what of the rescue work I had anticipated doing in medicine (psychiatry, to be precise)? I heard the answer—such work would be done through the Twelve Steps. This would be my instrument to help others who, like myself, were suffering. Unlike professional psychiatry, there would be no pretense that I was the well one, while they were the sick. No superiority or profit interest should color my work. God was cleaning all that out in order to make me more truly of service to others, and healthier within myself.

When I got off the train in Stony Brook I was in an exultant state. As I write these words now on Christmas morning I am reminded of how that day the whole world felt like Christmas. I'd been given the gift of a brand-new life. Years, no, decades of obsession about how I'd *have* to be a doctor (though I never wanted to) had been swept away on that train-ride home. I got to be who I wished, who I was. I found myself, hokey as it seems, hugging a dog, marveling at the beauty of trees, and singing over and over, "Amazing Grace, how sweet the sound that saved a wretch like me. I once was lost, but now am found, was blind but now I see."

And that brings me to a third getting-out-of-prison vignette. Years later, having found a job as a college teacher (things unfolded with ease and direction after that first day) I was well satisfied with my new career. But still miserable in life. I mean bordering on suicidal. Racked with depression and self-hatred. A nonprofit Twelve-Step-based organization I had been a part of for years had booted me out of its membership. More accurately, I had been "asked to resign." Who could blame them? I wasn't recovering, wasn't working the Steps, wasn't contributing to or supportive of the group's mission. But the problems went deeper I now see, to my obsessive guilt. I was tearing myself to shreds, and no matter how I wrote endless inventories or prayed, I couldn't or wouldn't stop the pain. God seemed as absent as He could be. The power of death was everywhere, filling our house with its musty odor. I was stymied. When even the God-stuff doesn't seem to work, what's left? It was December, the days growing cold and short, and bringing with them a profound desolation. Then a thought occurred to me, "Why not ask for help from Jesus?"

To gauge the desperation of this maneuver you have to place yourself in the shoes of a nice Jewish boy, brought up to associate Jesus with Christianity, and hence pogroms, inquisitions, forced conversions, and TV preachers. But in reading the Bible and talking with friends, I had come to a very different impression. Jesus, I realized, wasn't a Christian, but a Jew. He was a reform Rabbi, his teachings steeped in Torah. Anyway, I wasn't primarily concerned with theological reflection just then. I was trying to save my life. And Jesus (or Yeshua, to use his Hebrew name, not the Latinized form) seemed my last hope. It was there in his name—"Yeshua" means "God saves." Another of his names, "Emmanuel," means "God is with us." I needed a saving God right there with me, as I'd met in Washington Square Park, and on the LIRR, but had so lost since. Maybe Yeshua could turn the key, open the door to my own soul. He was the repository, by many accounts, of great healing power. And he had come to make this power manifest first and foremost (by his own account) to fellow Jews. Particularly those most in dire straits—the blind, the crippled, the paralyzed. That's exactly how I felt. He was the Last Chance Motel at the end of the line.

Though it was cold December, that meant Christmas was approaching. In preparation I prayed that Yeshua be born within my heart, singing the Christmas carol based on Isaiah 9:6, "For unto us a child is born, unto us a son is given: and the government shall be upon his shoulder: and his name shall be called Wonderful, Counsellor, The Mighty God, The Everlasting Father, The Prince of Peace." I needed that God-birth within.

And the baby emerged, as any infant, from an orgy of blood and suffering. I'll never forget that horrendous time. But since then the process of the child's maturation has been slow but real. There's no single moment that captures it, unlike the Washington Square or LIRR stories. Yet, day by day, year by year, bones knit, muscles develop, and the infant grows into adulthood. My sense of God's saving power ever strengthens. And Yeshua, Emmanuel, helped unlock that power, and remains a conduit of grace to this day. I've since become a Quaker, but am proud to be a *Jewish* Quaker. I see no reason to convert to Christianity (Yeshua certainly never left Judaism), and I don't believe many of the theological tenets most Christians would accept. But I am nonetheless summoned to joy and gratitude this fine Christmas morning.

In such ways, and a dozen others, I've experienced God releasing this prisoner. And that brings me around to another prisoner with whom my life intertwined. "But when you *get out* of prison," H.B. had said, "you get out before you leave." No one exemplified this principle better than H.B. himself. From a two-bit addict and thief he had transformed himself into an acclaimed poet, essayist, and playwright. He had rebuilt his life on a foundation of core principles: Treat yourself and others with dignity, and demand the same back. Speak up the truth even when others remain silent. Language is our most precious gift; use it with care, caress it to life, don't let it slide into bullshit. Don't make friends too easily, but when you find one, stand by him for life. Acts of kindness are more precious than jewels: never let them pass unnoticed.

H.B. didn't articulate these messages so much as embody them in his actions. The very way he walked, slow and erect, proclaimed "I stand before you a free man." It didn't matter that every manuscript he sent out bore a penitentiary return address. He had gotten out of his prisons: an eighth-grade education, uncontrolled rage, a heroin habit, to name but a few. At night, while others slept, he had woven a zone of freedom using writing as his loom.

I remember the day he casually told me after class, "I've got AIDS."

"You're HIV positive?" I asked.

"No. AIDS. Full-blown. But don't get upset. It's not such a big deal."

He wasn't interested in sucking on the sweet teat of sympathy. His health was just starting to fail, with night sweats, lung-thickened plugs, and the other small purgatories that wear you down and presage the hells yet to come. But H.B. wasn't buying into this AIDS shit. He continued to write late into the night no matter what the next day's toll. When he told me I felt stunned and saddened. It seemed like a cliché from a badly written play—the convict who turns his life around only to lose it to deadly disease. Years ago, H.B. said, he'd been shooting up drugs obtained from a guard and had shared a dirty needle. Although he later got off drugs it was too late.

"No. Stop the presses!" I wanted to shout. This isn't the right ending to H.B.'s last play. He's not supposed to die, emaciated and forgotten in a prison ward, a guard picking his teeth in the corner. Something had to be done. But what, I wondered? The answer came welling up from within: "Try to get him out."

Yes, but how in the world to proceed? H.B. was in the ninth year of a thirty-five-year sentence for attempted murder, *without possibility of parole*. Yet surely, given his illness, his newfound celebrity as a writer, his power as an example of "rehabilitation" (that word Tony hates), he'd be the perfect candidate for a commutation. I tracked down a lawyer savvy in such matters. He confirmed that it was a long shot but not impossible. Still, I felt stuck. I wasn't sure what to do next, paralyzed by the responsibility. What if there was some way of getting him out but I botched the effort? He'd die in jail because of me. After my family history I was leery of this rescuing-lives type of thing and the guilt attendant upon failure. Should I back away from the whole thing? But that would only bring its own guilt and failure.

So I did some serious praying. "If it's your will that H.B. get out, you'd better show me what to do." In AA, God is sometimes said to stand for Good Orderly Direction. And that's what I received that day—a series of action steps to take in appropriate flowchart order. Follow up with the lawyer. Draft a petition. Contact appropriate signees, especially those well known or with possible influence on the governor. Etc. But it wasn't only these directions that set my mind at ease. There was also a message concerning the outcome. I found my thoughts drawn to Moses, of all people—how he stood on the mountain and surveyed the promised land but was not permitted to enter it. He died first. Why? One reason the Midrash gives is that Moses had earlier slain an Egyptian (Exodus 2:11–12). Even this man who led a whole people to freedom couldn't escape responsibility for his past. And I heard God saying, so it will be with H.B. He will see the promised land but will not enter because of the violence he has perpetrated.

I understood this to mean that my efforts to secure H.B.'s release would surely fail. Surprising as it might seem, I found this comforting. I didn't need to worry so about screwing up. No matter what I did, success was out of the question. But I still felt guided to go through with the attempt. This would allow H.B. to gaze at the promised land of freedom. He'd have hope. And even if that hope died, H.B. would still know his friends had stood by him until the end.

And so we did. Mike Bowler, who as op-ed editor for the *Baltimore Evening Sun*, had run pieces by H.B., now threw himself into gaining his release. Mike knew local politicos and friends of the governor and how to work with the governor's staff. Never mind that Governor William Schaefer almost never commuted sentences, and that when he had in the past, he had sometimes been burned. We had a strong case. We'd persuade him. An array of people participated who knew H.B. personally or through his writing. We sent the governor a letter with some twenty-five signatures, then kept the pot boiling with phone calls, individual notes, and new supporters.

Consideration proceeded with all the glacial speed characteristic of bureaucracy. As Tony said, "You could be sending out to the street for something positive or negative. You still going to wait." And so we, and H.B., waited and waited for word. Now and again our hopes would ascend—H.B.'s case has been remanded to the parole board for possible medical commutation!—only to be slapped back down again: he's not sick enough to qualify. For medical release, we were told, you've got to be incapacitated and on the verge of imminent death. That way you can't really do much damage on the street. I understand the logic. But it was like a cruel jest to H.B.: "When you're emaciated, demented, and at death's door, *then* you can have your freedom."

I tried to remind myself that the whole affair was hopeless to begin with. Remember that Moses message? But I had never shared it with H.B. It seemed that our efforts were raising his hopes only to leave them dashed. Had I done him a kindness or needless cruelty?

After weeks of up-again, down-again signs and confusion, one day a definitive message came through. The governor had decided to commute.

That's right. Commute. I was stunned, elated, and exhausted all at once. H.B. was actually getting out of prison. It soon became clear there'd be a number of conditions attached; most important, for six months H.B. would be stuck on home detention (or, as he put it, under house arrest), his every move monitored electronically. So what? Home is home. We planned a party to celebrate his return, with banners, music, and a whole lot of food. The invitation said it all: *"He's Out. Let's Eat!"*

But the party, it turned out, was for more than just H.B.'s release. That same week his new play won first prize in the WMAR-TV Black Playwrights contest. He became the only person to have ever captured this award twice. The first time he'd been unable to attend his own premiere. Not this time. He was going, and going in style.

These days, with all H.B went through since his release, it's nice to think back on that evening. The video of the prize-winning *Smooth Disappointment* was being shown to an invited audience prior to its telecast. H.B. was determined to do it up right. Maybe he was making up for the other premiere he had missed; for all those nights spent in a dingy prison cell; for a whole fucked-up life. Whatever. I remember, one, two, three stretch limos pulling up to his inner-city apartment, each white as snow, equipped with a TV, a personal bar (nonalcoholic beverages), and most of all, filled with family and friends. It was H.B.'s way of saying thanks to those who had stuck by him, and of celebrating his own freedom. Subsisting on SSI checks, and occasional writing sales, he didn't really have that kind of money. But this was of no concern that night. When you're not going to be around for too long, you grab the moment.

He accepted his award with customary flourish, dressed in a stylish black coat and beret. By special dispensation, he had been allowed out of home detention until 1 a.m. Violation could land his ass back in jail. As speeches went on and on, and H.B. lingered to shake hands, I remember nervously eyeing the clock. 12:15, 12:30, 12:45. I waited for that witching hour when the limos would turn into pumpkins, the drivers into white mice, and H.B. risked being thrown back in jail. But he would not be rushed. "We'll make it," he said, and he was correct. We arrived home right on the dot. Having gotten out of prison, he wasn't going back.

CHAPTER TWENTY-FOUR

Changing Selves

Malcolm X went through many different identities. Born in 1925 in Omaha, Nebraska, as Malcolm Little, he joined the Black Muslims while in prison (1946–1952) for robbery. He later became the organization's national minister, preaching black separatism and nationalism until a trip to Africa and a pilgrimage to Mecca changed certain of his views. He left the organization and converted to orthodox Islam before his tragic assassination in 1965. What is your true self? How do you change identities? How do you make the new self stick? Malcolm's life raises these questions for the men.

Double Identity

For evil to bend its knees, admitting its guilt, to implore the forgiveness of God, is the hardest thing in the world. It's easy for me to see and to say that now. But then, when I was the personification of evil, I was going through it. Again, again, I would force myself back down into the praying-to-Allah posture. When finally I was able to make myself stay down—I didn't know what to say to Allah.

For the next years, I was the nearest thing to a hermit in the Norfolk Prison Colony. I never have been more busy in my life. I still marvel at how swiftly my previous life's thinking pattern slid away from me, like snow off a roof. It is as though someone else I knew of had lived by hustling and crime. I would be startled to catch myself thinking in a remote way of my earlier self as another person. (Malcolm X with Alex Haley, *The Autobiography of Malcolm X*, 170)

O'Donald: The first time I got locked up I was ten. I was in training school, and I didn't know nobody and I was scared, terribly scared, but I didn't want nobody to see it. A priest came in and was telling us how we could give our life to Christ, and at night when we went back to the dorm, I stayed up and prayed. And after that I was able to go to sleep. When I woke up that night the fear was gone. It's like I had peace inside.

Tray: I received that type of freedom too. I was over at the Supermax and I was plagued with so many problems and secrets in my heart. . . . I don't want to share them with you now because it would take a week. I felt like I was going crazy. It was New Year's night, the start of the nineties, and I was going to be locked up for another decade, and the bitch—sorry, Doc, I mean my girlfriend—had left me, and I was just praying for the strength to make it. And I think I called God by about ten different names that night—Allah, Yahweh, Jesus—because I'm not of any specific religious discipline. And as I prayed and said so many things my heart came to the surface. And after I got up from my knees it was like a great big burden off of me. The walls of Supermax didn't seem as restricted. I stopped smoking during that period. I was freed from so many things, the walls, the smoking, the hollering that hits you every night, all of it just left and I felt calm.

Maybe I need to be burdened by those problems again so I can get back in that form. [*laughter*]

Mike: I remember when I first got in this situation, I picked up a book, and it had a little quotation. It said, "Sometimes when the spirit goes a'riding on the wind alone and unguarded, you commit a wrong to others and therefore unto yourself, and for that wrong committed you must wait unheeded at the gate of the blessed." Something like that, I probably quoted it wrong. But it meant something to me instantly, because all my life it seemed like I had been walking in the company of angels. I been cut, stabbed, hit by cars, and people be falling around me, but I was always getting out lightly. Go to prison, but get out. Then all at once, I got all these charges. Major stuff. I was broken up. But it was like something was saying, "Look, I'm tired of fooling with you. You're not getting the message. I've been giving you subtle things, but you're not picking them up. So now I'm just going to *smash* you. Then maybe you'll get the message." And now I'm a different person, view things different. And I think that's what it really took.

Drew: *The Autobiography of Malcolm X* gives a lot of examples of times when his sense of identity radically shifts. It raises the question of who your true self is.

Tray: Ever since I can remember, even when I was stealing out of the stores, I always felt that I'm destined to do better than this. It's like some kind of divine force inside me, and I just haven't found the answer yet. I'm better than a murderer, a thief, or a drug dealer.

Selvyn: For me, I pretty much fluctuated between two different personalities. Growing up in my family, I was this religious, nice, humble, preaching, spreading-the-word person. But outside, I was ruthless and coldhearted. In front of the congregation I'd put on one hell of a show, belt out a good sermon. When I got finished, I'd go out and light up a joint.

Tony: You have to adapt to the environment. Like, in my neighborhood where everybody knew you, and everybody might whup your behind, I had a certain persona in order to *survive.* You wanted to keep your rear in good shape!

Mike: And it all depends what street you're on. Like Malcolm X, when he was on the streets of Harlem, his standard of behavior was that of a hustler—the costume, mannerisms, actions. But when he enters prison and hears some profound truths, he gravitates toward it. It's like the old saying, "A man functions on the level of his understanding."

Q: But you have to be yourself at all times. When you fake your identity, the consequences are very, very great. Prior to me coming to prison, if you told somebody I'd be charged with conspiracy to narcotics, they would never believe it. Because I wore a suit and tie everyday, woke up, got my briefcase, got in the car, and drove to Washington. You'd say this guy is probably a banker. I think that fake identity is the most painful thing because you have to constantly act. Then, boom, you get charged with a crime, the façade falls down, and that's very painful.

Tray: Hey, I got a friend, he was my mentor, and he taught me everything about the code: "Don't tell the law on nobody—and every sixty days, Tray, you got to hit somebody in the head because you're my trigger and if you're perceived as being weak our whole empire is going to fall." Well, about two years ago, he got shot up real bad. And he went to the police on the guy who shot him. And I think I felt more betrayed by that than the dude who did the shooting, because his words were my scriptures. And he couldn't even face me for over a year—I had to communicate with him by way of his wife. So them images, once you start lying, they hard to hold up.

Mike: This all brings to mind when I was working for an insurance company as a claims adjuster. And at the same time, I'm robbing banks and jewelry stores with these guys in Washington. And what they like about me best was I could put that suit and tie on, carry that briefcase, go right into the jewelry store, and say, "It's my wife's anniversary, I'm looking for something." Meanwhile, I could get the drop, and they'd come in and rob it.

But one day, I'm sitting there thinking why should I go in there with a gun? I can take my pen and do the same thing. So I'd go into the insurance company and started making fraudulent claims. And I'd sit in the company lounge, and the other guys would be reading the paper, saying "Crime is terrible." And I'd say, "Yeah, isn't it!" I was two different people to two different sets of individuals.

Drew: It sounds like in the criminal life there has to be a constant manipulation of appearance and reality. As a hustler, like Malcolm started out, you may have to appear even tougher or more violent than you actually are so no one will challenge you. But then in relation to other parts of the world, you have to pretend to be an upstanding citizen. So all of you are probably expert at constructing false identities.

Donald: I used to be good at that. But I wrote you a letter, Doc, and described to you some problems I was having holding up my image in prison. Do you remember that? I was in the shower and this other guy was trying to get past. I didn't want him to go behind me—you know what I mean—but he was trying to. So I popped him. But I was at a disadvantage of being naked and he got the best of me. He won the fight.

Anyway, we made arrangements to meet at the gym an hour later so we could really fight. But someone stopped me at the door and said, "Look, that guy's a fool, but I thought you were a thinking guy." So he made me stop and think, and I didn't do anything. But I was wrestling with it when I wrote you. I had this image once that used to protect me, but with the newer guys in here, it don't seem to work. Even some of the older guys felt like their image was threatened 'cause I'm considered one of their crowd. So I asked you for some advice, and you sent me a Hindu story.

> There was once a holy man who came to a village. The villagers warned him that he must not go along a certain path because a venomous snake, which had killed many people, always lay there. [But] the sage taught it to give up the idea of biting and killing. Soon the boys of the village discovered the change in the character of the snake. Knowing that it was now harmless, they would attack it with sticks and stones whenever it came out of its hole—but the snake would never strike back. After a while, the snake grew so weak from its injuries that it could scarcely crawl. When next the holy man came to that village . . . the snake expected to be praised for not resisting evil. To its great surprise, however, the holy man became quite cross: "How foolish you are!" he cried. "I told you not to bite. Did I tell you not to hiss?" (Swami Prabhavananda, *The Sermon on the Mount According to Vedanta,* 66–67)

Drew: The idea is, don't actually harm people, but you may need to keep up that image.

Making It Stick

> I wrote to Dr. Shawarbi, whose belief in my sincerity had enabled me to get a passport to Mecca. . . . "Never have I witnessed such sincere hospitality and the overwhelming spirit of true brotherhood as is practiced by people of all color and races here in this Ancient Holy Land. . . . There were tens of thousands of pilgrims, from all over the world. They were of all colors, from blue-eyed blonds to black-skinned Africans. But we were all participating in the same ritual, displaying a spirit of unity and brotherhood that my experiences in America had led me to believe never could exist

between the white and the non-white. . . . You may be shocked by these words coming from me. But on this pilgrimage, what I have seen, and experienced, has forced me to *re-arrange* much of my thought-patterns previously held, and to *toss aside* some of my previous conclusions. This was not too difficult for me. Despite my firm convictions, I have been always a man who tries to face facts, and to accept the reality of life as new experience and new knowledge unfolds it. I have always kept an open mind, which is necessary to the flexibility that must go hand in hand with every form of intelligent search for truth. (Malcolm X, *The Autobiography of Malcolm X*, 339–40)

Drew: Again we see Malcolm experiencing a change of thought and identity, a transformation. Were there any specific experiences where you felt such a shift?

Tray: I want to talk about something that happened in '86 that really had a profound effect on me. They had this little old white lady that used to teach English here, and I mean every time you saw her she was smiling and happy-go-lucky. She used to bring us the most singly boringest material and made us read it, and she was real insistent on it. That started me reading a lot of things that I still do, and to take pride in books.

But she also softened my heart up. One time I had a cold and she made me a cup of tea. No one has ever done that for me, especially in the heart of the penitentiary. It wasn't the tea itself, because I can get my own tea. But the thing was how gentle she was and the smile she always had. It's just the whole relationship was so unconditional. And it opened me up. I mean she was the first white person that I ever had a love for. No ideology could ever make me look at her in a poor light.

Wayne: Once when I was in the army I was on my way from Junction City to Topeka, Kansas, sixty miles on the highway. My alternator went bad and I pulled off on the side of the road but didn't notice the snow had covered a ditch. I was stuck. I tried to get some help—even took out money from my wallet and waved it to get someone to stop. Nobody stopped.

Then this white guy and his wife—he had two kids in protective chairs in the car—he stopped. He got all wet helping push me out. He even made me stop in town to make sure everything was cool. And it's funny because I saw people of my own race and they just kept going by. When I look back on things like that, I know I can't be a racist.

John: I was sitting here thinking about some of the things that effect changes in your life. The latest change I've been through one of the most significant ones, is about three years ago: I decided that I wasn't going to use or sell any more drugs. And the hardest part wasn't *not using,* but *not selling.* Because a great portion of my adult life I made all my money through dealing. My decision to quit was an accumulation of several things. Thinking about my children. Being near Charles had its impact, because Charles had stopped using. Then moving into a double cell with this little guy who really hates drug dealers. He was a stick-up boy, so that's a nemesis to a drug dealer.

Drew: Why?

John: Because they stick up the dealers, and the dealers may end up killing the stick-up boys—things like that. So we'd argue, and I'd rationalize that I was still dealing in prison so I could take care of myself, send money home to my kids. But when I finally got a single cell to myself I started thinking about what he was saying, and for some reason, I can't never put my hand on why, one day I said I'm not selling no more drugs.

Man, it's been hard. A lot of guys in here have this problem too. Once we get out of that lifestyle we don't know what to do. We really don't have a lot of confidence that we can be successful at other things. I'm adamantly against selling drugs. But what else can I make a living at? I'm trying to develop some skills and feel my way around. And I have to realize I'm going to suffer financially until I find my niche; it might be worse for a while, but I'm learning to live with and like myself.

Drew: Sometimes when we make those transitions to a bigger self, there's also a loss. We're not just birthing something new, but there's an old self that's dying. It's striking how quickly Malcolm is willing to let his old selves die off. But sometimes it's a very painful process.

John: I remember me and Charles was walking through the yard and this guy's telling us, "I can't wait to get the keys, and then I'm getting connected"—all that stuff. I hadn't given the life up, but Charles had, and he said, "Man I don't know what I'm going to do now that I can't sell no drugs." And it dawned on me that he wasn't joking. My whole life was designed around those activities. I was always traveling to get it, cutting it up, selling it, or collecting the money. Give that all up, and there's a void.

Drew: It sounds like in order to let go of the old sense of who you are, you have to find another option, envision something else.

Mike: And you also have to guard against slipping back. In the early seventies I was working for that insurance company as a claims adjuster, making in excess of $18,000 a year, engaged to a young lady who was a dentist. Unlimited possibilities. And a guy from way back called me and said, "Man, I got a problem." I helped him out and he appreciated what I did, so he offered me a blow. Cocaine. And I love that cocaine. He reminded me of that former self and I slipped right back in.

John: It's like when Malcolm got out of jail, Elijah Muhammad spoke to a crowd about how Malcolm had been living inside the bush where he'd been protected. No more. And in here we're protected from a lot of situations, and I don't think we're realistic about how we'd deal with them.

I'll give you an example. I was talking to my son's mother the other day; she's purchasing a house and talking about how much money she needed for the closing. She didn't know if she was going to make the deadline. Now this is family, and something to do with my child. In here I got an excuse—I'm in prison, I can't come up with no money. But I know John out on the street. He'd have said, "I can get two, three thousand real fast for you." Will I have the strength to pass it up? Or will I be like Mike, "Just this one time." Next thing you know, you're paying for it the rest of your life.

I've seen guys get out and do what they said they were going to do: start working with kids, making a little money, being happy. They suffered a little; they didn't have the car, and then had to get a used one. They couldn't get a house, they had to go live with Mom a few weeks. But they had their mind made up good.

Then I've seen guys do the other side of it too: go straight back to the game, get yourself a car and a couple girls. These guys are not out of prison a week before you start hearing their names ringing over the phone—"Your man out there getting money, he just got himself a new BMW, I saw him last night." And you say, "Goddamn, the man just got out yesterday! How could he get caught up in that?"

I had a heart-to-heart with my uncle the other day, and he asked me, if I get out what kind of person I'm going to be. I had to tell him, "If I haven't changed, if I go back to that old stuff, then I need to be left in here." I look at the suffering I caused my family, even my children. If I do that stuff again I ain't doing nothing but hurting people all over, and rather than putting everybody through that again why don't I just keep my dusty ass in here?

That's why I say to Charles, if I ever get the chance to roam I'm leaving the state. Otherwise, I don't think I'd make it. I got to go where nobody really knows me and I can just work at being a *square* for a while.

Charles: Yeah, you have to change people, places, and things.

O'Donald: I disagree. A lot of guys in here are smokers, and if they go on lock-up where they don't have any cigarettes, they say, "Well, I don't smoke anymore." But as soon as they're back they smoke. They really didn't stop. So I don't believe I've truly changed if I'm released from prison and have to move somewhere else, or disassociate myself from people. This isn't change—it's running. If I can be in the midst of these things and still not do them, that's *true change.*

Tony: Yeah, I came here from Texas to get away from anybody I knew. Then I got into the wrong kind of gang in Maryland!

Mike: But if you leave, it's easier to divorce yourself from unnecessary pressures. If I get out of here, I'm going to Atlanta. I ain't never been there, but I heard it's nice. Who knows? But I'll tell you something: I know countless guys that come out of these prisons and a guy pulls up in a Lexus or Mercedes, takes him to the shopping mall, buys him everything he wants, says, "Look man, here's my beeper number."

John: If you need anything—

Mike: —Just holler at me. So you don't holler. You're standing on the corner, catching the bus to wherever you're working at, but the guy keeps coming by. So it's best when we divorce ourselves from this madness, go somewhere else, start over where we don't know nobody to holler at.

Tray: If I'm trying to be a celibate, there's no need for me to be sitting in a room with a naked woman.

CHAPTER TWENTY-FIVE

Deaths and Births

Remaking a self is no easy matter. The chapter 24 dialogue shows that the men were aware of the consummate difficulties in so doing. As John says, "Once we get out of that lifestyle we don't know what to do." You were the Man—now you feel like a lost boy. And the day looms empty, without sensation or purpose. How can this inner void resist the gathering forces of the same old street, the same old dealers, the offer of free blow?

Does it have to happen? The men agree that it doesn't, though their strategies of resistance differ. Is it enough just to get out of inner prison or hadn't you also better get your butt far, far away from the street that had led straight to the Maryland Pen? H.B.'s return to the street raises all these questions, though it also leaves them unanswered for me.

An old friend had invited H.B. to share living space and split the rent in an apartment in the old neighborhood. For a time, all went well. H.B. came to loathe home detention, with its claustrophobia and petty humiliations, but he put up with it and still reveled in his freedom. We created a part-time position for him at Loyola with me as his supervisor. This gave him some small income, but more important, got him out of the house, put institutional resources at his disposal, and went some way toward restoring his dignity. I was used to seeing H.B. in prison; it was quite a switch see him sauntering into my office every Monday to settle down at the computer. He began writing a biweekly column on AIDS for the *Baltimore Evening Sun* and was hard at work completing his first novel, *Baltimore Badlands*. In the meantime, he was also being asked to participate in radio shows, speak in public forums, and address classes. This he did with determination and honesty, sharing openly about his past and his current battle with AIDS. Baltimore's Arena Players put on a production of *Smooth Disappointment* at Loyola. For the first time, H.B. saw live actors performing his play. The story of an addict who'd finally gone clean and righteous, it was, in many ways, H.B.'s own story.

But with time the frustrations came and, like sandpaper, began to wear away the newer self. H.B. found himself in fights with his roommate, though still annoyingly dependent on him. For a time, H.B.'s daughter moved in with them, a dream of restored fatherhood come true. But she was a handful and it just didn't work out. She moved back with her mom. Then too, there were constant money difficulties attacking from the outside, and from the inside, the progressive disease eating away at the man. H.B. struggled with painful tooth problems, difficulty breathing, untreatable skin sores, periodic exhaustions, and near blackouts. His physician ended up prescribing opiates—Tylenol with codeine, and the like.

Whatever the cause, H.B. picked up. Heroin, that is. It was all around him on the street, and the pain and temptation wore down any resolve. It was many months before I knew, but I sensed the return of an older H.B. before I had any explanation. He seemed more distant, more manipulative, more . . . irritating. Continually borrowing money, cadging rides, showing up and disappearing mysteriously. Maybe that's one reason they call it "using"—I felt used by H.B., and grew to resent it. But with my anger came guilt. Here was a sick man struggling to survive. Why was I so lacking in the sweet milk of human compassion?

When I heard thirdhand that H.B. was using, it was almost a relief. The confused puzzle sorted itself into place. I could understand his erratic behavior, and my own building rage. I was dealing again with an addict. My Twelve Step training gave me guidance as to what to do, though I didn't particularly wish to. It took great prayer to confront a dying friend with "tough love."

But I did, challenging H.B. directly, and he gradually came clean. It started, he said, with the painkillers. He had become addicted to them and had later turned to street drugs. Then too, there was the factor Tray and others had mentioned—H.B. was back in the old neighborhood, amidst old connections. "If I'm trying to be a celibate, there's no need for me to be sitting in a room with a naked woman." H.B. had talked about moving to Florida for the weather (he felt he could no longer survive the cold) but never had the money. In Baltimore, that naked lady was strutting her stuff.

Whatever the reason, H.B. got hooked, and had entered the hospital to begin a methadone program. He'd found that his worn-down body couldn't take it: the methadone just made him sicker. But how long, I wondered, would he survive street drugs? He told me he'd even thought of an intentional OD. One fix and the pain's over. Images of my family suicides shot through my body like my own OD. Had H.B. really gotten out of prison? Had I?

We both did our best to wrestle this demon to the ground. I did the tough-love thing. H.B.'s life was up to him, but as his supervisor I'd have to fire him unless he stayed clean and proved it with biweekly urinalyses. But for H.B., it wasn't just a matter of keeping the job; more important, he said, and I believe him, was to win back my trust. He didn't want to go out no "smooth disappointment." And soon thereafter H.B. cleaned up—I started receiving the evidence each week by fax.

But the truth is, I never felt the same. I'm not proud of this lack of compassion for a dying man. But there it is. Maybe it wasn't just H.B.'s relapse, understandable in the circumstances, that so pissed me off. Maybe it was also the very fact that he was dying. Hadn't he been my pet project, my rescue fantasy? I couldn't save my mother from cancer, my brother and father from their descent. But I had, by God, gotten H.B. out. Maybe he was a surrogate for all the other living dead in my life, and even for myself struggling toward freedom.

But the joke was on me. I hadn't saved shit. Any glorified intervention on my part was again too late, way too late. The needle was in the arm, the virus in the vein, before I even knew the man, and now I had to watch him slowly die. It was a constant reminder in Cinemascope of all the other deaths I had previously witnessed or missed. To see him gradually consumed in a holocaust—emaciated, covered with sores, nearly toothless, and finally, addled with AIDS dementia—and to be powerless in the face of it all, was absolutely infuriating. H.B.'s drug relapse was a convenient pretext for me to distance myself, and to have a target for my rage.

But witnessing his struggles, I also better understood that Moses message that H.B. would see, but not enter, the promised land. I had originally taken that to mean that H.B.'s commutation would be denied. Now I saw it differently. H.B. did secure his physical freedom, but that wasn't *the* promised land. H.B. wasn't fully free. He still was enslaved by the AIDS contracted in prison and the addict's instinctive responses to pain.

It took H.B. a long, painful time to die, just as it had for him to start living. By depressed T-cell counts, and other objective criteria, he should have succumbed far sooner than he did. But H.B., stubborn until the end, would not go gentle into that good night. By the time death came, it was almost a relief: for me, for his loved ones, maybe even for H.B. Plato says that the body is a kind of prison for the soul, and death the great escape. Who knows? Maybe H.B. had finally gotten out of prison.

His funeral was alternately a somber and joyous affair. It was held at the Grace African Methodist Episcopal Church. Outside was a small park where I went wandering, in search of release. A sign, nailed up on a stick, caught my eye: ADDICTS: PLEASE CLEAN UP YOUR NEEDLES!!

Death and disappointment seemed everywhere. Around that time, another big blow fell: the Omnibus Crime Act shut off monies for prison college education. For over two decades these programs had been made possible by Pell Grants that help fund higher education for those with low income. Since the start, prisoners, whose income is effectively zero, had been eligible to apply for Pell Grants. This money paid for colleges to establish extension programs that sent books and professors into the prisons. Over 35,000 inmates were enrolled around the country.

But the crime bill ended all that. A barely noticed provision made prisoners unable to receive Pell Grants. Senator Jessie Helms had long led the charge for such a cutoff, but the recent get-tough-on-crime mood finally put it over the top. Without federal money, prison programs across the country have had to close. Since I functioned as a volunteer leading a noncredit workshop, my own course wasn't directly affected, but pretty much all else at the Maryland Penitentiary was. No more Baltimore City Community College courses. No more Coppin State University extension program. Close the books, say goodbye to the teachers, forget about the degree. Want something to do in long years ahead? Play basketball. Lie in your cell.

It makes no sense to me. People were outraged about public funds pouring in to convicted felons. But prisoners accounted for less than one percent of Pell Grant funding; they did not knock anyone else off the rolls (since these grants are an "entitlement" program for all those who meet the criteria) and they received no more than $1,500 a year in college expenses. By way of contrast, it costs greater than ten times that amount, $20,000 or more, to jail the offender. And without education, many more inmates come back to jail. A series of studies have found a 30 to 70 percent reduction in recidivism for those who latch on to some higher education. They've got the training and the diploma that open doors. Order the teachers out, and the doors begin to shut. Who will inmates study with—each other? What will they learn about—criminal techniques? The crime bill was supposedly geared toward crime prevention. In fact, it killed one of the few effective prevention programs we have. I think that crazy, but then nobody asked my opinion.

I gave it anyway, writing an op-ed that appeared in the *Washington Post* and elsewhere. From that, I was on radio interviews, and felt the ego-boost of (temporary and minor) celebrity. But more important, like the prisoners I was able to transmute my anger, turn it into a voice. I also had to accept that this voice was dissonant with the prevailing chorus. I wanted to talk about the possibilities of building a new self in prison, but the public had grown skeptical. Better instead to build more prisons.

And this we are doing with a vengeance. From 1990 to 1995, 213 new state and federal prisons were constructed, and the boom continues unabated. It doesn't correlate with an increase in criminal behavior: over the past eight years the number of incarcerated people has risen by 50 percent, even as violent crime has *fallen* by about 20 percent.

And it has become a big business. The building of new prisons, along with the provision of "services" to the inmates, is a tremendous growth industry. In the past twenty years, spending on corrections has increased *fivefold*, now totaling some thirty-five billion dollars a year. Just as hoteliers need to fill their rooms, so companies and communities, and increasingly state and local governments, need inmates to fill the cells.

But where in the world do we find all these criminals? As Eric Schlosser writes in his *Atlantic Monthly* article on "The Prison-Industrial Complex"

(December 1998), "Crimes that in other countries would usually lead to community service, fines, or drug treatment—or would not be considered crimes at all—in the United States now lead to a prison term, by far the most expensive form of punishment." For example, because of the "war on drugs" and mandatory sentencing, the proportion of prisoners locked up for drug offenses has increased dramatically from one in fifteen in 1980 to now one in four. These are the people, disproportionately African American, with whom we can fill those cells. Two-thirds of federal antidrug funding goes into law enforcement. Not treatment. Not prevention.

In the words of Franklin E. Zimring, director of the Earl Warren Legal Institute, "No matter what the question has been in American criminal justice, prison has been the answer." About 70 percent of inmates in the United States are illiterate. Some 200,000 may suffer from a serious mental disease. Some 60 to 80 percent have a history of substance abuse. So many problems and questions. One answer: prison cells.

Another factor feeding the prison binge is the trend toward longer and longer sentences. Parole boards are toughening up, releasing fewer inmates. Fifteen states have even eliminated parole boards entirely. No doubt the public rage toward criminals fuels this trend. But again it's interesting to "follow the money." In 1994 the federal government passed a law providing grants for prison construction, but only to states that require inmates to serve at least 85 percent of their terms. Forty states that now comply can get at those bucks.

Here in Maryland, we're seeing a version of this don't-let-'em-out trend. Governor Parris Glendening, a moderate Democrat, announced an unexpected decree: he would henceforth refuse parole for all inmates with life sentences for murder or rape, except in cases of old age or terminal illness. Time served, prison record, educational attainment, parole board review—none of it mattered. The governor would simply turn down any favorable recommendations.

I assume this sudden move was motivated by political expediency. Very few lifers were getting out anyway—an average of six a year in Maryland from a total of more than 1,700. But as a political/media researcher said about the announcement, "It probably helps [the governor] a little bit. Democrats in general have a 'wimp' image when it comes to crime." Beyond politics, there are also legitimate concerns. A third of those in prison for violent crime are rearrested within three years of release for another violent crime. Why take the risk of setting murderers free?

But I couldn't help thinking about the actual men I knew—like Tray, or John, or Selvyn, or Donald—who were painstakingly working themselves up the ladder only to have that ladder abruptly pulled out from under them. Just as the Pell Grant cutoff seemed to me misplaced, so this sudden edict, and in much the same way. It didn't slam the guy who sits on his butt in prison or piles up tickets picking fights. Such a person wasn't going to enroll in college or see the street anytime soon. No, the guy hit hardest is the one most serious about change. Before, there had been incentives and rewards. Get through the GED, and there's a college program ahead. Get through that, and someday there may be a job. Build a clean record and there's a hope of release. Build a new person, as Malcolm X had in prison, and you may gain a new life. But now that hope was taken away with a one-size-fits-all rule—*no parole, period.*

This local policy is under court challenge. After all, judges sentenced inmates to prison for life *with possibility of parole*, not knowing that later a governor would change this to *no* parole. And after three years of study, a Maryland commission has recommended against this no-parole policy. Still it remains in effect. Lifers aren't getting out.

And around this time, I found I could no longer get in. I was barred for many months from the penitentiary. Why? After the Pell Grant termination, the inmates, and some of us at Loyola had come up with a response. We would train college-graduate inmates to lead seminars for the other prisoners. Men like John, Tray, and Q were poised to take the lead. They would design and run courses that in turn would be overseen by Loyola professors like me. It wouldn't really be a college program and couldn't grant degrees, but it would empower the prisoners themselves to keep alive the spirit of higher education. We could take the cutoff of resources not just as crushing defeat, but as challenge and opportunity.

A national crime reporter from the *Chicago Tribune* was intrigued by our plan and wanted to meet the prisoners and witness a workshop in action. The school principal and I decided to prepare a count-out for her to enter the class as a guest. This wasn't proper procedure—all reporters were supposed to go through cumbersome official channels to get any prison admission approved. We took the short cut and, like the prisoners, paid for it a long time. When it was discovered, the principal was removed from his position. I was summarily escorted out of the prison, forbidden indefinitely to return. An investigation of the incident proceeded with due gravity and at the customary slow pace. It all seemed to me rather like using a shotgun to subdue a flea. But as month after month slipped by, I also experienced a certain pleasure at my banishment. I felt burned out on teaching the course-that-will-not-end (almost no one ever graduated), and even more so by the constant snubs, inefficiency, disregard, and obstacles attendant on volunteering in a maximum security prison. Being booted out was a little like being released.

But this pleasure was also saturated with guilt. Wasn't I, after all, to blame for what had happened? In my urge for press coverage and glory, hadn't I jeopardized all we had built together? I stewed in that death-dealing guilt for a good while, and then finally screamed "Enough!" My intent in inviting the reporter had not been heinous, nor had I been able to anticipate the results. I wasn't a bad guy. No more self-hate. That guilt was my own prison, and I wasn't going to be locked up again.

I did, however, return to the Maryland Penitentiary. Once the investigation was completed and I'd apologized profusely to the warden I was permitted back in. Sort of. One week the document to let me in hadn't been properly prepared. Turned away at the gate. Another week the prisoners' count-out wasn't properly prepared. I was asked to leave. We couldn't seem to get things restarted. And then suddenly everything was topsy-turvy because of the wide-scale transfers. This was the time of the penitentiary's conversion from maximum to medium security. I showed up one day to a skeleton crew. Most of my men had been dispatched to Jessup.

As I earlier said, it felt like another death. But when I prayed about my next move, the message was life-giving. There was a reason, I sensed, that everywhere doors were being slammed shut. Just as I had once been summoned into the prison, I was, for now, being summoned out. Accept it. Once again, this voice sounded consonant with that of my deepest desires. The truth was, I needed a break, and it was the right time for one. Our taping for this book was in the can. The group I had worked with was now disbanded. And a new character was coming on the scene, one who would demand concerted time and focus. My wife and I were adopting a baby.

Nothing quite so cheerful awaited the other men. Most were transferred to the House of Corrections Annex in Jessup, a new maximum security prison built to help relieve Maryland's prison overcrowding. But soon the solution became part of the problem: by 1997 the Annex was stuffed with 1,800 prisoners, twice as many as the facility was built to hold. And there wasn't much to do there except suck air. The prison offered little in the way of recreational or educational programs, and equally little in the way of hope. The majority of inmates were lifers, many young, and staring at an endless term, especially given the governor's no-parole policy. Is it any wonder that the Annex was soon a scene of violence? One day in 1997 a melee broke out in the mess hall, injuring seven inmates and twelve guards. The next day, three correctional officers were attacked and seriously injured. One was stabbed seventeen times in the head, neck, back, and shoulders. The prison went into long-term lockdown, prisoners confined to their cells. From little to do, soon there was *nothing* to do. By comparison, the Maryland Pen was a hotel.

Still, as I hear from the inmates there, and ones transferred elsewhere (the Annex has moved many out to reduce overcrowding), any notes of despair are still tempered by hope's sweet music. Many of the men, like Malcolm X, are still about the business of building a new self even within the frozen world of prison. Charles Baxter has been certified as a tutor teaching illiterate prisoners to read. "I enjoy my job," he writes, "but it's more an opportunity to help and give service to my comrades in the struggle for freedom of the mind." Donald Thompson feels that he has won that struggle: though "most of my legal options have been exhausted . . . I am already experiencing the only true freedom there is—an unshackled mind." Tony Chatman-Bey is the editor of his prison writer's club newsletter, and a new grandfather to boot. O'Donald Johnson, no longer the young tough perpetually in lock-up, writes that he has "found my true heritage and faith. I profess to be a Hebrew Israelite, believer in the almighty Yah and my saviour Yahshua and follower of the Torah." Talk of a new self!

Q is building his new self outside of prison walls. Incarcerated on a drug charge, he was recently released after winning a reduction of sentence. At the moment he is working two jobs, one of which involves assisting youths in trouble, finding alternatives to imprisonment. On top of that he's enrolled in a graduate program at a well-reputed local university.

Here, I was poised to write of Gary Huffman, persevering despite severe liver, kidney, and heart disease that might long ago have done him in. Then just today I received a letter informing me of his death. His cousin writes, "He said that he was blessed to know you, thankful for love and support, and that he would see you on the other side." I never got to know Gary that well. (I don't even have enough information to write a biographical note for him as I did for the other men.) He joined our group late, and his participation had been restricted by illness. Still, receiving that death note felt like a punch in the stomach. He had always been warm and gentle toward me. Yet along with the grief, I felt something almost akin to quiet celebration. Here was a man released from so much prison time, so much disease and suffering, who by his own account was heading to "the other side." Maybe he will find a new and better self there.

Tray Jones isn't going anywhere, at least physically. He recently received a bitter disappointment when his writ of habeas corpus was denied. He writes, "I've been experiencing tremendous sensations of melancholy and anger, but I've been reading the [Bhagavad] Gita, and it has been very helpful. There is a consequence to the horrible things I've done, and I shall face it with dignity and honor. I admit: it hurts like hell— and I desperately want to be home with my wife, and be among other family and friends that are warm and comforting. But if it's not meant to be, then it is not meant to be."

His wife? Yes, about a year ago Tray got married. He had known Francine way back when he was fourteen, before dealing and prison took him away. They met again when Francine was visiting a family member in prison. She was struck by the change in Tray: "He was softer." Communicating through letters, phone calls, prison functions, personal visits, they gradually fell in love. The wedding was a spare ceremony—four guests allowed from outside, no cake, and needless to say, no honeymoon. No subsequent conjugal visits. But no regrets, either. Francine and Tray seem verily smitten.

And that brings me back to my own blessed event that helped pull me out of the Maryland Pen—the adoption of a child. My wife and I had run the gauntlet of the infertility game. We had grieved for the child we would never have, and opened our heart-gates to a new one. We settled on adopting through China. There were tens of thousands of girls there abandoned to orphanages, largely due to that country's one-child-per-family policy and the widespread preference to make that one a boy. My wife, a feminist philosopher, could feel for these gender discards. And for me, the baby came bearing a thousand meanings. Some of them floated to the surface and clarified as we waited for our assignment (bureaucracy again). For example, there was the baby as magical reversal of the past. I had failed to save Mom, Dad, or Scott, even H.B. In each case, I felt I had abandoned them. But here was someone I could really rescue, someone who herself had been abandoned. If my family was wiped out, here was family restored. She was all those I had lost, resurrected in a twelve-pound package.

And then too, she was *me*. I, like her, had been orphaned, and knew the fear, pain, rage, of abandonment. In taking her into my arms I was not only rescuing others, but somehow rescuing myself.

Yet this rescue mission also seemed fraught with dangers. I struggled again with an unfocused guilt. I had to wrestle it to the ground like Jacob wrestling the angel, before it would reveal its meaning. It was that old serial killer scenario again. By daring to start a new family, I felt myself again killing off the old one. (I know this makes no sense, and is the opposite of what I said above, but the unconscious doesn't follow linear logic.) I was abandoning my family of origin to embrace a new beginning. But wasn't that how I'd murdered them to begin with? Daring to leave—for Yale, for the West Coast, now for China—to start anew and claim my independence. If I did it again, who else would die? Perhaps Janice, or myself, or the baby—punished as in the plot of a Greek tragedy. Maybe there was a reason I wasn't meant to have children. Why tempt fate? The ancient demons did a circle dance in my brain.

Screw it! Such was my sophisticated reply. I'm not turning back. I'd won my case on retrial—remember?—so don't go pinning discredited charges on me. If I remained imprisoned by fear and guilt, how could I liberate my daughter? She was waiting in some Chinese orphanage in serious need of parents. We're coming, little girl, hang on! We just have to find out who you are.

Finally, we did. She was five-month-old Gao Hua Hua, "Double Blossom," and we would go to Nanjing to receive her. Her American name, we'd already decided, would be Sarah. After all, the biblical Sarah had also been handed a new identity: "And God said to Abraham, 'As for your wife Sarai, you shall not call her Sarai, but her name shall be Sarah.'" (Malcolm X didn't start the name-changing trend.) And it was Sarah who, in later life, past the time when it was naturally possible, was granted by God the gift of a child. The same was happening for us, in our forties and infertile. Abraham and Sarah's new life began when God said, "Go forth from your native land and from your father's house to the land that I will show you." Nanjing for us? Baltimore for our daughter?

The ordeal we passed through there and back is not easily summarized, and would be material for a different book. Impatience, terror, exhaustion, hotel rooms. Language difficulties, illness, boredom, twenty-seven-hour trips. What matters is that somewhere along the way a baby was thrust into our arms. She stared at us, and we at her. Who the hell are you? That was all we had in common.

At that moment, Janice and I changed selves forever. We were now Mommy and Daddy. But Sarah's changes seem unimaginable. From Gao Hua Hua overnight she became Sarah Chang-Ye Leder. Left as a one-month-old outside the orphanage, she had gone from her mother to the Gaoyou Welfare Home; then to Nanjing, to Guangzhou, to Shanghai, to Tokyo, to Los Angeles, to Baltimore in a few days. But she copes, don't ask me how. All's fine as long as she has some formula, a good nap behind her, and a sufficient quorum of adults to adore her.

No problem assembling that! With a father's objectivity, I can declare her the cutest, brightest, sweetest thing going. Culled from a nation of 1.2 billion, she was definitely *the one*. And she has definitely made a change in me. People comment on the goofy smile I now seem to wear around town, an unaccustomed accoutrement. It's not that I was miserable before. All the work of getting out of prison had dismantled much of that time-worn pain. But as the inmates say, giving up an old self is hard; you don't know what to put in its place. Now I do. I squeeze my daughter like a sponge; I tickle her little Buddha-belly and see her giggle; I watch her watching me with the perplexed fascination of an alien scouting out human life-forms—and I laugh. She is my heart, blooming and beating alive.

The prisoners, in some small way, shared in our journey to China and what we brought back. Tony wrote, requesting (no, demanding) his first picture of Sarah. On receiving one, Charles replies, "May (God) bless her with the joy and happiness to have a wonderful life as the cuteness, and smartness, and gladness that shines from her golden smile lights up your life and your wife's life with joy." It does. John writes, "You can take it from a person that knows. A daughter is a precious jewel who will give you great joy." Tray and his wife sent Sarah a sweet flowered frock. And Selvyn writes, "You have a wide variety of races in your family. First, you are Jewish, your daughter is, or was Chinese. . . . You also have an African American member of the family, me. Do you plan on having any more kids? Why stop at one? You can have my share of kids. That way you get to enjoy fatherhood for me."

And so we fill in the missing pieces for one another. I am touched by Selvyn's sense of our diverse family and by the surrogate fatherhood he claims. And I have felt something similar in the writing of this book. What is a book but itself a kind of baby? This one was gestated by an unlikely group of men, some dead or dying, some killers, many lifers, each shut up in a barren womb designed to prevent any issue. But issue there was, albeit bloody and flecked. As I write these last words I have the curious sensation of slapping the manuscript on its little butt, hearing a cry, cutting a cord, and sending it out into the world. May it speak not just of violence and death to you who read it, but proclaim "L'Chaim!" (as the Jews say)—to life!

Notes on Method

It may be helpful to clarify the method I used in editing and reconstructing the inmate dialogues. In class discussion we often spent two one-hour periods on any given text. These were then transcribed word-for-word by a number of invaluable helpers. I worked directly from these transcriptions, at times returning to the original tape to clarify muddled speech. My task then involved boiling down a large amount of material into a relatively brief and compelling dialogue.

A number of principles guided my editing process. First, I tried to select those comments I found most insightful or revealing about the text at hand and its relation to the inmates' lives. Needless to say, my choices were sometimes difficult. Much rich stuff was cut in the interest of brevity.

I also tended to retain comments that followed one from another in a rich and logical flow. Tangential points, interesting as they might be, were often dropped. My ideal was something like a Platonic dialogue wherein the reader could follow the thread of argument whether it led one finally down a blind alley or into an illuminating space.

In the classroom I had naturally tried to channel these discussions through questions and remarks. In the editing process, I often, though not always, cut out my voice. I felt that I more than have my say in the alternating chapters where I comment on the preceding dialogue. In the dialogue itself I wanted to let the voices of the men stand forth.

As a result of my prunings, each dialogue-chapter usually represents less than a quarter of our actual classroom discussion. From an hour session I might have used material treated in the last twenty minutes, discarding my introductory lecture, student questions, and initial responses, as well as topics that, while fruitful, seemed less suited to the book. Having focused on a topic, I then inevitably did further cutting. I often retained the comments of certain men while eliminating those of others. In a few cases, I moved the comments around to better represent a logical flow of ideas. (The give-and-take of a classroom, teacher calling on students as he sees their hands, is not always conducive to linear argument.) Usually, though, I tried to retain the original sequence of comments. I didn't want to construct "pretend" dialogues through unlimited cutting and pasting, but to stay reasonably faithful to the discussion that actually occurred.

At the same time, I had to keep the poor reader in mind. One has little patience, scanning the printed page, with all the digressions, hemming and hawing, broken grammar, and repetitions that characterize off-the-cuff speech. When including a man's comments, I often tried to edit them down to the essential point and most telling example. A page of transcribed speech might be cut to a few lines. Then too, I struggled with the issue of how much to "fix up" the comments I chose. Some of the men spoke more crisply and grammatically, others less so. I wanted to remove impediments so that everyone's ideas came through clearly. However, I didn't want to make them all sound like me, a highly educated, upper middle-class white. My imperfect solution was to seek a middle ground. I tried to retain some of the flavor of "street talk" and the vivid turns of phrase that made each voice distinctive, but also cleaned things up into more standard grammatical form.

I am acutely aware of the dangers of this editorial power that chooses which issues and voices to foreground, and even how these voices are to sound. I gave all the men the chance to go over the manuscript. If any felt my editing had in any way twisted his meaning or misrepresented his voice, he was free to change the text. For whatever it says, I received a number of enthusiastic comments and very little in the way of alterations. The few changes that were requested were simply to correct grammar further or clarify meaning.

In closing, I will give a sample of a word-for-word transcription of a snippet of conversation, followed by the way it appears once radically edited down for the book. My selection of this particular sequence to focus on is rather arbitrary. I am not using it to make any special point. Simply, the reader is entitled to peek behind the curtain and see the editing process at work.

Original Transcription

Drew: It brings up a question that I wanted to ask, which is what kind of effects does an institution like this, this panopticon type of institution, have on individuals and how does it affect people psychologically or spiritually? Does it tend to reform these individuals in a sense or quite the opposite?

H.B.: The effects of the panopticon are more or less to keep you docile, to keep you under control, make it easier for the guards to come into the prison and fill their day and get out. But I want to go back a little bit, where we were a moment ago. When you asked how does the theme of the panopticon play out in this particular prison, my mind immediately went back to the torture period and it began to roll forward back this way, rather. And my mind immediately I thought about what Foucault said about the docile subordinate regime that they try to turn the human being into and then I began to think that it's no longer just an architectural structure the way a particular office may be located or etcetera. They're using human beings to serve the same purposes now. You have more informers, okay, in the prison system today than ever before because it's more widely accepted today than it used to be. There was a time when it was totally corrupt. There was a time when it was a disgrace to stand up in a court of law and say I'm guilty of anything. You had your rights and you used those. But now this is acceptable because plea bargain, copping out, looking out for number one, all those things. So what you have in here now, in this prison, is you have almost [unintelligible] for what Foucault is talking about when he speaks about the dismantling of this human being and the erection of this structure for the purposes of the state. And it's not even necessary to build a guard tower in the center of *this* particular yard because there are so many informers. And some of them do it simply because they don't have anything else to talk about, they don't have any ideas handy. So they start talking about people. You've heard the expression "Big men talk about ideas. Little men talk about each other." So you get a lot of that going on. And as a result of it, a lot of the guards who come in here to work, they don't come in here, at least the impression I get, is that they don't realize that they're coming to work in a dangerous environment. They come in, and maybe it has something to do with survival mechanisms, you know, damned if you do, damned if you don't. Ha, ha, ha. But they come in here as if they're coming to a playground or a kindergarten, a yard with a lot of kindergarten kids running around and that says to me that it's working, this use of the human being as a machine. So that same purpose as that guard tower serves. . . .

Drew: So human beings are effectively controlled.

John: Thinking about certain things that Skinny was just mentioning. I concur with him to some extent, but I disagree. I think the panopticon is effective if the person's in control of you because I've been in here a while and I've seen different administrations come and go. But I know there's one chief, the way he approaches things and the way he does things, it always has an effect, what Skinny was saying, to create not just a docile individual in here sometimes, but to create an individual that does things that aren't rational, to appease this person. I've seen him here when he was first in here, and this was a tough penitentiary and guys still did the same things then. And then seeing him leave, it seems like guys try to pull themselves together, then I seen him come back in again and I seen the same kind of effect. And I think, I don't know if he studied this stuff, or if he just on his own intuition if he knows how to make intimidation or what other tactics he's learned are most effective. But he uses these tools better than others in the same position. 'Cause some get in that position and they're so nonchalant, it's just a day's work, that we don't pay that stuff no mind. We don't care, guys don't even think about it right. But once someone comes in who's effective, you have two options: back up or be very conscious of what your activities are and like in here you got blind spots everywhere. One thing you do on the tour of the Project Turnaround, we show the kids that come here the different blind spots around the penitentiary that you could lose your life or something could happen to you and the guard would never see it until they come find you or they hear you. So there's always ways of getting around and ways of doing things, but just getting back to panopticon, I think it can be a very effective tool of control, monitoring and creating, but as Skinny said, but I think whether they're in control, it has to be someone who knows how to use this tool. Because if someone in control doesn't know how to use this tool, like any other tool it's not effective at all, it's just in place.

As Edited for the Book

H.B.: The panopticon in this prison is not just an architectural structure, or the way an office is located—they use *human beings* to serve the same purpose. You have more informers in the prison system today than ever before. There was a time when being an informer was considered totally corrupt; now it's acceptable 'cause of plea bargaining, copping out, looking out for number one. It's not even necessary to build a guard tower in this particular yard because there are so many informers. And some of them do it simply because they don't have anything else to talk about, no ideas handy. You've heard the expression, "Big men talk about ideas. Little men talk about each other."

John: But the panopticon's only as effective as the person in control. Not all chiefs know how to use the tools. And you got blind spots everywhere. We show kids from Project Turnaround the blind spots around the penitentiary where you could lose your life and no one would ever see.

References

Alcoholics Anonymous (New York: Alcoholics Anonymous World Services, 1939).

Bollnow, O. F. "Lived-Space," *Philosophy Today* V (1961), pp. 31–39.

Buber, Martin. *The Way of Man According to the Teaching of Hasidism* (Secaucus, N.J.: Citadel Press, 1966).

Campbell, Joseph (with Bill Moyers). *The Power of Myth* (New York: Doubleday, 1988).

Foucault, Michel. *Discipline and Punish: The Birth of the Prison* (New York: Vintage Books, 1979).

Heidegger, Martin. *Being and Time* (New York: Harper and Row, 1962).

Johnson, H. B., Jr. "At Last, the South Wing Falls!" *Baltimore Sun*, May 13, 1993, 21.

Malcolm X (with Alex Haley). *The Autobiography of Malcolm X* (New York: Ballantine Books, 1973).

Minkowski, Eugene. *Lived Time: Phenomenological and Psychopathological Studies* (Evanston, Ill.: Northwestern University Press, 1970).

Moore, Thomas. *Care of the Soul* (New York: HarperCollins, 1992).

Nietzsche, Friedrich. *A Nietzsche Reader*, ed. R. J. Hollingdale (London: Penguin Books, 1977).

Swami Prabhavananda. *The Sermon on the Mount According to Vedanta* (New York: New American Library, 1963).

Tolstoy, Leo. *War and Peace* (Oxford: Oxford University Press, 1983).

Weil, Simone. "The *Iliad*, Poem of Might," in *The Simone Weil Reader*, ed. George A. Panichas (New York: David McKay, 1977).

West, Cornel. *Race Matters* (Boston: Beacon Press, 1993).

Index

About the Author

Drew Leder, M.D., Ph.D., is a professor of Eastern and Western philosophy at Loyola College in Maryland. He lives in Baltimore with his wife, Dr. Janice McLane, and their daughters, Sarah and Anna-Rose. He is the author of *Games for the Soul: 40 Playful Ways to Find Fun and Fulfillment in a Stressful World* (1998), *Spiritual Passages: Embracing Life's Sacred Journey* (1997), and *The Absent Body* (1990). His work with inmates has been featured in the *Washington Post*, the *Baltimore Sun*, the *Chicago Tribune*, and in the national media.